RURAL SETTLEMENT
AND FARMING IN GERMANY

RURAL SETTLEMENT
AND FARMING IN GERMANY

Alan Mayhew

Lecturer in Geography
Birkbeck College
University of London

BOOKS
10 East 53d St., New York 10022
(a division of Harper & Row Publishers, Inc.)

Published in the U.S.A. 1973 by:
Harper & Row Publishers, Inc.
Barnes & Noble Import Division

ISBN 06 4946703

Contents

List of Plates

facing page

List of Figures

page

The line illustration on page 65 is by kind permission of the
Hessisches Landesvermessungsamt, and the line illustrations on
pages 73, 156, 159 and 185 are by kind permission of
the Niedersächsischen Landesverwaltungsamtes-Landesvermessung
19.9.72 B4 282/72

Preface

A colleague and friend of mine maintains that all geographers start off as historical geographers, most subsequently become ' trendy ' and go into other branches of the subject and only the select few remain in historical geography. This book is written for the select few by one who has fallen by the wayside. I hope it will be of use to them.

The origins of this work lie in the two years 1963-5 which I spent working in the Geographical Institute of the University of Münster. My thanks are due to Professor W. Müller-Wille for making me so welcome in his Institute and for introducing me to the complexities of German *Siedlungsgeographie*. The year 1965-6 spent at the University of Göttingen was also most fruitful.

In England it was Professor Gordon East at Birkbeck who encouraged me to write this book. He read the whole script and made numerous helpful comments. I thank him for this and for his continual goading, which persuaded me eventually to complete the text. The responsibility for the inadequacies of this book is, however, entirely mine.

The maps were drawn with great care by Geoff Davenport and his staff in the drawing office at Birkbeck, and the manuscript was quickly and efficiently typed by Mrs Jill Wadie. I appreciate very much the work they have done.

Finally I would like to thank Kurt and Annette, Tim and Irmgard, Hans Kleinn, Eichhörnchen, Dieter, the Schmidts, Wolfgang and of course above all Hildegard, together with all those other friends who made those years at the Universities of Münster and Göttingen both fruitful and happy.

Introduction

This book is an attempt both to discuss the main body of work in German settlement geography and to give a chronologically ordered account of the development of settlement forms and farming in Germany. I hope it may therefore, be of some use both to those looking for a brief analysis of the major academic controversies which have arisen this century, and to those who wish for a more or less factual account of developments in Germany at some particular period.

The first chapter is a discussion of what has been the major debate in German *Siedlungsgeographie* this century; namely the original Germanic settlement form. This has been a most inconclusive debate but it has not been a sterile one. The vast amount of research which has been put into the solution of this problem may not have brought us any nearer to finding out about the original Germanic form of settlement but it has produced a great wealth of material on the historical geography of the high and late medieval periods and of the early modern period.

In this book the cover of the subject becomes sketchier and more selective the later the period. I have attempted to deal with the high and late medieval periods fairly thoroughly for there is a real gap in the English language literature on this period. The final chapter on the modern period from about 1800 is, however, very brief and selective. In a short book of this nature it is impossible to deal with many topics at length and I felt that it was in the modern period that I could save most space, for there is already some literature in English on the subject. This chapter is therefore brief and deals most inadequately with just one or two major topics.

I am very conscious of the fact that I have not attempted to tie the results of German research into the problems of research in historical geography in Britain. There are two reasons for this.

Firstly it seems to me that until very recently there has been a clear and significant difference between the approaches to research taken in German *Siedlungsgeographie* and British historical geography. Siedlungsgeographie has concerned itself very much with the description and classification of settlement forms and patterns and of field patterns. In historical geography more emphasis has been placed on the study of the progress of change and development and little formal work has been done on settlement forms and field patterns. Recently in Germany the study of these processes has come more to the forefront but it remains very difficult to relate the German work to English problems. The second reason is more simple; it is my own ignorance of recent trends in research in historical geography in Britain.

I am also conscious that there may be a slight bias towards using material derived from research in north Germany, in spite of the fact that I have tried to draw on research done in other parts. The bibliography has a definite and intentional bias towards the North. I have included in this bibliography most of the basic works on settlement geography, with material covering the whole of Germany. In addition I have included a few more obscure references on the North, which illustrate minor points made in the text and which may be of use to anyone just starting work on this area. My own doctoral thesis has even more obscure references to the North, though these are concerned largely with the modern period. On south Germany the reader will find more references in the work by Schröder and Schwarz, *Die ländlichen Siedlungsformen in Mitteleuropa.*

Note

The reader should note that I have used the terms early, high and late medieval periods in the usual continental manner. The early medieval is that period from the *Völkerwanderungen, c.* A.D. 375-550 until the end of the Carolingian period (say until A.D. 900-1000). The high medieval, which saw the great expansion of settlement in Germany, lasted until around A.D. 1250-1350. The late medieval is that period of great settlement desertion and takes us up to the start of the early modern period at about A.D. 1450-1500.

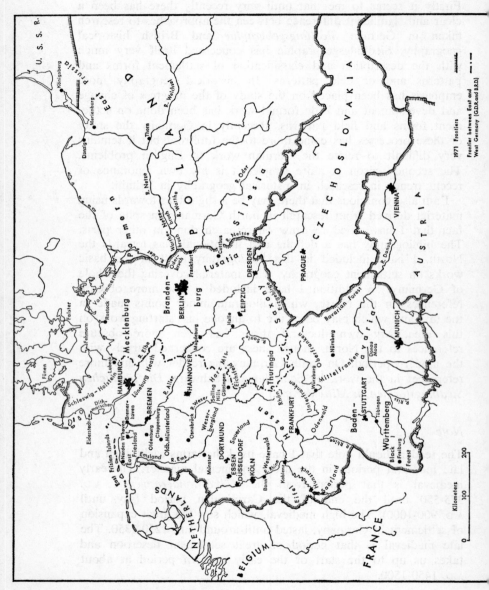

Fig. 1. General location map of Germany

1 The Great Folk Movement and the colonization of the German lands

The movement westwards of the Germanic tribes began as early as the third century before Christ. By the middle of the following century the Roman Empire in Germany was crumbling and Germanic tribes had been settled to take over frontier defence. The westwards and southwards migration continued until the end of the fifth century, by which time Germany west of the Elbe, Gaul and large parts of Britain and the Iberian peninsula had been occupied. Behind the Germanic tribes the Slavs had moved west to settle the lands east of the Elbe.

The first five centuries A.D. were unsettled and dangerous years. in which wars were frequent, and destruction widespread. The population declined to reach a nadir in the late fifth or sixth centuries. The seventh century, with the initial Germanic settlement completed, marks the beginning of a period of increasingly centralized power culminating in the empire of Charles the Great and considerable population growth. Pressure on the land increased and the settled area was extended. By the mid-tenth century a movement back to the lands in the east, now occupied by Slavs, had begun, and within the next three centuries Germanic settlers occupied all the land between the Elbe and Oder and penetrated deeply into Silesia.

The Völkerwanderung

The Germanic tribes moved westwards and southwards from their tribal areas in Scandinavia and between the Weser and Oder. Three groupings are usually recognised, the North Germans who remained in Scandinavia, the East Germans who moved from Scandinavia to occupy the area east of the Oder, and the West Germans occupying the North German Lowlands between the Weser and the Oder. In the east the Goths moved south and east to reach the Black

Sea about A.D. 200 whilst the West German tribes came increasingly into conflict with the Roman Empire along the Rhine and Danube. The ambition of the Romans to extend the bounds of their Empire eastwards to the Elbe was finally extinguished by the victory of Hermann (Arminius) and his Germanic tribes over Varus in the Teutoburger Wald in A.D. 9. Throughout the following three centuries the Roman *Limes* along Rhine and Danube was held and for a short period extended eastwards, but the attacks of the Germanic tribes became more frequent and more dangerous.

The *Völkerwanderung* was borne largely on the shoulders of the East German tribes. In A.D. 375 the Huns moving in from the east destroyed the Empire of the Eastern Goths. The East Germans moved westwards and southwards to break the power of Rome and establish empires in Gaul, Spain, Italy and North Africa. The West German tribes, notably the Franks and the Alemans, intensified their attacks on the *Limes*, so that the Roman Empire in Germany was crumbling long before the final collapse in A.D. 476. The Germans occupied and settled the areas west of the Rhine and south of the Danube, moving on into Gaul and, in the case of the Angles, Saxons and Jutes, into England. Behind the Germanic tribes the Slavs moved westwards to roughly the line of the Elbe and Saale rivers.

The *Völkerwanderung* was a time of unrest, destruction and plague. There had almost certainly been a steady decline in population between the time of the early assaults on the *Limes* in the second century after Christ and the gradual return to stability in the sixth century. By this time the area west of the Elbe was occupied by German farmers, who had created new settlements and broken new agricultural land. They were spread very thinly. Müller-Wille has estimated that the probable density of population around A.D. 500 in the area of the present Federal Republic was only 2.2 persons per square kilometre[1]. This estimate may be on the low side, but there is general agreement that the density was not above 3 per square kilometre.

There were of course even in A.D. 500 areas of denser settlement. Müller-Wille divided the regions of Germany into six groups according to settlement density. The most favoured areas of settlement on this basis he found in the loess-covered *Börden* from the Cologne Bay into the Leipzig Bay and parts of the

---

[1] Müller-Wille, W., ' Siedlungs-, Wirtschafts- und Bevölkerungsräume im westlichen Mitteleuropa um 500 n. Chr. ', *Westfälische Forschungen* Vol. 9, 1965, pp. 5-25

Rhine Rift. Almost as favoured were the valleys of the Rhine Uplands and the limestone plateaux of southern Germany. On the other hand, the wet sea marshes and peat bogs of the North German Lowlands, the Hercynian blocks of the Mittelgebirge and the Pre-Alps were very sparsely settled. Large areas remained virtually empty (Harz, parts of the Black Forest, and the Erzgebirge, for instance) until the expansion of settlement several centuries later. These results are for A.D. 500 and it should be noted that the relative placing of a few of these regions (notably the North Sea Marshes) would have been different if a slightly earlier or later period had been chosen.

The beginnings of German agriculture

The Germans were basically an agricultural people, without traditions of urban life. Some of the Roman towns managed to survive with a much reduced Romano-German population (Cologne and Trier) but a very large number disappeared altogether. With no specialized demand for food from a non-agricultural population and therefore no organized trading in foodstuffs, early German agriculture was on a very small scale and served a subsistence rather than a market economy.

The scale, type and organization of farming around the middle of the first millennium are extremely difficult to reconstruct because of the lack of both contemporary written sources and archaeological evidence. Several researchers have attempted to estimate the average size of arable land per farm using a variety of methods from pollen analysis to the projection back of written and map material from a somewhat later period. The conclusion reached in many of these investigations is that each farm had on average between 1.5 and 4 ha. This area will have varied from region to region and it is true that most of the research to date has been done in north and west Germany. The research has suggested that most early Germanic settlements consisted of only two or three farms at this time, so that if these findings are reasonably accurate the settlements were associated with at the most 20 ha of arable land.

Written evidence of value on the type of farming practised and the crops grown for this early period is found in legal codes such as the Lex Salica, Lex Alamannorum or Lex Baiuvariorum. Rye, oats, barley, wheat, spelt and millet are all mentioned in the Lex Salica, together with roots, beans, peas, lentils and flax. All of these were grown as field crops. Unfortunately nothing is said about the rotation of these crops, nor is there much about the size and number of fields, though it is clear that they were fenced and that there was already some scattering of ownership parcels in the individual fields. Both a plough with ploughshare (*carruca*) and a simple form of rake (*aratrum*) were used to break the ground and the Lex Salica also mentions the harrow and two-wheeled trailer.

The great detail with which the early legal documents treat livestock points to their importance at this time. Abel speaks of a 'pig terminology' in the Lex Salica, which distinguishes more than a dozen types of pig in its list of fines for stealing[2]. Horses already played an important role in agriculture; they were regarded as the most important livestock and were used for pulling the heavy plough, where this implement had penetrated. Cattle, sheep and goats are also mentioned in these documents. Excavations show the relative importance of these species to have varied in the different regions, cattle being particularly dominant in the North-Sea-Marshes and sheep rather more important in the heath-lands. Besides pastoralism, these excavations have also shown that hunting still contributed a high proportion of the food supply in many settlements at this time.

The initial Germanic settlement form

What form did the settlement of the Germanic peoples take? This question has stimulated much research in Germany since Meitzen published his *Siedelungs-und Agrarwesen der Westgermanen und Ostgermanen, der Kelten, Römer, Finnen und Slawen* in 1895[3]. It is doubtful whether the question can ever be satisfactorily answered. This is partly because of the lack of documentary and archaeological evidence for this early period, and partly because it is unlikely that there was one particular Germanic settlement form.

Documentary evidence in Germany which throws light on early Germanic settlement forms is rare. The early legal codes have been mentioned but little unequivocal evidence can be gained from them. There is the history of Gregory of Tours completed at the end of the sixth century, the lives of the Saints written in the sixth

[2] Abel, W., *Geschichte der deutschen Landwirtschaft vom frühen Mittel-alter bis zum 19. Jahrhundert*, Stuttgart, 2nd ed., 1967
[3] Meitzen, A., *Siedelungs- und Agrarwesen der Westgermanen und Ostgermanen, der Kelten, Römer, Finnen und Slawen*, 3 vols. and Atlas, Berlin, 1895

and seventh centuries, and later collections of letters[4] and short items of important news, but none of these sources helps us to determine the early settlement patterns. The earliest important sources for our purpose are the records of the monasteries founded under the Carolingians. These begin to appear in the early ninth century (*Annales Fuldensis*, the records of the Abbey of St Gallen) and later the *Traditionsbuch* of the Monastery of Corvey). It is not, however, until considerably later that solid, indisputable evidence can be gained from written sources.

Archaeological evidence rarely gives the right to generalize about settlement form, for as a rule this is areally restricted because of the cost and time involved. In one landscape of Germany, however, the scope of excavations makes it reasonably safe to draw conclusions about the history of settlement and agriculture. This is the North-Sea-Marshes, in which specially favourable conditions for excavations exist. The settlements on artificial mounds had to be raised with each rise in sea level and these settlement horizons can be investigated separately today. As many of the mounds were deserted in the sixth century and were not subsequently reoccupied there are many suitable sites for archaeological investigation. It would not be safe, however, to generalize the findings here to other Germanic areas where no excavations have been made.

Too frequently research workers have simply projected the settlement forms found on detailed maps of the late eighteenth or nineteenth centuries backwards in time without considering the vast changes which have taken place in the late medieval and modern periods. Müller-Wille's 'topographical-genetic' method of investigation, demonstrated by him in his 1944 paper, also starts with these late maps and tries to discover the core of the field pattern and the original settlement form through the use of field pattern analysis, place and field name evidence, document-ary evidence, thickness of the humic layer, carbon 14 dating and the history of individual holdings[5]. This is a more refined method of investigation but, like all attempts to reconstruct settlement form and field patterns in the early medieval period, it does not give us any definite evidence.

The discussion really began with Meitzen's great work at the

---

[4] For instance, the correspondence of Pippin and Charles the Great with the Pope, and those of the missionary Boniface

[5] Müller-Wille, W., 'Langstreifenflur und Drubbel. Ein Beitrag zur Siedlungsgeographie Westgermaniens', *Deutsches Archiv f. Landes- u. Volkskunde*, Vol. 8/1, Leipzig, 1944, pp. 9-44

end of the nineteenth century. Meitzen thought that variations in the settlement forms of Europe could be explained by ethnic differences. He considered the isolated farms with a block field pattern the original forms associated with a Celtic population, which were taken over by Germanic settlers. Strip field patterns and small hamlets were therefore secondary forms. The original Germanic forms according to Meitzen were the dense, nucleated settlements of south Germany (*Haufendörfer*) with their large open fields (*Gewannflur*). Meitzen's theories found general acceptance for a generation but were then disputed in a number of research papers based on work done in north-west Germany. It was found in the area between Weser and Ems and in Westfalen that the oldest settlement form was not the isolated dwelling with a block field pattern, as Meitzen had stated, but the small hamlet (*Drubbel*) and the long-strip field pattern (*Langstreifenflur*) on the infield (*Esch*)[6]. Since then there has been continuous debate on the age and origin of the *Esch* and *Drubbel* and their relationship to the *Gewannflur* and *Haufendorf*.

DRUBBEL AND ESCH

In north-west Germany at the beginning of the nineteenth century, there were two contrasting forms of settlement and types of farming. The isolated farms with their enclosed blocks of land around the farm buildings, as described by Meitzen, were mixed in with small hamlets which had all their arable land on the *Esch*. As will be seen later, the majority of the isolated farms were founded in the late middle ages or in the modern period, and are of more recent origin than the *Drubbel* settlements. These dispersed farms had no arable land on the *Esch* and generally no claim to use of the common land. The farms in the *Drubbel* held both land on the *Esch*, and had rights to graze on the common pastures. Often they also held land in blocks immediately surrounding their houses.

The *Drubbel* was initially a loose grouping of farmsteads (roughly varying between 3 and 15) but by the beginning of the nineteenth century it had often been infilled. Nevertheless even today many of the *Drubbel* have retained some of their original characteristics. The heart of these hamlets is still often formed by the small open green with several great oak trees spreading out over the surrounding farm buildings. Even today the centre of the settlement has a spacious feeling about it completely unlike the compact, congested *Haufendorf*. There was no set arrangement of

[6] See note 3 on page 60

farms in the *Drubbel* and, whilst the type clustered around a small green described above is quite common, there are also settlements where the farms are strung out along a path or around the edge of the *Esch*. In the case of Gross Hesepe on the Ems (plate 1) the original *Drubbel* can be seen clearly in the loose grouping of farms around an open space in the south-east corner of the picture. The village of Gross Hesepe occupies a position in relation to the river and the arable land common to many *Drubbel*. It lies on a high, dry sand dune overlooking the flood plain of the river, which can be seen on the right of the photograph to the north of the settlement. To the north and south of the village the arable land of the *Esche* also lies on the dry sands. To the west the commons stretch away into the peat bog of the Bourtanger Moor. Immediately to the west of the arable land on the *Esch* there has been some settlement of the common land at a later date.

Within the *Drubbel* there was an important social and economic distinction made between the classes of farmer. The earliest established farmers, the *Vollerben,* had full rights to use of the common land, they had all their arable land on the *Esch* and normally their farmhouse in the original hamlet settlement. Where farms had been divided among heirs, the rights attached to the farms were also divided, so that a group of farmers developed with only partial rights, the *Halberben* and *Drittelerben.* With the rise of population in the period from the tenth to the thirteenth centuries, a large class of people grew up with no rights to land at all. These were generally the non-inheriting sons of farmers in an area where undivided inheritance prevailed. They were sometimes allowed to settle as cottagers (*Kötter*) close to the original *Drubbel* but more frequently built their houses close to the land granted to them on the commons. As land became scarcer the generosity of the *Vollerben* towards these new classes of settler became less marked. Finally a group of people, the *Heuerlinge,* were settled with no rights in the *Mark* but the right to use some land of a *Vollerbe* in return for their working on the farmer's land for an agreed period of the year.

These distinctions were maintained into the twentieth century in some cases, though they had no legal importance after the commons had been divided. The rigidity of these distinctions and the fact that land parcels were in private ownership and were not periodically redistributed, means that it is possible to reconstruct in some cases a picture of the *Drubbel* and the lands associated with it for the period before the eleventh century. Such reconstructions, however, are not based on firm evidence and some doubt must remain. They are also only possible where a fairly strict system of undivided inheritance has prevailed.

The *Vollerben* held their arable on the *Esch*. The *Esch* was generally located on a dry site and this often meant on top of a sand dune. The problem of continuously cultivating this poor soil was solved through an annual system of manuring known as *Plaggendüngung*. This involved the pasturing of sheep on an area of heath or peat bog, and the subsequent cutting and transport of the sods together with the collected manure onto the *Esch*. The *Esch* land was therefore able to support crop after crop of cereal – generally rye (the agriculture of the *Drubbel* in the nineteenth century is often referred to as *ewige Roggenbau* – continuous rye cultivation). The addition of heath sods to the *Esch* each year led to the development of a deep humic layer deepest at the centre of the infield and thinning out towards the edges on the more recent additions to the *Esch*. In this way the characteristic rounded profile of the *Esch* was produced. The system of manuring used severely restricted the area of the infield, for it was necessary to maintain a certain relationship between the area of the *Esch* and the area of the common lands, and between these and the size of the flocks of sheep which were kept. Once turves had been cut a long period was required for the heath to recover; according to Niemeier thirty years[7], or ten to twelve years according to a contemporary source Arends[8]. Slicher van Bath estimated a recovery period of only seven to ten years on which basis he calculated the necessary relationship between arable and commons yielding turves to be as follows[9]:

Ratio of arable area to turf area in percentages

Humus Restored	Number of loads per hectare of arable			
	40	60	80	100
in 7 years	33.8 : 66.2	25.4 : 74.6	20.3 : 79.7	16.9 : 83.1
in 10 years	26.3 : 73.7	19.2 : 80.8	15.2 : 84.8	12.5 : 87.5

[7] Niemeier, G., 'Eschprobleme in Nordwestdeutschland und in den östlichen Niederlanden', in *C. R. du Congrès Internat. de Géog.*, Amsterdam 1938, Vol. 2, 5. Leiden, p. 38

[8] Arends, F., 1818-1820, *Ostfriesland und Jever in geogr., statist. und besonders landwirtsch. Hinsicht*, Emden, 1818-20

[9] Slicher van Bath, B. H., *The agrarian history of Western Europe A.D. 500 to 1850*, London, 1963

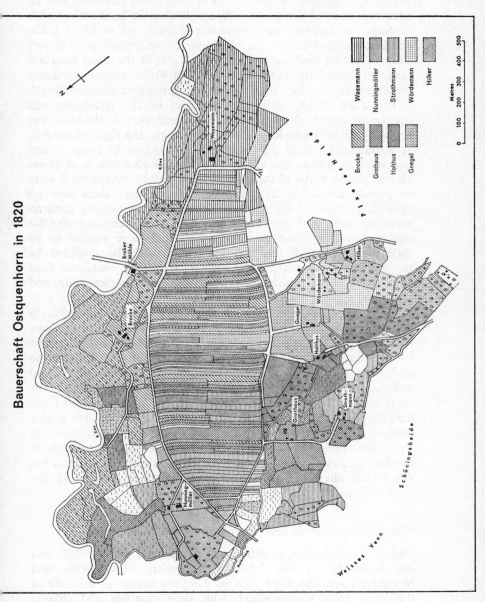

Bauerschaft Ostquenhorn in 1820

Fig. 2 The Esch at Ostquenhorn, 1820 (after Hambloch)

Whilst the majority of settlements in north-west Germany had an adequate ratio of arable to common land even in the nineteenth century, the farmers were extremely careful not to allow indiscriminate settlement on the commons or to permit new settlers from obtaining land on the *Esch*. At Lohe in the Soesteland not far from Papenburg on the Ems the eight *Vollerben* prevented any settlement in the *Mark* until its division in the nineteenth century[10].

The *Esch* which, until the enclosure of the commons, was simply an island of arable land associated with a *Drubbel,* was generally divided into long and narrow strips, the *Langstreifenflur*. A particularly simple *Langstreifenflur* is shown in figure 2 and two such complexes are visible in the aerial photograph of Gross Hesepe to the north of the village. Land parcels on the *Esch* were in private ownership in the nineteenth century; there was no periodic rotation of the strips and there appears to have been no recurring pattern of strip ownership. The strips were all accessible without crossing other private land so that there needed to be little organization of farming. The strips could be extended by the individual owners, but the farmers frequently reclaimed land around the *Esch* which then went into private ownership and prevented further extensions to the strips on the *Esch*.

Figure 2 shows the *Esch* at Ostquenhorn near Gütersloh in Westfalia. Each farmhouse lies in the centre of enclosed blocks of land on which their meadows are situated, and has direct access to its land on the *Esch* via the perimeter road. Beyond the enclosures lies the common land with both peat (Weisses Venn) and sandy heathlands (Schöningsheide and Pixeler Heide). A short study of the ownership pattern on the *Esch* will soon show that the farms of Hilker and Wördermann have very little arable land in strips. It is therefore unlikely that these two farmers are *Vollerben*. They are in fact *Kötter* who were allowed to settle in the late medieval period. Strothmann falls into the same class but this is not obvious from the ownership pattern because he has been able to buy up a large area of land on the *Esch*.

The Eschkerntheorie and the origin of the Gewannflur

The *Eschkerntheorie,* as introduced at the end of the 1930s and the beginning of the '40s by Niemeier, Müller-Wille and Mortensen, sees the *Esch* with its *Langstreifenflur* as the core of the open fields (*Gewannflur*), with their complex and chaotic

[10] Schwalb, M., 'Die Entwicklung der bäuerlichen Kulturlandschaft in Ostfriesland und Westoldenburg', *Bonner Geog. Abh.,* Vol. 12, 1953, p. 59

short-strip field pattern[11]. The *Gewannflur* has, according to this theory, developed from the *Esch* and its *Langstreifenflur*, whilst the densely built-up, large village often associated with the *Gewannflur*, the *Haufendorf*, has grown from the *Drubbel*. This theory was built up on research done in north-west Germany and applied elsewhere in Germany, with only very superficial investigation of the origins of the field patterns in these other areas. The reasons for the development of the *Gewannflur* from the *Esch* in some parts of Germany were given by Müller-Wille. He argued that whereas the favourable climate, the Frankish invasion bringing a new form of plough, a new inheritance system (partible inheritance) and the desertion of settlement and the subsequent concentration of the remaining people in large villages had favoured the development of *Gewannflur* from the *Esch*, in the north-west, where these factors were of no importance, the original forms of *Drubbel* and *Langstreifenflur* had been preserved[12].

The results of research in north-western Germany were supported by work done in East Prussia. The initial settlement of Lithuanian immigrants under primitive family relationships in the fourteenth century was studied by Mortensen through a fairly complete documentation[13]. The initial settlement took place in small family group hamlets and the land was divided amongst the members of the extended family. As the population increased with the need for more land and as relationships became more complex the arable land was divided into long narrow strips similar to those of the *Langstreifenflur* in north-west Germany. The settlement form after the earliest period of development was similar to the *Esch* and *Drubbel* in the north-west. This research provides some evidence that the small hamlet settlement with a *Langstreifenflur* can be an early form of settlement in a primitive colonization of new land. It in no way answers the criticism that the *Eschkerntheorie* was applied to south German areas without thorough local investigations.

More recent research into the origin of the *Gewannflur* has cast doubt upon the validity of the *Eschkerntheorie*. Since the end of

---

[11] Niemeier, G., 'Gewannfluren, ihre Gliederung und die Eschkerntheorie', *Petermanns Mitteilungen,* Gotha, 1938, pp. 57-74
Müller-Wille, W., *op. cit.,* 1944
Mortensen, H., 'Fragen der nordwestdeutschen Siedlungs—und Flurforschung im Lichte der Ostforschung', *Nachr. d. Akad. d.* Wiss Göttingen, 1946, pp. 37-59
[12] Müller-Willie., W., *op. cit.,* 1944, pp. 35-44
[13] Mortensen, H., *op. cit.*

the second world war a large number of detailed studies of field patterns have been completed in southern Germany and many of the new works in north Germany have come to different conclusions. These new findings suggest, on the one hand, that the *Gewannflur* has developed from block field patterns or wide strips and not from the *Langstreifenflur* and on the other that even in north-west Germany the *Esch* and the *Drubbel* may not be the original settlement form.

In lower Franconia, Krenzlin and Reusch investigated the origin of the *Gewannflur* in fourteen parishes[14]. Their findings are supported by Matzat working in the Odenwald and the adjoining Bauland[15]. In south Germany it is essential to use a different methodology to discover earlier forms of field division than that used so successfully in north and east Germany. In the north-west most investigations have been based on an analysis of land held by different social strata together with field research in the depth of humus on the *Esch*. It proved possible to separate the land of the *Vollbauern* from that of the more recently settled groups (*Kötter, Brinksitzer, Heuerlinge*). In south Germany these distinctions cannot be drawn and partible inheritance has made the ownership pattern on the open fields extremely complex. It was, however, found possible to reconstruct the old ownership unit, the *Hufe*, which had existed in the late medieval period but which, by the nineteenth century, had completely disappeared. The last references to these units appear in records made between the sixteenth and eighteenth centuries (the *Salbücher* and *Lagerbücher*). The individual land parcels of each *Hufe* are recorded with size, owner, location and, occasionally, to which *Hufe* the parcel originally belonged. With this information a picture of the field pattern before the development of the *Gewannflur* can be obtained.

This method and the results obtained can clearly be seen in an example taken from the work of Krenzlin and Reusch[16]. Altbessingen is a parish on the Wern-Lauer Platte just north-east of the Main in Lower Franconia. This is in general a fertile region with some loess material and rich Keuper loams (fig. 3). The village is first mentioned in 804 in a register of the monastery at

[14] Krenzlin, A. and Reusch, L., 'Die Entstehung der Gewannflur nach Untersuchungen im nördlichen Unterfranken', *Frankfurter Geographische Hefte*, 35/1, Frankfurt/Main, 1961
[15] Matzat, W., 'Flurgeographische Studien im Bauland und Hinteren Odenwald', *Rhein-Mainische Forschungen*, 53, Frankfurt/Main, 1963
[16] Krenzlin and Reusch., *op cit.*, pp. 17-26

Fulda. Here it is called an old settlement so that one can assume that the village dates back considerably further. The field pattern in Altbessingen in the early nineteenth century was a fairly typical *Gewannflur*, though made less regular through the pattern

0 ▬▬▬▬▬▬▬▬ 500 Metres

▦	Johanneshub	▥	Böheims Erb	▦	Thüngenscher Hof
▤	Reishub	▦	Marxer Lehnhof	▦	Kleines Keyls Erb
▦	Pfisters Hub	▦	Brönners Erb	▦	Grosses Keyls Erb

Fig. 3. The Gewannflur at Altbessingen (after Krenzlin and Reusch)

along the small stream west of the village and the existence of vine slopes with their characteristic degree of fragmentation. The small *Haufendorf* was surrounded by open fields divided into a chaotic mixture of generally short and narrow parcels. There was no obvious *Langstreifenflur* at the heart of the fields but if this was the original field pattern one would expect it to be unrecognisable after centuries of land division. But in fact a reconstruction of the ownership parcels of the old *Hufen* suggests that a *Langstreifenflur* was not the predecessor of the *Gewannflur*. The map shows clearly the existence of blocks of short strips belonging to the *Hufen* (in Altbessingen divided into the *Huben* and *Erb*), which have subsequently been divided. The *Gewannflur* is therefore a secondary form (not primary as Meitzen suggested), which has developed rapidly since the end of the medieval period from a block or wide strip pattern.

The village itself is also a recent creation. The plan of Altbessingen (fig. 3) shows a complex arrangement of buildings at high density. Many *Haufendörfer* show considerably greater congestion. In the case of Altbessingen it has been possible to reconstruct some of the farmyard areas of the old *Hufen*. These have been divided up subsequently and in the case of the Grosses Keyls Erb seven separate plots have been produced from the original farmyard areas. It has been estimated that this particular farm originally had a farmyard in the village, of 2,875 square metres, whereas the average size of farmyards in the village by the beginning of the nineteenth century was only 862.5 square metres[17]. Prior to the rapid growth of the village the settlement must have consisted of a loose grouping of farmhouses around the church. The expansion has been produced by the division of plots among heirs and by the settlement in the eighteenth and nineteenth centuries of large numbers of cottagers.

Krenzlin sees the main reason for the creation of the *Gewannflur* in the rapid growth of population. She points to three main periods when this process of *Vergewannung* took place: the eighteenth century, the sixteenth century, and the period between the eleventh and thirteenth centuries. Each of these periods was marked by a rapid rise in population. Although she suggests that a large number of open fields with *Gewannflur* were created within the last 250 years, it is clear that there must have been far earlier examples of this field pattern occurring. Krenzlin quotes work done by Jost in the Wetterau north of Frankfurt am Main, where in the fourteenth century three quarters of the parcels were smaller

[17] Krenzlin and Reusch., *op cit.*, p. 85

than 1.5 acres (2½ *Morgen*) and a third were smaller than 0.62 acres (1 *Morgen*)[18]. Planned *Gewannfluren* were also established in Slav areas when the Germanic settlers moved east in the twelfth, thirteenth and fourteenth centuries. Presumably these were based on a knowledge of existing patterns in western Germany. Nitz also found strong evidence of planned *Gewannfluren* on the Upper Rhine, which were laid out by the Carolingians for their soldiers as early as the ninth century[19].

During these periods of rapid population growth, the practice of partible inheritance led to the break up of farms into many smallholdings. This division of the land took place only where the largest growth rates of population were associated with a prosperous and expanding economy. It was confined therefore, according to Krenzlin, to those areas of highly productive soil, which had been occupied very early by the incoming Germanic tribes. These were also generally the regions in which urban development was most rapid. In the areas which were first settled in the high-medieval period, there was not the economic prosperity to allow the division of the land to such a great degree.

But Krenzlin also considers that the development of the *Gewannflur* is connected with the spread of the three-field system of agriculture. This accounts for the division of the block parcels to a higher degree than would have been necessary simply for the functioning of a system of partible inheritance. Krenzlin agrees that there are inconsistencies in this theory, but she argues that these can be simply explained in the majority of cases. In Messbach in the Odenwald for instance, in spite of the three-field system being used in the nineteenth century, there is little indication of the *Vergewannung* – the creation of a *Gewannflur*. This is explained by the lapse in time between the adoption of a system and the changes in the field pattern to take account of it. In Messbach the three-field system was only adopted in the nineteenth century and the *Vergewannung* has not had a chance thoroughly to change the field pattern.

Krenzlin's research, on which these findings were based was carried out in a small area in south Germany. She claimed that her theories could be applied throughout south Germany, but she also claimed that the *Langstreifenflur* on the *Esch* in northwest Germany was also developed from an original block-field

[18] Krenzlin and Reusch., *op. cit.*, p. 105
[19] Nitz, H. J., 'Siedlungsbeiträge zum Problem der fränkischen Staatskolonisation im süddeutschen Raum', *Zt. f. Agrargeschichte und Agrarsoziologie*, Vol. 11, 1963, pp. 34-62

pattern. In other words, throughout Germany the early field pattern, which developed after the initial settlement of the Germanic tribes, was the *Blockflur* or the wide-strip field pattern.

The early German settlements may have been small hamlets or isolated farms with a field pattern divided into blocks, as the most recent research both in south and north-west Germany suggests. Given the fragmentary nature of the evidence and the inadequate research technique, wide, generalizing conclusions cannot be drawn. In spite of this most research workers have claimed universality for their findings. The lack of substantial evidence to test the theories which have been promoted means that we shall never have complete certainty that these theories approach the truth. The crude generalizations of Meitzen have been refuted by research done throughout Germany, but the enormous effort which had been put into the search for the early settlement forms since Meitzen wrote, has borne relatively little fruit.

Settlement on the North Sea coast

Settlement studies have, however, brought substantial results in one particular area of Germany. The form of settlement in the North Sea coastal area from around the birth of Christ until the fifth and sixth century has been successfully reconstructed through excavations. So numerous are the excavations and so clear is the evidence that generalizations can indeed be made for this small part of Germany.

The *Marsch* is a low plain spreading inland up to twenty kilometres to the edge of the peat bog or sandy *Geest*, which themselves rise only a few feet above sea level[20]. The *Marsch* stretches further inland along the Weser and Elbe rivers. The area did not become free from flooding until the dikes were built from the eleventh century onwards, and even then there were numerous dike breaches during the later medieval period, when some of the great coastal embayments were formed. During the centuries immediately before the birth of Christ serious floods were relatively rare but during the first century A.D. a period of increasingly severe flooding set in. The relative rise in sea level continued throughout the first millennium A.D. with only a slight respite during the eighth and ninth centuries.

The relative movement of sea level is reflected in the form of

[20] The word *Marsch* is used in Germany to describe the area of clays and silts running parallel to the coast or along the coastal rivers.

settlement. In the first century B.C. the settlements in the *Marsch* were at ground level for flooding was not a great danger. As flooding increased in frequency and severity in the first centuries A.D., so the inhabitants were forced to raise their settlements on artificial mounds, above the level of the *Marsch*. Through the centuries the mounds were continually raised and enlarged, until many of them, if not all, were deserted in the fifth and sixth centuries A.D. Many of the mounds seem to have been reoccupied during the eighth century and some new ones were constructed. With the building of the dikes it became unnecessary to site farms on artificial mounds and many new settlements were founded at *Marsch* level. The old sites continued, however, to function as settlement sites and in the Krummhörn, north-west of Emden, almost all building is still confined to the old mounds.

These mounds remain obvious topographic features in the flat *Marsch*, whether occupied or deserted. They presented obvious objects for excavation. With settlement continuity over as long

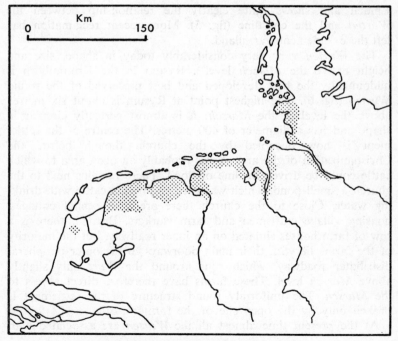

Fig. 4. The distribution of Wurten in north-west Europe

a period as seven centuries and with the mounds divided into several settlement horizons, more has been learnt about early Germanic settlement form, agricultural economy and society in the *Marsch* than about any other region in Germany. For this reason it is important to discuss at some length the results of research on these mound settlements, called in Germany *Wurten* or *Warfen* and in the Netherlands, *Terpen*.

The distribution of the *Wurt* settlements is shown in figure 4. They spread in a more or less continuous belt from the eastern shore of the Ijssel Meer through to southern Jutland, with a small isolated area in Noord Holland. This line is only broken where the *Geest* reaches the coast, that is at the Jadebusen and near Cuxhaven or where the *Marsch* has been reclaimed from the sea since the construction of the dikes as in Noord Holland, the Harlebucht and the Oste Marsch. To understand the location of the *Wurten,* it is essential to reconstruct the coastline as well as is possible at approximately the period when these settlements were founded. This has been done for the Krummhörn north of Emden and shows quite clearly the relationship between the *Wurten* and the coastline (fig. 5). More recent reclamation has left these settlements far inland.

The *Wurten* vary very considerably today in shape, size and height above the *Marsch* level[21]. Rysum in the Krummhörn is undoubtedly the best developed and best preserved of the round Wurten (fig. 6). The highest point at Rysum is about six metres above the level of the *Marsch*; it is almost perfectly circular in shape and has a diameter of 400 metres. The centre of the settlement is now occupied by the church, though before the Christianization of the area it was probably an open area to which cattle could be driven in time of flood. There remains next to the church a small pond, which was used to provide cattle with drinking water. Close to the church there are many small cottages, housing village craftsmen and farm workers. Beyond, there is a row of farm houses situated on an inner roadway, but the majority of the farms lie with their main doorways to the outer peripheral distributer roadway, which runs around the *Wurt* only slightly above *Marsch* level. These farms have therefore direct access to the *Marsch*. The uniformly round structure of the settlement is broken only by the open site of the former castle.

At the present time almost all the *Wurten* are associated with

[21] Reinhardt, W., 'Studien zur Entwicklung des ländlichen Siedlungsbildes in den Seemarschen der ostfriesischen Westküste', *Probleme der Küstenforschung im südlichen Nordseegebiet,* Vol. 8, Hildesheim 1965

a field pattern consisting of small blocks, with a considerable degree of fragmentation. Where the farmers on the *Wurten* hold polderland, this is generally divided into strips. The degree of fragmentation varies between settlements near the coast and those

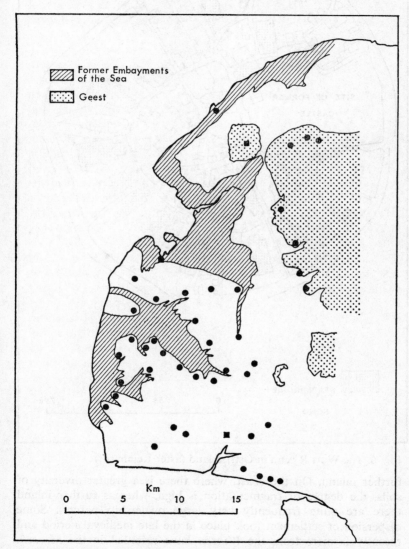

Fig. 5. The relationship of Wurt location and the former coastline (after Wildvang)

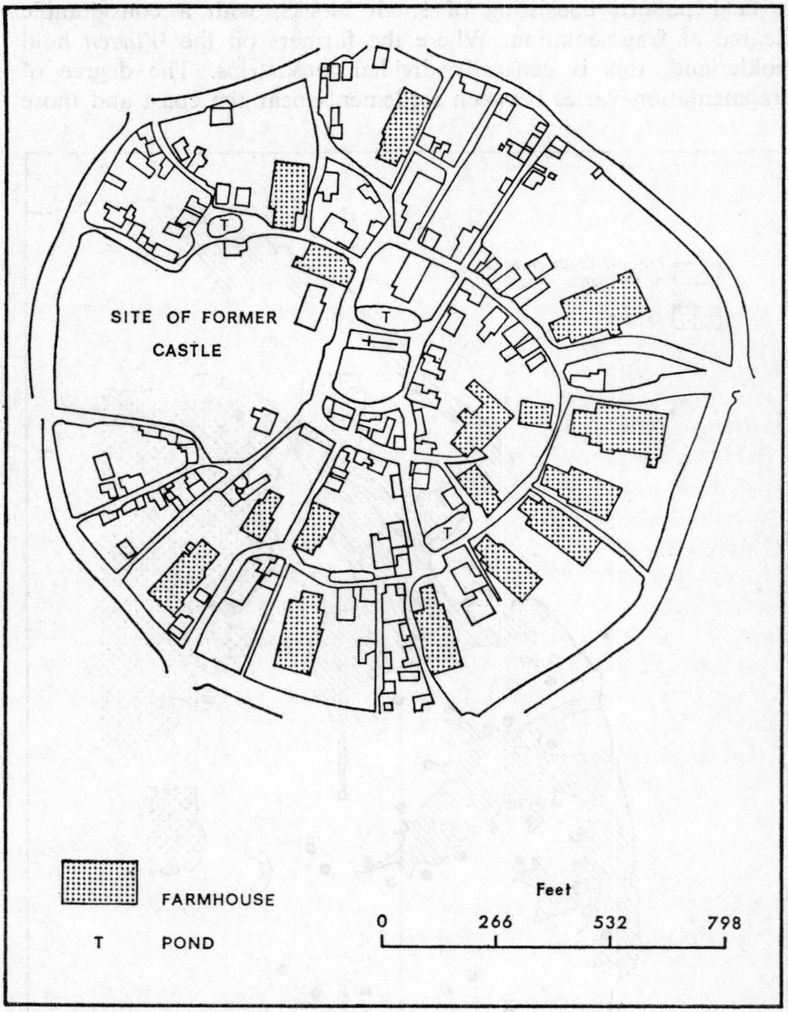

SITE OF FORMER CASTLE

FARMHOUSE

T POND

Feet

| 0 | 266 | 532 | 798 |

Fig. 6. The Wurt Rysum in Ostfriesland (after Reinhardt)

further inland. On the coast, where there is a greater diversity of soils, the degree of fragmentation is high, whereas further inland there are quite frequently very large ownership parcels. Some dispersion of settlement took place in the late medieval period and recently farmers from the *Wurten* have resettled in the *Marsch*. In both cases the farmland was consolidated and fragmentation cut to a minimum. The *Wurten* remain, however, farming centres

and the fragmentation of ownership parcels is a serious problem.
The origins of settlement in the *Marsch* have been traced to at
least the late Neolithic period through excavations in Holland. In
Germany, it is at Jemgum, south-east of Emden on an old arm
of the Ems, where the most interesting evidence of early settlement has been found[22]. The settlement of Jemgum spans the
period from the end of the Bronze Age to the early Iron Age and
was given up apparently because of severe flooding in the fifth
century B.C. This was an isolated settlement or at most
a very small hamlet. Unlike the farmhouses found in the Iron
Age settlements in the *Marsch*, at Jemgum house and barn are
separate buildings. The house was surrounded by a fence to separate it from the farm buildings. There was no sign of buildings to
house cattle, though evidence for the existence of cattle at the
settlement was discovered. It is also certain that there was some
arable cultivation and that the main function of the farm buildings
was as storehouses for the grain crop. Many of the findings at
Jemgum are supported by those at a recent excavation of a contemporary settlement at Hatzum, some seven kilometres down-
stream from Jemgum[23]. There appear to be two main differences,
however; firstly Hatzum was a far larger settlement covering at
least 2 hectares and secondly the dwelling and the barn are under
one roof. The unit farmhouse here is similar to the Lower German
House, which occurs very frequently today in northern Germany,
and to those houses found in excavations of settlements of the
late-Latène period.

A recolonization of the *Marsch* seems to have started in the
first century B.C. This finding draws support from almost all
excavations from the first important one by van Giffen at Ezinge[24]
to the most recent and most illuminating by Haarnagel at
Feddersen-Wierde[25]. Feddersen-Wierde is a deserted *Wurt* in a line

[22] Haarnagel, W., 'Die spätbronze-frühneuzeitliche Gehöftsiedlung
Jemgum bei Leer auf dem linken Ufer der Ems', *Die Kunde* (Neue Folge),
Vol. 8 1-2, Berlin, 1957
[23] Haarnagel, W., 'Die Untersuchung einer spätbronze-alteisenzeitlichen
Siedlung in Boomborg/Hatzum, Kreis Leer, in den Jahren 1963 und
1964 und ihr vorläufiges Ergebnis', *Neue Ausgrabungen in Niedersachsen*,
Vol. 2, Hildesheim 1965
[24] van Giffen, A. E., 'Der Warf in Ezinge Provinz Groningen, Holland,
und seine westgermanischen Häuser', *Germania*, Vol. 20/1, Berlin 1936
[25] Haarnagel, W., 'Die Grabung Feddersen-Wierde und Ihre Bedeutung
für die Erkenntnisse der bäuerlichen Besiedlung im Küstengebiet in dem
Zeitraum vom 1. Jahrhundert vor bis 5. Jahrhundert n. Chr.' *Zeitschrift
f. Agrargeschichte und Agrarsoziologie*, Vol. 10/2 pp. 145-157, 1962
Haarnagel, W., 'Die prähistorischen Siedlungsformen im Küstengebiet
der Nordsee', *Erdkundliches Wissen*, Vol 18, 1968, pp. 67-79

of *Wurten* to the east of the Weser, marking the edge of a former flood plain. It rises just under four metres above the level of the surrounding *Marsch*, has a diameter of 200 metres and covers some 4 hectares. It was possible to separate seven different settlement horizons, covering a time span from the first century B.C. to the end of the fourth or start of the fifth century A.D.

Like the settlements at Jemgum and Hatzum, the earliest settlement here was at *Marsch* level. Van Giffen proved this also at Ezinge. The first artificial mounds were built in the first century A.D. when flooding had become quite serious. They were small but long *Wurten*, rising to about one metre above ground level. With their construction the form of settlement changed completely. Whereas the settlement had previously been a linear one, now the individual house mounds were constructed radially around an open space. This then remained the form of settlement until the desertion of Feddersen-Wierde. There was a considerable expansion of the village in the second and third centuries A.D., when a ring of new houses was built around the original ring. Gradually the increase in the number of mounds and the need continually to raise them yet higher above the *Marsch* led to the coalescence of the many individual *Wurten* into one large oval village mound (*Dorfwurt*). This form has been preserved to the present day in the *Dorfwurten* of the Krummhörn and at Ziallens in the Jeverland, north of Oldenburg, but elsewhere in the German *Marsch* the movement of some farmers into the *Marsch* has led to a change in the form of settlement.

The excavation at Feddersen-Wierde revealed a clear picture of the economic life of the settlement and produced interesting evidence about the social structure. Both arable and pastoral farming were practised but the bones of wild animals, antlers and a fish-net prove that hunting and fishing were also carried on. Beans, oats, barley and flax were certainly cultivated and some idea of the location of arable cultivation and the size and form of the fields could be gained. The fields were always located on the relatively dry sandy banks of the small streams which flow through the *Marsch* (*Priele*). The same position was chosen when the fields had to be moved to accommodate an expansion of the settlement. The arable was divided into small irregular blocks, the length of which was determined by the distance between the streams, while the width appears to have fluctuated between 30 and 50 metres. Unfortunately, it has not yet been possible to establish the area of arable land associated with the village or with any one particular farm.

The farmhouses at Feddersen-Wierde were at all periods of the Lower German type, both the dwelling and the cattle stalls under one roof. The living accommodation was separated from the cattle stalls and the small working area by a partition. The cattle boxes were separated from each other by small wicker divides. The number of cattle boxes varied from house to house, showing that there were considerable wealth differences in Feddersen-Wierde. There were houses 30 metres long by 5.5 metres wide, which could house 30 to 32 head of cattle, while at the other extreme the small 10m by 4.5m houses had room for only 2 to 4 head.

The farmhouses are found in all the horizons at Feddersen-Wierde in groups, each group being surrounded by a fence to divide it from the next. The groups consisted of a larger farmhouse and one or more smaller houses. This suggests that the social structure of the settlement was based on the extended family group and that within the family there was one more important and wealthier farmer. The relationship between the leader of the group and the other members cannot be ascertained from the excavation. Differences occurred not only within the group but also between groups. The number of houses within the fenced enclosures varied as did the size of the house.

From the first century after Christ, one farm stands out above the rest in each settlement horizon. This farm is distinguished by the larger number of buildings associated with it and by its size. The cattle were not housed in the same building as the living accommodation, but in a separate building which was probably serviced by labourers, rather than the farmer himself. By the third century, this farm had been separated from the rest of the village by a sturdy oak fence and by a ditch. The location of the village hall immediately next to this farm rather than in the centre of the village suggests that the owner of the farm had a rather special position in the social and economic life of the village. Close to this compound, a large area was used for the working of iron and bronze and this area grew larger through the centuries. The position of this craft area and the existence close by of large food-storage buildings suggests that the large estate owner kept a group of craftsmen who were not engaged in farming on their own account. At the same time it is obvious from the finds of Roman coins and other products that the estate owner was also engaged in trading beyond the local area. In most of the late medieval *Wurten*, a castle on the eastern side of the *Wurt* was characteristic (figure 6). This suggests a continuous development from a large farm or estate in the first centuries after Christ to a castle by the end of the first millennium. Any line of development was, however, broken in Feddersen-Wierde and in most other *Wurten* by the complete desertion of the settlements in the fourth and fifth centuries A.D.

The reason for the desertion of these settlements could conceivably have been the increasing severity and frequency of flooding. It is possible that both the pasturing of cattle on the *Marsch* and the cultivation of the arable on the sandy areas between the *Priele* became extremely difficult and that eventually the population was forced to move inland. The population in the *Marsch* may also have been caught up in the great folk movements. It was not until the seventh or eighth centuries that the old *Wurten* were reoccupied or new ones constructed. Several of these new generation mound settlements had a completely different character from the agricultural *Wurten* of the pre-fifth century A.D. period. There appeared now long narrow mounds on which the buildings were very small craftsmen's houses closely packed together. These were some of the great trading centres of early medieval Europe, the *Wike*, whose trading links were especially well developed with the great cities of the lower Rhine. Although today the *Wike* settlements like Emden, Groothusen and Nesse lie some way inland, they were located on arms of the sea or navigable river channels at the time of their foundation[26]. Their origin as trading and craft centres is supported not only by the type of house which was built on them, but also by the finds of Rhineland pottery, which have been made during excavations at Emden and Groothusen[27].

The importance of the **Wurt** settlements is that through the favourable circumstances for archaeological investigation, it has been possible not only to trace the form of settlement and the house forms, but also to learn a great deal about the economy and the social order. Since, in the rest of Germany, one can only conjecture about the form of settlement and the economic and social life of the times up to the ninth century, the evidence from the *Wurten* is all the more important, although one must beware of assuming that the findings here can be applied elsewhere.

[26] Reinhardt, *op. cit.*
[27] *ibid.*, pp. 96-97

2 The spread of settlement in east and west

In the first chapter it was mentioned that the *Wurten* were reoccupied in the seventh and eighth centuries and new settlements were founded. Evidence for the spreading of settlement and the colonization of new areas has been collected for many parts of Germany at this time, so that it is reasonable to assume a general upward trend in population and extension of settlement.

The most frequently quoted figures used to demonstrate this expansion in the Carolingian period are perhaps those for Hailfingen near Tübingen, where the investigation of grave sites suggested a population of only 20 for the early sixth century but 250 for the early eighth century[1]. In Angeln, the north-eastern corner of Schleswig-Holstein, Jankuhn has proved conclusively that the region was suddenly deserted in the fifth and early sixth centuries, but that a new settlement began around A.D. 800[2]. In the Mosel region, Lamprecht demonstrated an increase in population from A.D. 800 until the mid-thirteenth century[3]. The expansion of population and settlement in the period from the eighth to the thirteenth centuries was seen in the expansion of old established villages and in the colonization of new lands. New colonization, we shall see, took place both in western Germany on the fringes of the settled areas but also in eastern Germany, the areas which though formerly occupied by Germanic peoples were now settled by Slavs.

The expansion of existing settlements

The size of settlements about A.D. 800 will have varied quite

[1] Dannenbauer, H., *Bevölkerung und Besiedlung Alemanniens*, 1958
[2] Jankuhn, H., ' Die Entstehung der mittelalterlichen Agrarlandschaft in Angeln ', *Geografiska Annaler*, Vol. 43, (1/2) 1961, page 159
[3] Lamprecht, K., *Deutsches Wirtschaftsleben im Mittelalter, Vol. 1*, 1886

considerably, but the evidence which is available suggests that there were already large villages in existence. Dannenbauer's example of Hailfingen, mentioned above, suggests that the settlement had a population of around 250 in the eighth century. In the Bauland, east of the Odenwald, the Monastery at Lorsch received such large areas of land in gifts from the settlement Seckach that it is certain that Seckach must have consisted of more than fifteen farms. It is of course not clear whether these farms formed a nucleated settlement or whether they were dispersed throughout the parish[4]. Perhaps it was only in the most favourable areas for settlement that large villages occurred, elsewhere smaller hamlets being more general. In the Weser-Ems *Geest* in the far north of Germany, the small hamlet settlements, the *Drubbel*, rarely had more than three or four farms at this time and they were mixed in with a large number of *Einzelhöfe*. There was also still a very large area of unused land between the settlements, so that the density of settlement was very low[5].

What is clear is that throughout Germany the existing settlements expanded rapidly from about A.D. 800 onwards. The expansion took place both through the growth outwards of the built-up area and of the fields and also through the founding of daughter settlements some way from the old settlements. On the fertile loess plain (*Gäulandschaften*) surrounding the Odenwald, the settlement pattern which we know today was almost complete by A.D. 800, but from this date the village expanded in area and daughter settlements like Leutershausen near Weinheim were founded[6]. The period between the reoccupation of the *Marsch* and the large-scale construction of dikes was also a time when the settlements on the *Wurten* were expanded and many new *Wurten* constructed[7]. These daughter settlements are especially common in the *Marsch* and perhaps reflect the difficulty of transport on the heavy clay soils. When the population increased it would have proved difficult to farm extra land on the edge of the existing fields because of the long transport distance involved.

[4] Matzat, W., 'Flurgeographischt Studien im Bauland und Hinteren Odenwald', *Rhein-Mainische Forschungen*, Vol. 53, Frankfurt/Main 1963, p. 35
[5] Clemens, P., 'Lastrup und seine Bauernschaften', *Schriften der wirtschaftswissenschaftlichen Gesellschaft zum Studium Niedersachsens*, Vol. 40 1955
[6] Nitz, H. J., 'Die ländlichen Siedlungsformen des Odenwaldes', *Heidelberger Geog. Arb.*, Vol. 7. 1962, pp. 19-20
[7] Reinhardt, W., 'Studien zur Entwicklung des ländlichen Siedlungsbildes in den Seemarschen der ostfriesischen Westküste', *Probleme der Küstenforschung im südlichen Nordseegebiet*, Vol. 8, Hildesheim, 1965

To cut the transport costs new small mounds were constructed for just one or two farms on the edge of the cultivated area. From the old *Wurt* of Eilsum near Emden, for instance, the settlements of Hösingwehr, Mittelstewehr and Uiterstewehr were founded.

In those areas which had been settled early by the Germanic tribes therefore, both the size of the existing settlements and the density of the settlement pattern increased. During the period of five centuries after A.D. 800 many of the large nucleated *Haufendörfer* came into existence. The term *Haufendorf*, as used here, has no generic significance, nor is its use regionally restricted. It is simply a convenient term for describing a large village, with densely packed houses and with no obvious planned origin. The farm buildings lie cramped on narrow lanes, and where roads widen out buildings stand often chaotically in the middle of them. It is quite frequently observed even today that the edge of the *Haufendorf* is clearly marked by roads or a path and that beyond this perimeter no development has taken place at all. In most cases the *Haufendorf* is a secondary settlement form having grown from a small village or hamlet. But the reasons for this development and the time at which it took place vary very much from area to area.

An interesting example of *Haufendörfer* which must have developed at an early period are those of the Hildesheimer Börde (loess plain) in north Germany. In fig. 7, it can be seen that here the villages are large with a very definite perimeter marked by a path and that beyond this path little development has taken place. The interesting thing is the position of the church in the oldest settlements. In Gross Himstedt, for instance, the church is on the edge of the village. This is a rather unusual position, for wherever possible the church was placed at the centre of the settlement. On the *Wurten* for instance, most of which were in existence when the area was Christianized, the open space at the centre of the *Wurt* was used for the construction of the church, in spite of the usefulness of this open area for herding cattle at times of flood. This suggests that in Gross Himstedt the *Haufendorf* as it exists today may have been more or less complete at the time of the Christianization in the ninth century. It will be noticed that Klein Himstedt, a daughter settlement of Gross Himstedt, developing far later, has the church at its centre.

Krenzlin also sees the period from the eleventh to the thirteenth centuries as one during which the *Gewannflur* was created. The rise in population coupled with a limitation on the area of new land which could be taken into cultivation may have led to the

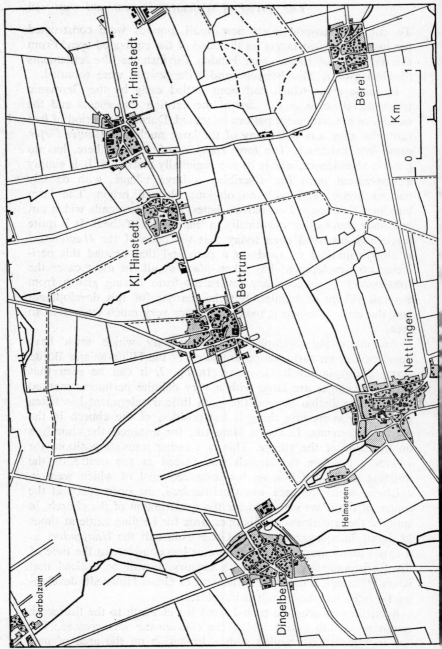

Fig. 7. Villages in the Hildesheimer Börde (from the 1:50,000 topographical map of Germany)

division of existing land parcels into much smaller units[8]. But this process of expansion both in the settlement and in the field pattern will only have affected some of the most fertile areas. These may well have included the Hildesheimer Börde, and the *Gäulandschaften*, mentioned above, both of them fertile loess lowlands. Elsewhere the development of the *Gewannflur* and the *Haufendorf* (the two need not necessarily occur together) came far later after the period of settlement desertion in the fourteenth century.

In north-west Germany the period from the eleventh to the thirteenth centuries was also one of settlement expansion. For the first time there appeared ' half-entitled ' farmers, the *Halbbauern*, who only had half the rights on the commons which the *Vollbauern* had. At the same time cottagers begin to be mentioned in documents around the twelfth century. These people had only a very small area of arable land on the *Esch* and very restricted rights to use of the *Mark*. The early cottagers were however ' *Erbkötter* ', that is they were allowed to leave their holding to their heirs, without interference from the *Vollbauern*. The *Halbbauern* were almost certainly to some extent the result of the division of fully-entitled holdings as land became scarce. Occasionally holdings may have been founded with only half rights from the beginning. It seems probable in the case of the *Erbkötter*, that they may have been the non-inheriting sons of farmers, who were given a small area of the home farm and were eventually recognized as independent farmers. Both of these new classes of farmer strove to attain a higher status in the hamlet and this they occasionally did, in spite of the general resistance to change of the established farmers. A few centuries after their establishment, it is not uncommon to find *Erbkötter* counted as *Vollbauern*. With the addition of these groups, the old *Drubbel* began to grow and in many cases the infield was extended somewhat, though this was limited by the size of the outfield. Fields were also taken into private ownership on the common land and especially in the valleys, where private meadows could be created. Even on the relatively poor *Geest* soils therefore, expansion of the existing settlements took place during the high and late medieval period.

Not only did existing settlements expand, but also daughter settlements were founded. The concentration of the growing population within the existing villages, which Krenzlin suggests

[8] Krenzlin, A., ' Zur Genese der Gewannflur in Deutschland ', *Geog. Annaler*, Vol. 43, 1961, p. 195

as the cause of the division of the fields into small parcels, was frequently not the whole story. The daughter settlements in the *Marsch* and on the loess in both the *Gäulandschaften* and in the Hildesheimer Börde have already been mentioned. These new settlements were probably an attempt to reduce the transport costs of reaching the edges of the village fields, enlarged many times in the centuries after A.D. 800. But there is also evidence of the disintegration of some existing settlements and the creation of a dispersed pattern of *Einzelhöfe*. For the same reason, the growth of existing settlements often seems to have been in the form of *Einzelhöfe*, loosely arranged around the margin of the old village. In Westfalia some villages were deserted as the farmers moved out to build *Einzelhöfe*.

Only a part of the population increase was accommodated in the areas of existing settlement, however. From the areas of early Germanic settlement, farmers spread out both into the unsettled areas of western Germany and into the area beyond the Elbe occupied by the Slavs.

Land-holding, the nobility and the peasant in the high middle ages

Before we look at the process and pattern of colonization, it is essential to discuss the pattern of land-holding in the Carolingian period and after[9].

The Frankish emperor owned all the land in the empire. The amount of land under his control grew very rapidly, through the conquest of the other Germanic tribes. The additions were particularly extensive during the reign of Charles the Great. By the time of his death the empire stretched from the Pyrenees and Brittany eastwards to Austria and the Elbe and south to beyond Rome. In his reign of almost 50 years he conquered the Saxons and the Bavarians and established some degree of control over the Slav peoples living east of the Elbe and Saale. There was no shortage of land; it was people rather than land which were scarce.

To administer and defend this vast empire the emperor needed a reliable system of organization. To his followers who took on the responsibility of organization he gave large areas of land, both as a reward and to increase their dependence on himself.

Large areas of waste were given over to the control of territorial lords and to the Church. This land was quite frequently of little value when it was first granted to the lord or monastery, but later

9 Abel, W., 'Die drei Epochen der deutschen Agrargeschichte', *Schriftenreihe für ländliche Sozialfragen*, Vol. 37, 1962, pp. 24-30

as the population rose and the area of settlement expanded, it became more valuable. In these largely unoccupied areas, the ruler was able to state the conditions of settlement to anyone wishing to settle. In the older settled areas, which came under the rule of the territorial lords, more or less free farmers became subject to the rule of the lord and were forced to make payments and perform services for him. The processes through which this legal situation was altered are not completely clear, but it is probable that there was a mixture of force, persuasion and free decision involved.

It should be made clear that though the farmer had to make payments in kind or money to the lord, he had more right to his land than simply a tenant would have. Abel speaks of a sort of double ownership of land; the lord was the superior owner and the farmer the inferior owner[10]. The farmer had a right to his land, in spite of attempts by many lords to alter the legal situation. These attempts often led to serious conflict between lord and farmer, which culminated in the farmers' wars of the early sixteenth century, which led in practice to the extinction of many of these traditional farmers' rights.

The large-scale land-holding typical of the Frankish period began to change into a pattern of smaller holdings about the end of the first millennium. The territorial lords in the Frankish period employed local officials, the *Meier*, to cultivate their farms and to gather the payments made by the farmers. The *Meier* lived on the lord's farm, the *Fronhof*, and was essentially a farmer. In many cases the *Meier* became very powerful and eventually usurped some of the rights of the territorial lord. Sometimes the lord turned his relationship with his officials into a landlord-tenant relationship to work against the move towards independence of his *Meier*. With the break up of the old system of the territorial lords, the place of the *Meier* was taken by the knightly vassal, more interested in the hunt than in farming. The lord therefore lost interest in farming his own land and in general the *Fronhöfe* became smaller or were closed and the rents that were paid became the main interest.

It is most important to appreciate the relative importance of the territorial lords and the settlers in the colonization of the waste and of the east German lands. This was an operation which was organized, controlled and financed by very large and wealthy landowners, and was not simply a spontaneous movement out from the old areas of settlement by farmers seeking new land. This is

10 Abel, *op. cit.*, p. 24

often not fully appreciated. It is very clear in the east German colonial settlements, that there was a high degree of organization and leadership, which is reflected in the regularly planned village forms and field patterns. But even in the western parts of Germany, where there seem to be fewer planned settlements, we shall see that most of the colonization in the high and later middle ages took place under the control of territorial lords or of local rulers, who had obtained permission from the territorial lord to settle farmers on the land.

New settlement in western Germany

Abel quotes the chronicler Lampert von Hersfeld to give some idea of the emptiness of many areas in Germany in the later middle ages. Lampert, describing the Harz as ' an enormously large forest ', went on to write about a column marching ' through the primeval forest for three days without anything to eat on a narrow path, which was only known to a very few. This path had been discovered by the leader, a hunter, who had found it while exploring the remote parts of the forest. On the fourth day they reached Eschwege, completely exhausted through hunger, the night watches and the rigours of the long journey '[11]. This journey was made in 1073 and we must assume that almost three centuries earlier at the beginning of the ninth century, many of the upland areas of Germany, the forests and scrub, the marshes and peat bogs were unsettled. The population of Germany was concentrated on the more fertile low-lying areas.

The rise in population from the ninth century onwards and the consequent demand for more land gave the territorial lords a chance to increase their incomes through the settlement of the lands, which they had been granted by the emperor. The settler had to pay land-taxes to the lord (*Grundzinsen*) and was frequently forced to perform services on the lord's land. Apart from this there were the church taxes to pay (*Zehntabgaben*) which in the later middle ages were often collected by the local lords. For the settler additional taxes had to be paid to the local representatives of the landowner – payments for local defence were often paid to the *Vogt* (*Vogteiabgaben*) for example. Frequently a few years free of taxes were granted to the settler to allow him to establish himself, but from then on he gave a proportion of his produce (and generally it was a large part of his total production) for taxes

[11] Quoted in Abel, W., *op. cit.*, p. 16, from Lampert von Hersfeld, *Annalen*

to the individuals who held positions of authority over him.

Of all the large landowners, it was the Church which perhaps played the major part in the settlement of the waste during the earliest periods of colonization. Under the Carolingians, and especially during the reign of Charles the Great, the Church received gifts covering enormous land areas. The great Benedictine monasteries founded in the eighth and ninth centuries like those at Reichenau on Lake Constance (A.D. 724), Fulda (A.D. 744), Werden on the Ruhr (A.D. 796) and Corvey on the Weser (A.D. 822) rapidly acquired large territories, as did some of the Bishops like those of Würzburg, Mainz, Cologne and Paderborn. The bishop of Würzburg had a large area of Hessen at the end of the eighth century, stretching north to around Höxter on the Weser (in Nordrhein-Westfalen today), while Corvey gained control over land not only on the Weser in the vicinity of the monastery, but also in East Friesland and the Weser-Ems Raum[12]. Through the settlement of the areas granted to them, the monasteries and dioceses became extremely wealthy and it was not until the break-up of all central control and the loss of rights to the local representatives of the large landowners in the twelfth century (fall of Heinrich der Löwe in 1180) that the star of the monasteries and of some bishops began to wane.

An example of the colonizing work of the monasteries is provided by the activities of the Monastery of Lorsch, founded about A.D. 760 on the Bergstrasse between the present towns of Darmstadt and Heidelberg[13]. This monastery played an important part in the settlement of the Odenwald, which in A.D. 800 was unoccupied. Around 800, the Odenwald was passed from the direct control of the king to the church or to secular rulers. In 766 Pippin gave a large part of the northern Odenwald to the monastery at Fulda, and Charles the Great gave the western and southern parts (Heppenheim and the Heppenheimer Waldmark) to Lorsch in 733. Ludwig der Fromme, the son of Charles, gave the southeastern part of the Odenwald to a private individual, Einhard, but he in turn left this area of the Michaelstädter Mark to Lorsch at his death. The southern area, the Ladenburger Mark fell to the Bishop of Worms and much of the eastern Odenwald probably went to the monastery at Amorbach, which had also been founded in the eighth century. Most of the Odenwald was therefore in the hands of ecclesiastical bodies by the first half of the ninth century.

[12] Metz, W., ' Mainzer, Fuldaer und Würzburger Einflüsse an der oberen Weser ', *Kunst und Kultur im Weserraum 800-1600,* Münster 1966, pp. 122-6
[13] Nitz, *op. cit.,* p. 21ff.

The Benedictines in Lorsch received land in large quantities not only from the emperor but also from small farmers and large secular rulers. Nitz cites the case of Handschuhsheim, near Heidelberg, where more than a hundred individuals gave land within a generation[14]. Some gave their whole farm. They probably joined in the settlement of the Odenwald, which was being carried on by Lorsch. Another source of colonists undoubtedly came from the gifts of unfree peasants, which were made by the larger landowners to the monastery. Lorsch received, for instance, 64 villeins in one gift in 790 and even as many as 102 in another gift in 877. With the financial might and the organizational skill of the monastery behind them, the settlers had a good chance of establishing themselves in the Odenwald.

The colonization of the Heppenheimer and Michaelstädter Marken followed a course typical for most of the regions settled first by the Benedictines. Following the river valleys into the uplands, the monastery established large farms in key situations to serve as local colonization bases (*Klosterhöfe*). In the Heppenheimer Mark for instance *Klosterhöfe* were laid out at Mörlenbach and Fürth, both of which lie at key points for the settlement of valleys leading up to the high Odenwald. Both became centres of administrative districts (*Villikationen*), Fürth having nine settlements in its area. By the end of the eleventh century almost all of the Odenwald in the hands of Lorsch had been settled. The colonies had been given over to officials of the monastery to administer, and all the colonies were contributing to the financial wellbeing of both these officials and the monastery itself. When the power of the monastery began to decline in the middle of the twelfth century, only a few small areas were left for the rising local aristocracy to colonize.

Yet not all the land owned by the Church was colonized by a central power like Lorsch[15]. In the southern Odenwald, the Bishop of Worms allowed local lords to undertake the colonization. The bishop founded a Cistercian abbey at Schönau in 1142 but it is not clear whether the monks were responsible for any colonization. Probably by this time much of the forest had been cleared by local lords and settled, with or without the permission of Worms. They laid out small groups of settlements close together, so that there was no settlement planning on a large scale as was practised by Lorsch.

The importance of local feudal lords for the colonization of the

14 Nitz, *op. cit.*, pp. 22-23
15 Nitz, *op. cit.*, pp. 27-29

waste areas grew as the power of the territorial lords and the monasteries and dioceses declined. In the twelfth, thirteenth and early fourteenth centuries small groups of settlements were being founded in western Germany in place of the regional colonization by the large landowners in the ninth, tenth and early eleventh centuries. Monasteries (especially the reformed Benedictines, and Cistercians) were still engaged in clearing the forest and establishing new settlements but they were now of no more significance than a very large number of secular rulers.

A certain amount of regularity in the form of the settlements was assured through the use of settlement planners by the landowners. These planners (the *Reutmeister* or *Lokatoren*) were responsible for the design of the settlement and very frequently for the recruitment of settlers. They played a major part in the early success or failure of the colony and sometimes they were rewarded with a large holding in the new settlement. Occasionally these skills were sought from the experienced ecclesiastical circles. The Dukes of Schaumburg for instance invited the *Propst* of the Cistercian monastery at Rinteln to plan a settlement (Propsthagen) in the thirteenth century[16]. The use by numerous landowners of the same group of people to plan the new settlements led to the small-scale regularities in the new settlements in west Germany and the considerable degree of uniformity in the colonization of eastern Germany.

The influence of the large landowners on the high and late medieval colonization of the waste has been emphasized. But how much new settlement was carried through by individual farmers moving out of the old areas of Germanic settlement? Habbe maintains that the central Black Forest is an area where colonization by private individuals is dominant. Habbe points out that in this area the land belonging to some farms crosses the boundary between two feudal territories; this would have been unlikely if the settlement had been planned by one or other of the landowners[17]. On the North Sea coast too, it would appear that at least some of the late medieval settlement and reclamation of land was achieved through the collective efforts of the local farmers. And even where the local lord invited the Dutch to come into his territory and reclaim and settle the land, these settlers were

---

[16] Blohm, R., ' Die Hagenhufendörfer in Schaumburg-Lippe ', *Schriften der niedersächsischen Heimatbundes,* Vol. 10, 1943
[17] Habbe, K. A., ' Die " Waldhufensiedlungen " in den Gebirgen Südwestdeutschlands als Problem der systematischen Siedlungsgeographie ', *Berichte z. dt. Landeskunde,* Vol. 37, 1966, pp. 47-52

accepted as freemen for several centuries at least. Nevertheless in spite of these examples of individual initiative on the part of the farmers, it is true that by far the greater part of the colonization at this time was guided and financed by powerful landowners.

The clearance of the waste and the establishment of new settlements continued in western Germany from the eighth and ninth centuries through to the first half of the fourteenth century. As more and more land was cleared restrictions began to be placed on new forest clearance. The Duke of Homburg, for instance, ordered the Cistercian monks at the monastery of Amelungsborn, near Holmzinden on the Weser, to restrict their clearances to very small areas[18]. The colonization had been on a tremendous scale, and by the fourteenth century almost all the settlements of modern Germany had been founded and a good many which had been founded were to disappear shortly after in the period of settlement desertion. Abel quotes Wilhelm Koppes' description of the Bungsberge area between Lübeck and Kiel to emphasize the rapidity of the landscape changes in this period of settlement expansion. Whereas in the middle of the twelfth century this area was untouched forest, by the beginning of the fourteenth century ' the face of the country around the Bungsbergen had undergone a rapid change. Around the end of the thirteenth and the beginning of the fourteenth centuries there was a close network of villages, in the middle of arable land, on which rye, barley and oats and occasionally also wheat and peas were grown. The remains of the forest were grazed right up to the boundary with the neighbouring parish, unless the lord had a reason for prohibiting this '.[19]

The expansion of settlement was not confined to the wooded uplands of Germany. On the North Sea Coast a ' golden ring ' of dikes was constructed and for the first time protected large areas of *Marsch*, rather than individual settlements. In relative safety behind the dikes new settlements could be laid out. The first dikes were probably constructed around A.D. 1000 though the first references to them in western Germany are found in twelfth century documents. Often it was not until considerably later that a complete sea dike was constructed round a large area of coastline. In the area around Norden in East Friesland for instance, the first major continuous dike was not built until 1375. For the Land Hadeln,

[18] Jäger, H., ' Entwicklungsperioden agrarer Siedlungsgebiete im mittleren Westdeutschland seit dem frühen 13. Jahrhundert ', *Würzburger Geographische Arbeiten*, Vol. 6, 1958, p. 10

[19] Abel, W., *Die Geschichte der deutschen Landwirtschaft, vom frühen Mittelalter bis zum 19. Jahrhundert*, Stuttgart, 1967, p. 67

however, east of Cuxhaven, Hövermann recognizes dikes which were completed as early as the eleventh century, although Bierwirth disputes the accuracy of Hövermann's data[20].

Diking was common in the Netherlands long before the first sea dikes were built in Germany. As with other methods of reclamation or improved colonization in the *Marsch* and peat bogs of northern Germany, it was probably through Dutch immigrant settlers that the Germans became aware of the possibility of continuous dike protection. Though it is probable that dike construction and reclamation in some areas were carried through by local farmers, even here the idea probably came from the work of the Dutch elsewhere. Hövermann considered the settlement and reclamation in Land Wursten on the lower Weser to be the work of local nobles, who merely regularized the procedures of local farmers, who had been reclaiming land and laying out new settlements for a long time before the nobility took over[21]. But the work of Kersting and Mangels suggests that in the areas immediately surrounding Land Wursten, it was indeed Dutch settlers, invited by the great landlords (including the Bishop of Bremen and Hamburg) and given the privileges of Dutch law (Hollerrecht) who reclaimed and settled the land[22].

Not only did the Dutch build dikes and found new settlements behind them, they also drained and settled marshy areas along the coast and along the wide glacial melt-water channels (Urstromtäler). A document dated 1106 gives particulars of the agreement between the Archbishop of Bremen and Hamburg and Dutch settlers for the cultivation of fen land on the lower Weser. It lays down both the size of the holdings which were to be created (48 ha) and the taxes due to the Archbishop[23]. Several early documents record grants of land to colonial entrepreneurs or to colonists themselves on the basis of Dutch law. In 1149 for

[20] Hövermann, J., 'Die Entwicklung der Siedlungsformen in den Marschen des Elb-Weser-Winkels', *Forschungen zur deutschen Landeskunde*, vol. 56, 1951, map 10
Bierwirth, I., 'Siedlung und Wirtschaft im Lande Hadeln, eine kulturgeographische Untersuchung, *Forschungen zur deutschen Landeskunde*, Vol. 164, 1967, pp. 14-15
[21] Hövermann, *op. cit.*, pp. 80-81
[22] Kersting, W. C., 'Das Hollische Recht im Nordseeraum aufgewiesen besonders an Quellen des Landes Hadeln', *Jahrbuch der Männer vom Morgenstern*, part 1, Vol. 34, 1953; part 2, Vol. 35, 1954
Mangels, I., *Die Verfassung der Marschen am linken Ufer der Elbe im Mittelalter*, Bremen-Horn, 1957
[23] Helbig, H. and Weinrich, L., *Urkunden und erzählende Quellen zur deutschen Ostsiedlung im Mittelalter*, Darmstadt, 1968, pp. 42-45

D

instance, the Archbishop of Bremen and Hamburg granted un-drained land on the lower Weser (Stedingen) to two men for the founding of new settlements according to the rights and duties of the Dutch living in the area of Stade[24]. A further document from 1171 records the granting of badly drained land south and south-west of Bremen by Heinrich of Saxony and Bavaria to Friedrich of Mackenstedt, who was allowed to settle colonists again on the basis of the Dutch law[25]. These documents and several others point to both the direct participation of the Dutch in the coloniza-tion of fen land, but also their influence on colonization under-taken by Germans alone.

The colonization of east Germany

The expansion of Germanic settlement eastwards from the old area of Germanic colonization in western Germany began as early as A.D. 800. The most spectacular advances were, however, made in the twelfth and thirteenth centuries when German settlers pressed into east-central Europe through Poland to the Baltic states and south-eastwards into Silesia, Moravia, Bohemia and western Hungary. The Germans transformed the economy of central Europe, settling the waste, opening up mines and creating trading networks[26].

The earliest movement was by the Bavarians in southern Germany. They pushed down the Danube from their territory on the Enns and began the opening up and settlement of the eastern Alps. This colonizing movement was strengthened from the second half of the tenth century, when large areas in Austria were settled. In the north, Heinrich I of Saxony defeated the Slavs in 928-9, and in 933 the Hungarians were defeated at Riade, south-east of the Harz. These victories were followed up by the establishment of the frontier *Mark* organization, which affected the whole area east to the Oder and Neisse rivers. Several new bishoprics were established as centres from which the conversion of the Slavs could be achieved (Schleswig, Oldenburg, Havelberg and Branden-burg in 948, Meissen, Merseburg and Zeitz in 968, Prague in 973 and Olmütz in 975). Yet there was little Germanic settlement during this period, and in 983, the Slavs rose against the invading Germans and expelled them from the lands east of the Elbe.

[24] Helbig, and Weinrich, *op. cit.,* pp. 46-49
[25] *ibid,* pp. 48-51
[26] Perhaps the best account of the colonization of east Germany in English is by Hermann Aubin in the *Cambridge Economic History of Europe,* Vol. 1, 2nd ed., Cambridge, 1966

Fig. 8. The high-medieval German colonization in the east (after
W. Kuhn)

Colonization had to wait for more permanent conquest.

The famous call of Pope Urban II in 1095 for the conquest of
the Holy Land (Deus lo volt) was followed 13 years later by a
similar exhortation to the Germans to attack and destroy the
heathen Slavs. The ecclesiastical and secular rulers of eastern
Saxony recorded the ill-treatment of Christians by the Slavs in
gruesome detail, and then, comparing the situation with that of
Jerusalem, they called on the Germans to rise up and conquer
for the sake of the Church. They also mentioned that there was
good land to be occupied (Quapropter, o Saxones, Franci,

Lotaringi, Flandrigeni famosissimi et domitores mundi, hic poteritis et animas vestras salvificare et, si ita placet, optimam terram ad inhabitandum acquirere)[27]. This call was soon followed. The election of Lothar of Saxony in 1125 gave the Empire a ruler, who developed a powerful *Ostpolitik* and gave a new impulse to the conquest and settlement of the east. The territorial lords became the leaders of the eastwards movement on behalf of the emperor. Albrecht der Bär (from 1150 Markgraf of Brandenburg) and Heinrich der Löwe pushed the boundary of the empire eastwards. Heinrich der Löwe led numerous campaigns against the Slavs in what is often called the Wenden Crusade. By the middle of the twelfth century he had succeeded in making the Slav princes of Mecklenburg and Pommern vassals of the Saxon emperor and colonization by German settlers soon followed on the advances of the German armies. By the end of the twelfth century the area up to a line running from just east of Lübeck to Berlin and on south to the Elbe had been settled[28].

The twelfth century conquest and colonization prepared the way for a rapid movement eastwards in the thirteenth century, when the German colonization reached its peak. By the end of this century, the area of German colonization reached deep into Silesia and east far beyond the Oder. The settlement of Silesia was almost complete and there were German settlers around the Riesengebirge in the Hirschberger Kessel and in the Grafschaft Glatz. There was a band of German settlement along the Oder, stretching to between 50 and 100 miles east of the river. Far in the east the *Deutscher Orden* (Teutonic Order) had been granted the Kulmerland on the lower Weichsel as a bridgehead for the conversion of the Prussians. Here the settlement of German farmers began around the middle of the thirteenth century, after the area had been made thoroughly safe by the Order. It was not until after the final defeat of the Prussians in 1283 that Prussia itself was settled.

The fourteenth century saw the end of the German colonization. Nevertheless before the end came, extensive new areas were settled. The main areas of settlement were in eastern Pommern (which had remained in Slav hands until 1294 and was finally divided up amongst the German claimants in 1308) and East

[27] Helbig and Weinrich, *op. cit.*, pp. 96-103
[28] A clear and short account of the progress of colonization, ordered chronologically, appears in *Die Ostgebiete des deutschen Reiches*, G. Rhode, (ed.), Würzburg 1955. The relevant chapter is entitled ' Der Gang der deutschen Besiedlung ' and was written by W. Kuhn.

Prussia. In East Prussia some new settlements were founded towards the end of the fourteenth century or even into the fifteenth (e.g. Tannenberg in 1410), but the pace of colonization had markedly begun to run down after the first 30 years of the century. Large areas remained for settlement south of the Njemen river and the Order of Teutonic Knights was determined to go on with the colonization. It was the flow of settlers which gave out rather than the will to colonize. The Order had been forced throughout the early years of the fourteenth century to settle more and more Prussians in their colonies, but by the middle of the century, even this source of supply had given out.

This enormous task of colonization necessitated much organization and a large amount of capital investment. The colonists had to be recruited, transported and supported for the first few years until they could make a living from the land. The initiators and entrepreneurs of the eastern colonization were therefore powerful secular and ecclesiastical rulers. The organization of the colonization was in many ways similar to that in the new areas of settlement in western Germany. What was different in the east was the scale of the operation, partly a function of its distance from the core area of German settlement in the west.

Again the Church played a great role in the colonization process. The role of the Church had been extended from simple colonization in order to raise its income, to the conversion of the heathen Slavs and the establishment of Christianity in eastern Europe. The dioceses founded in the tenth century were active centres of the colonization, from which monasteries were established deep in the Slav areas. Whilst the Benedictines had dominated the early colonization in many parts of western Germany, in the east it was the Cistercians and the Praemonstratensians who were at the forefront. In the twelfth century Cistercian monasteries were established far into Pommern and Poland. In 1175 they settled at Oliva near Danzig at the invitation of the Pommeranian Prince Sambor, and were immediately granted seven villages and the fishing rights along the coast[29]. Others were founded in Poland up almost to the middle Weichsel.

The Cistercians certainly played a role in the settlement of large areas with German colonists, but they were perhaps even more important for the introduction of new management methods on the land. Often the land made over to the monasteries was already in cultivation and the work of the Cistercians was to make it pay better. Sometimes to achieve this they drove the peasants

[29] Helbig and Weinrich, *op. cit.*, pp. 380-3

from the land, which was then consolidated and run in large-scale enterprises or granges. The workers were largely lay brothers, whose numbers sometimes ran into several hundred or even thousands. The role of the Cistercians as innovators is disputed, but not so the high quality of their management, especially in the twelfth and thirteenth centuries. The Cistercians not only reclaimed and settled land for agriculture, they also built mills, they were great maltsters, and they exploited stone and minerals. The salt deposits around Lüneburg were, for instance, being used by almost a dozen Cistercian abbeys in the mid-fourteenth century.

In the eastern colonization it was not only the bishops and monasteries who represented the efforts of the Church to convert and colonize. The orders of knights, basically religious orders, which played such a large part in the crusades to the Holy Land, were also very important in the eastern colonization. The orders of knights combined the ascetic ideals of the monk, with the military function of the knight. Whilst the Knights of St John and the Templars played a role, it was the knights of the Teutonic Order who organized the colonization of the largest area. The Teutonic Order was founded in 1198. The Order was requested by Konrad von Masowien to help in the conquest of the heathen Prussians and in 1226 it was granted Prussia by Friedrich II. From bases at Thorn (1231) and Kulm (1233) crusades were made against the Prussians and after many setbacks the whole country was pacified finally in 1283. The last quarter of the thirteenth century marked the zenith of the Order's development, yet it went on for another century colonizing deep into Latvia and Estonia. By the end of the next century a great state had been created (*Ordensstaat*), stretching from the Neumark and western Prussia to Estonia in the north.

The Order settled extensive areas with German farmers, they planned and built towns and developed a very profitable trading relationship with the Baltic countries and the western parts of Germany. Planning of settlement was generally on a grand scale. Grants of land were made by the Order of as much as 1,440 *Hufen* or 93 square miles[30]. The settlement which ensued was carried out frequently by consortia of wealthy knights or urban capitalists, with the aim of maximizing profits. This led to extreme uniformity in settlement forms.

Secular rulers also played an important role in the settlement of

[30] Ordensmeister Friedrich von Wildenberg made over 1,440 *Hufen* to a consortium of knights according to Prussian Law in 1321; Helbig and Weinrich, *op. cit.*, pp. 508-513

the east, partly as the agents of the ecclesiastical authorities but also as colonizing lords in their own right. Many of the great rulers founded monasteries to help them in the exploitation of the land which they had been granted by the Emperor. But it was not only German Dukes and Princes who founded German settlements. The Slav rulers were also aware of the chance to increase the income from their lands. Where they lived in peace with the German nobility and accepted Christian teaching, they remained largely unmolested by the Teutonic Order and the other colonizing authorities. Through invitation by local Slav rulers German settlers penetrated far beyond those areas firmly under control of the German authorities. They came into western Hungary and into the Siebenbürgen in modern Rumania. But on the edges of the German Empire it becomes more and more difficult to distinguish settlements of Germans from settlements founded under the German legal code.

As in western Germany, the detailed planning and the establishment of most of the new settlements were left to a *Lokator*. In some cases the colonizing lord managed the job himself and in some regions (especially in southern Bohemia) *Lokatoren* do not seem to have been used. But even where a *Lokator* was not employed, the lord generally copied forms of organization and plans of settlements used by *Lokatoren* in other settlements. The *Lokator* generally came from the *Bürger* classes in the towns and had been able to accumulate some wealth. He brought to the area of new settlement not only his skill as an organizer and businessman but also his wealth, which he invested there. The rewards the *Lokator* could expect from the lord who hired him were by no means small. Apart from a considerable area of land in the new colony, often free of dues, he was also given the *Schulzen* position in the village, with legal jurisdiction over the colonists and the right to pocket fines. He also sometimes received the monopoly right to trade in the area and to set up mills, smithies, inns and so on. Finally the *Lokator* often received a part of the revenue in dues and taxes from the colonists. This generosity towards the *Lokator* allowed him in many instances to rise to a position of considerable importance.

The rewards which the *Lokator* received for his work from his employer were certainly generous. On the other hand, he performed a service which needed great skill and he put his own capital at risk. Frequently it was not just one village which was planned and built but a whole group of villages and a central town. This was a tremendous planning operation for the time.

Large numbers of settlers had to be attracted and transported, transport between the villages and the town planned, churches built and so on. The risk was also not small, for some of the settlements founded in the east declined and died, so that the *Lokator* received little return on his capital investment and in some cases even lost his capital in the venture.

A major task and problem for the *Lokator* was the attraction of colonists to the new area of settlement. Some of the earliest settlers were Dutchmen who founded new villages in areas where draining or diking were essential before settlement was possible. They played a similar role therefore to that in western Germany discussed earlier. A document from 1152 confirms the rights of Dutch settlers in Flemmingen just south-west of Naumburg on the Saale[31]. Another from 1154, written for the Bishop of Meissen gives the village of Kühren between Leipzig and Meissen to settlers from Flanders and at the same time praises their work of reclamation and clearance in the area[32]. By the twelfth century a great deal of the work of drainage and reclamation was almost certainly being done by German settlers, bringing the technology from the west. Numerous documents exist making land awards in badly drained areas to Germans, although often the territorial lord would grant them the privileges of settlement under Dutch law.

The vast majority of the colonists came from the old areas of settlement in western Germany, and later on from existing colonies in the east. In many instances Slavs were also accepted in colonies, where German settlers were not available. There is considerable evidence that many of the early settlers in Mecklenburg came from Westfalia, and especially the areas of the *Geest* between the Ems and Weser. Benthien quotes the contemporary writer Helmold, who wrote in his *Slavenchronik* for the year 1162 that Heinrich, Duke of Ratzeburg, brought a large number of people from Westfalia and settled them on the land of the Polaben. He concludes the *Slavenchronik* by saying that ' the whole Slav region as far as Schwerin is now (1168) settled by the Saxons (Westfalia was as the time part of the Saxon empire) and towns and villages have been built '[33]. Elsewhere in the east settlers from other parts of western Germany were used and there are frequent mentions of ' Frankish ' settlers in documents dating

[31] Helbig and Weinrich, *op. cit.*, pp. 54-57
[32] *ibid.*, pp. 58-61
[33] Benthien, B., *Die historischen Flurformen des südwestlichen Mecklenburg*, Schwerin, 1960, pp. 95-96

from this period. Increasingly the flow of settlers from western Germany was replaced by Germans from the older colonies in east Germany. The colonists had experience of the conditions and problems of the east German areas, not possessed by those coming from ' old ' Germany.

In the twelfth and thirteenth centuries in the areas under the control of German lords, there was considerable effort made to keep the German settlers completely separate from the local Slavs. Around 1400 the Hochmeister of the Teutonic Order published a memorandum to those officers responsible for the settlement of the East Prussian wilderness. These instructions demonstrate the degree of Apartheid which the German colonizing agents were trying to achieve. No German in town or country was allowed to employ a Prussian servant and no Prussian was allowed to serve beer in a German inn. Nor was it allowed that a Prussian be settled on a German farm[34]. The Teutonic Order especially, however, was forced to employ Prussian settlers with increasing frequency as the supply of Germans began to fall well below the demand. In those areas colonized in the early fifteenth century, settlements including mixed German and Slav or completely Slav colonists were founded. Under the Slav princes there had frequently been a mixing of the nationalities long before this. As a result of this intermixing of Slav and German in East Prussia, the whole population of the area, irrespective of origin, soon began to be called Prussian,

The majority of the colonists did not apply for settlement in eastern Germany nor did they just drift there. They were attracted by the advertisement made by the *Lokatoren* and they were moved east by the same person. This was a complex piece of organization, though in some cases a lord could send out peasants from his estates in western Germany. The great attraction of the east, was almost certainly the terms offered by the *Lokatoren* for settlement there, in relation to the restrictive controls on peasants in the west. The colonists were essentially free and could leave their land at will and their land could also be passed to their heirs, male or female, at death. The inheritance was subject to a small quit rent, but the land only passed back to the lord when no heir could be found. Dues had to be paid to the lord, and although these were not insignificant, they could usually be afforded with little difficulty. Dues had to be paid only after the early ' free years ' had come to an end. The peasants were not

[34] Helbig and Weinrich, *op. cit.,* pp. 530-531

generally required to provide service on the lord's land as they often were in western Germany. At the time of colonization and during the years following therefore, the colonists held the land on favourable terms compared to their counterparts in the west.

The colonists in the east were often given a large land holding. This was not always one *Hufe*, there are records of settlers being given 2 *Hufen*, especially in Brandeburg and the Ordensland of Prussia, and somewhat less than one *Hufe*, for instance in Lower Lusatia[35]. The question of size is made more complicated because the *Hufe* varied as a measure of area from region to region. In the area colonized by the Teutonic Order it was 16·5 ha, on the other hand, the Dutch *Hufe* in the colonization of Flemmingen near Naumburg has been calculated at 23 hectares[36]. A very different *Hufe* seems to have been used in the early (1106) colonization of the undrained land on the lower Weser; Abel has calculated its area at 48 ha[37]. The area of the *Hufe* may well have varied according to the supply of land and the quality of the land. Whichever *Hufe* is used, however, these colonial holdings were large compared with those in the west.

The German colonization of the lands east of the Elbe and Saale was of fundamental significance in the economic development of these regions. Areas were cleared and drained and made productive. New methods of production and organization in agriculture were introduced. Social organization and the legal framework in the village were distinctively different in the east and they led to the development of the major economic, social-political contrasts between east and west, which lasted until the twentieth century. The eastern colonization also brought new settlement forms, just as the colonization of the waste in western Germany had done. It is these forms, which will now be discussed.

The settlement forms of the German colonization

It has already been suggested that many of the settlement forms of German colonization in the late medieval period were planned forms developed and executed by the *Lokatoren*. It is these large-scale planned forms which have received most attention in the literature. It is, however, clear that over quite extensive areas,

---

[35] Most grants of land in Germany in the medieval period were measured in Hufen.
[36] Helbig and Weinrich, *op. cit.*, p. 57
[37] *ibid.*, p. 43

and especially in west Germany, it is not these forms which were dominant, but rather single farms or small hamlets, with often quite irregular field patterns.

THE WEILER

The regularity of the new settlement forms depended to a large extent on the organizational structure under which they were set up. In the early colonization of the Odenwald and in the Ordensland of East Prussia and Latvia, the territorial lords, including the Teutonic Order, took a direct interest in the foundation of colonies and the colonizing process was on a large scale. In these areas planned and extremely regular patterns emerged. In many areas the part played by the territorial lord was small and it was the local lord, or urban businessman, who was responsible for the founding of settlements. Where no *Lokator* was employed, the founder contented himself often with bringing the settlers to the area to be cleared and leaving them to organize the work as they wished. In this way hamlets (*Weiler*), often with the farms spread at low density over a wide area (*Streudörfer*) and numerous isolated farms (*Einzelhöfe*) were founded. Associated with them were irregular block-field patterns. These settlements changed considerably over short periods of time, for there was no rigidly enforced social or economic organization. The individual was generally free to use his land as he wished and to add to his land by further clearance. So with the division of farms and the establishment of new holdings the *Einzelhöfe* grew to small hamlets and some of the hamlets developed into small villages.

In the south-western Odenwald, a large number of these irregular settlements were laid out by relatively insignificant local rulers like the Vögte von Leutershausen and the Herren von Strahlenberg[38]. *Weiler* are typical of other areas of high and late medieval colonization in western Germany, though they do not all have the same origin as those of the Odenwald described by Nitz. In the Lallinger Winkel, north of the Danube and northwest of Passau, Benedictine monks from the monastery of Niederalteich settled a large area of woodland before 900 with some one hundred *Weiler*[39]. Habbe contends that the settlement of the central Black Forest is a pattern of *Einzelhöfe* and not of linear villages and that these *Einzelhöfe* were settled freely by farmers without the control of local secular or ecclesiastical

[38] Nitz, *op. cit.*, pp. 35-49
[39] Fehn, H. 'Kloster Niederalteich und der Lallinger Winkel', *Topographischer Atlas Bayern*, München, 1968, pp. 182-3

rulers[40]. Engel, writing on the Ohrnwald, north of Stuttgart, considers the *Weiler* to have been typical of the period of medieval forest settlement[41]. Even in the areas of eastern colonization *Einzelhöfe* and *Weiler* occur quite frequently. Both Krenzlin and Kötzschke, for respectively Mecklenburg and Saxony, also describe the irregular *Weiler* as a colonial form[42].

The small irregular hamlet settlement and the *Einzelhof* (from which the former sometimes developed through the division of holdings) were therefore characteristic forms of many areas of colonial settlement. In the west, perhaps the greater part of the upland areas were colonized with these forms, showing a minimum of planning. In the east it is probable that many of the Slav settlements took this form before the German colonization. Some of the Slav *Weiler* remained intact during the period of German settlement and perhaps some were occupied by German settlers. As the period of colonization progressed, the settlement forms became more regular and the percentage of regular colonial forms to that of the *Weiler* and *Einzelhof* increased.

The term *Weiler* refers merely to the small size and irregular arrangement of these settlements[43]. There is no other common feature to them, although perhaps the majority were originally associated with a block-field pattern, though this pattern may have subsequently been broken up into a strip pattern through division of the blocks. There are, however, other forms of settlement in the colonial areas which are characterized by their small size and the arrangement of the farms into regular patterns. Perhaps the two main forms which should be discussed are the *Rundling* and the *Fortadorf*.

[40] Habbe, K. A., ' Die " Waldhufensiedlungen " in den Gebirgen Südwestdeutschlands als Problem der systematischen Siedlungsgeographie ', *Ber. z. dt. Landeskunde*, Vol. 37, 1966, pp. 48-49

[41] Engel, A., ' Die Siedlungsformen im Ohrnwald ', *Tübinger Geographische Studien*, Vol. 16, 1964, pp. 15-17

[42] Krenzlin, A., ' Dorf, Feld und Wirtschaft im Gebiet der grossen Täler und Platten östlich der Elbe ', *Forschungen zur deutschen Landeskunde*, Vol. 70, 1952, pp. 38-47
Kötzschke, R., ' Landliche Siedlung und Agrarwesen in Sachsen ', *Forschungen z. dt. Landeskunde*, Vol. 77, 1953, pp. 191f

[43] This term has been used in the past genetically to describe high and late medieval colonial settlements with a block field pattern. The author considers is preferable not to attach such a meaning to the term. The author also considers it more appropriate to use *Weiler* to describe the small hamlet found in north-west Germany and called in this text *Drubbel* (see page 9). *Drubbel* has been retained here as it is part of the terminology used in discussions on the primary Germanic settlement form and the origin of the *Haufendorf* and it will be met commonly in published material on this subject.

The only thing which has really been agreed about the *Rundling* is its distribution and its form. Discussion on its origin continues. The *Rundling* is a small settlement form generally consisting of less than a dozen farms, to which a few cottagers' houses were added (fig. 9). The farms are arranged tightly around a small open space, the large main doors of the lower German farmhouses facing onto the open space. This arrangement is in contrast to that on the round *Wurt* settlements, where the living accommodation faces into the centre of the settlement and the doors of the agricultural part of the house face outwards onto the *Marsch*. There is only one track which leads into the centre of the *Rundling* and this is generally extremely narrow. The land immediately around the settlement is divided up radially, so that each farm receives a segment of close pastures and woodland. Whilst fig. 9 shows the

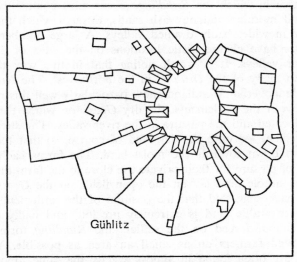

Fig. 9. The Rundling Gühlitz (after Schulz-Lüchow)

pure *Rundling* form, there are many associated forms which differ only slightly from that described. In the German literature, these associated forms have been classified in extreme detail, but it seems unlikely that these fine distinctions have much importance to a discussion of the origin of this settlement form. In some settlements the narrow neck of the *Rundling* is drawn out (*Sackgassendorf*), elsewhere the complete rounding of the *Rundling* has not been achieved.

Rounded settlement forms appear in several parts of Germany, but it is in the area where the early eastwards colonization by the Germans took place along the middle Elbe that the classic *Rundling* and associated forms are dominant. In the eastern parts of Lower Saxony, in the Hannoverian Wendland, and in western Mecklenburg, the *Rundling* exists almost alone, being mixed with only a few other settlement forms. To the north of this area in north-western Mecklenburg and southern Schleswig-Holstein and to the south in Thuringia and Saxony, the *Rundling* occurs with a large number of other distinctive forms. The *Rundling* is therefore concentrated in a north to south zone running through central Europe from the Baltic coast into the central Hercynian uplands, with outliers occurring even as far south as Marburg a. d. Drau. This distribution, coinciding roughly with an area of early Slav-German mixing, pointed to simple explanations of origin, which have, however, not been supported by recent detailed research.

The area in which the *Rundlinge* occur most commonly is one of ground moraine and outwash sands, through which the rivers meander in wide, badly drained valleys. A large number of the *Rundlinge* have characteristic locations on the edge of dry land and river valleys. It is worth noting that in this way they are similar to many of the *Drubbel* in the north-west. The *Rundlinge* in the Hannoverian Wendland show particularly well this relationship between the settlements, the dry *Geest*, on which the arable land is located and the pasture in the river valley. The street from the settlement led onto the dry land of course, so that the farmyards ran down towards the moist land. The farms each had a segment of pasture for their private use close to the farm therefore, while the arable land lay on the open fields on the *Geest*. Some authors have suggested that the position of the settlements, in an area where arable land is extremely precious and badly drained land common, forced on the settlers the *Rundling* form which concentrated farmers on as small an area as possible. Yet the *Drubbel* are often found in almost exactly the same topographic position and have a rather different form!

The first explanation of the origin of the *Rundling* generally involved a defensive function. Either they were Slav forms built for protection against the Germans or they were German forms built against the Slavs. The central open space could be used to herd the cattle and the one road entrance could be closed off. A variation of this reasoning was applied to defence against wild animals. Why though should the *Rundling* be concentrated in this particular area along the middle Elbe, while these same conditions existed elsewhere, where other settlement forms are dominant?

Krenzlin considered the *Rundling* to be a secondary settlement form and a colonial form[44]. It has developed from the small Slav hamlets, initially often in the form of a short linear settlement. Two main processes helped produce the final form. The first was the forced consolidation of settlement under the Germans to satisfy the needs of the newly introduced three field system of agriculture. Krenzlin declares that the *Rundling* was only developed on land which was relatively productive, sufficiently extensive to support the three-field system and with a high density of Slav population. But she also argues that the *Rundling* is . . . the nucleated settlement form of medium size, which best fits the needs of pastoral farming . . .' The farmers have the maximum area of near pastures, through the segmental division of the land around the settlement. The *Rundling* is therefore a compromise between the needs of the arable system introduced by the Germans and the old Slav pastoral economy.

Schulz-Lüchow comes to much the same conclusion in dealing with the forms which occur in the Hannoverian Wendland as does Krenzlin in Lusatia[45]. Schulz-Lüchow takes the view that the *Rundling* developed from small group settlements, sometimes admittedly arranged in a half circle. The transformation took place through the processes of farm division and settlement consolidation. The division of property led to an increase in the number of farms and the size of the settlements. The farmyards were often divided into two and from a small settlement of three farms grew a rounded one with six. Settlement consolidation under the influence of the German settlers was, however, a critical factor, and it was this that led to the final rounding off of the *Rundlinge* according to Schulz-Lüchow. Of course a simple amalgamation of settlements could take place in a variety of forms. Schulz-Lüchow suggests that the circular form may have been used because of the need to pack as many of the settlers on as small an area as possible and to give them areas of pasture.

An interesting and well documented case of amalgamated settlements is that of Satemin in the Hannoverian Wendland[46]. A small Slav hamlet existed on this site before the German occupation. Around 1400 two Slav hamlets were amalgamated on the site. The Satemin farmers retained their farms and land and the farmers from the hamlet of Prilipp were settled so as to

[44] Krenzlin, *op. cit.*, 1952, p. 109 ff.
[45] Schulz-Lüchow, W., Primäre und sekundäre Rundlingsformen in den Niederen Geest des hannoverschen Wendlandes ', *Forschungen z. dt. Landeskunde*, Vol. 142, 1963
[46] Schulz, W., ' Der Rundling Satemin im hannoverschen Wendland ', *Luftbildatlas Niedersachsen*, 1967, pp. 118-19

round off the *Rundling*. Each group kept its identity through spatial separation of both its farmhouses and its land. The amalgamation was ordered by the German lord, with jurisdiction over this part of the Wendland, almost certainly with the purpose of intensifying the Slav farming system and perhaps to prevent any attempt by the Slavs to settle in the German towns.

It is interesting that there were two *Schulzen* in Satemin after the amalgamation of the two settlements. The two men took it in turn to exercise the duties and privileges of the office and they shared the land of the *Schulze* equally. The existence of this office in all the *Rundlinge* and the dominant position of the farm of the *Schulz* indicates the Germanic influence on the settlements, at least in their final form, for this is a German office and apparently was not known to the Slavs.

The arguments about the origin of the *Rundling* are continuing. Briefly evidence points to the fact that they are almost certainly originally Slav settlements, but that the final *Rundling* shape was not produced until the German colonization. Only rarely were *Rundlinge* planned primary forms[47]. The major factor in the rounding off of the settlement may well have been coercion by a German lord. The production of the final form depended on an increase in the number of farms and this was achieved through land division and village amalgamation. The *Rundlinge* were almost always associated with a three-field system of agriculture, but pastoral farming was still important and favoured by this settlement form. The three-field system was almost certainly introduced by the Germans and was a major reason for the amalgamation of settlements.

Another settlement form occurs in parts of Schleswig-Holstein, which bears some resemblance to the *Rundling* but which has a rather different origin. This is the *Fortadorf* (fig. 10). These settlements are very regular, with the farmhouses located around a central rectangular open space, the *Forta*. Each farmyard is surrounded by a stone wall or hedge and there are four main exits from the village at each corner of the Forta. These settlements occur in eastern Schleswig and especially on the island of Fehmarn, where of 42 villages, 40 are of this type. In Schleswig the village form has been so changed through settlement on the *Forta* and the adaption of the village to modern economic demands, that the original character of the *Fortadorf* has been lost. On Fehmarn changes have taken place too, but the majority

[47] Schulz-Lüchow found only five planned *Rundlinge* in the area of the Hannoverian Wendland.

of the villages still show to some degree the character of the planned *Fortadorf*.

The *Fortadorf* was considered by some to be a Slav form from

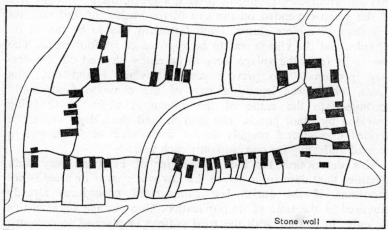

Fig. 10. A Fortadorf on Fehmarn

the period before the German colonization. This is most unlikely. It has, however, considerable similarity to planned Danish settlements. Hastrup considers the settlement forms of Fehmarn at some length and concludes that they are Danish planned forms[48]. The forms of Fehmarn are very similar to those of Falster in Denmark, also planned Danish settlements[49]. Evidence from the Fehmarn list in 'Kong Valdemars Jordebog' supports the thesis that these are planned village forms. The measurements given for the breadth of the plots facing the green are more or less constant in 15 villages which were investigated. Hastrup concludes that the Fehmarn villages are the product of a reorganization of rural settlements, carried through around 1200 under the supervision of the Danish king.

Hastrup considers the provincial laws to have been important in the creation of these planned forms. The same point is taken up by Bonsen in an investigation of the settlements in Schwansen in Schleswig, which is bounded in the north by the Schlei and in the south by the Eckernförder Bucht[50]. This law was passed in 1241,

[48] Hastrup, F., *Danske Landsbytyper*, Århus, 1964, cap. 2
[49] Hastrup, *op. cit.*, chap. 1
[50] Bonsen, U., 'Die Entwicklung des Siedlungsbildes und der Agrarstruktur der Landschaft Schwansen vom Mittelalter bis zur Gegenwart', *Schriften des Geographischen Instituts der Universität Kiel*, Vol. 22/3, 1966

E

but it is possible that it was a codifying measure, setting in writing common law. The Jutish law gave a detailed description of the way in which a settlement should be laid out. It laid down that all farmhouses should lie around a green, the *Forta*. The size of the green depended on the size of the settlement, but was not less than 28 metres across. Each farmyard was to be fenced on all sides and the village was to be approached by four roads. The four exits from the village were to be easily blocked off if necessary, presumably to prevent cattle straying in and out. The *Forta*, which was legally a part of the common land, could accommodate the cattle of the village at night, water being provided by small ponds. The land around the village was to be divided into several roughly similar fields, each of which was to be used uniformly for one crop only each year.

This description fits the *Fortadörfer* of Fehmarn very well. Whether they date from before the law was passed or after is not important, if the Jutish law summarized procedures already practised at the time of its publication. One passage suggests this strongly. In dealing with the road pattern in planned settlements, the law reads ' four roads shall lead to each village, as has been traditionally the case '.[51] It is interesting to speculate that if such a thoroughgoing reorganization of the settlement pattern and of village forms was possible under a Danish ruler, is it not also possible that a German ruler may have conceived a similar ' ideal ' settlement form and applied it to the middle-Elbe region? In this case the origin of the *Rundling* would also be sought in administrative pressures as suggested by Schulz-Lüchow and Krenzlin.

REGULAR HUFENDÖRFER

The colonial settlements of the greater part of eastern Germany but also of quite extensive areas in west Germany are linear in form. The regularity and large scale of many of these settlements have attracted the attention of many writers to such a degree that their importance in relation to other forms has often been exaggerated. Smaller, less regular and far earlier forms occurring in western Germany have been recognized by some authors as being forerunners of the later colonial settlement forms and these will be dealt with together with the regular planned forms in this section.

The planned linear settlements founded during the high and late medieval colonization are perhaps the simplest forms conceivable. The field-patterns associated with them are also generally

[51] Bonsen, *op. cit.*, pp. 127-8

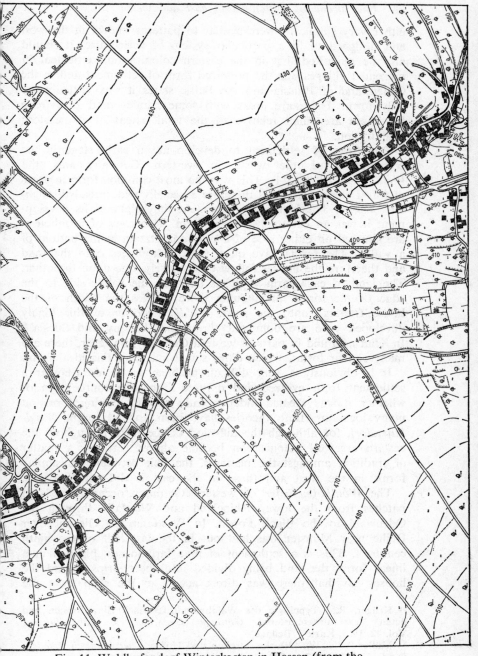

Fig. 11. Waldhufendorf Winterkasten in Hessen (from the topographical map 1:5,000)

either very simple or were similar to patterns known in the west and designed to fit a particular system of agriculture. It should also be remarked that in the eastern colonization, settlement in nucleated villages was the preferred form of settlement and in the Ordensland of Prussia and the Baltic states it was virtually the only form. There are areas with some hamlets and *Einzelhöfe* but these are small relative to the total extent of the eastern colonization.

One form of settlement to develop at an early stage in the colonization of the waste in western Germany was the *Waldhufendorf* (fig. 11). This was the most common form in areas of forest clearance and is therefore especially widespread throughout Saxony, Thuringia and Silesia. At the height of its development it was an extremely regular form. Two rows of farmhouses are situated on either side of a road and stream in the bottom of a valley. The farms have quite narrow frontages onto the road and therefore the houses follow quite closely, one upon the other. The land of each farm stretches back up the valley side to the edge of the forest, maintaining more or less the width of the house frontage onto the road. *Waldhufendörfer* of this highly developed type are dominant throughout Saxony and Silesia[52]. In Thuringia and in parts of western Germany, however, there are many similar forms, which differ somewhat from this ideal form.

It is obviously a very difficult problem to decide whether a settlement form evolved and diffused from one source area or whether it was created independently and in varying forms at many locations. Both theories have been applied to the *Waldhufendorf*, for although the diffusion of the form throughout the eastern areas of colonization became almost certainly a matter of tradition amongst the planners, the link between the similar forms in the west and those in the east is difficult to prove.

The *Waldhufendörfer* of western Germany occur in isolated patches from the lower Rhineland and Westfalia through the Odenwald to the Black Forest. In Westfalia the Gievenbecker Reihe near Münster was laid out in the last half of the ninth century[53]. This is a settlement of nine farmhouses, planned in a linear form, the land being divided into short strips behind the houses, so that there was direct access to the strip from the

---

[52] Krüger, R., 'Typologie des Waldhufendorfes nach Einzelformen und deren Verbreitungsmustern', *Göttinger Geographische Abhandlungen*, Vol. 42, 1967, Karte 1/Beilage 4

[53] Müller-Wille, W., 'Blocke, Streifen und Hufen', *Ber. z. dtsch, Landeskunde*, Vol. 29, 1962, p. 303

house. In the same area west of Münster, Mecklenbeck was originally very similar to Gievenbeck[54]. Here again there is a linear settlement with ten farms, the majority of which had direct access to a part of their land which lay in wide and short strips behind the farmhouses. It appears probable that these *Hufen* were not created at the time of foundation of the settlement but grew slowly by accretion. They eventually reached a length of about 400 metres, with an area of three to six hectares. These *Hufen* have therefore some resemblance to the *Waldhufen*, but they were not planned for by the Carolingian founders of these settlements. Other similar forms, which pre-date the full development of the colonial *Waldhufendorf* and which may therefore be early forms from which the fully colonial *Waldhufendorf* developed, have been found in the Delbrücker Land near Paderborn, on the lower Rhine, on the middle Weser, and in the Wiehengebirge in northern Westfalia[55]. All these early settlements have the direct access from farmhouse to *Hufe* in common, but no direct contact can be proved between the areas themselves or between these areas and those colonial regions with planned *Waldhufen*.

The colonization of the Odenwald also took place using forms of settlement similar to the *Waldhufendorf*. The monastery of Lorsch began to found settlements similar in form as early as the ninth century, and as time progressed the monastery went over to founding almost all their new colonies in this way. Probably the first proven occurrence of an early *Waldhufendorf* form is the village of Zotzenbach, founded in Carolingian times certainly before 877 and probably around 850[56]. Zotzenbach has two rows of houses with strips running up the valley sides behind the houses. Nitz estimates that the original wide strips had a length of only 300-400 metres and a width of between 90 and 150 metres, giving an area of some 3 to 6 hectares. The small size of the strips suggests that the clearance of the forest was completed before or at the original settlement rather than over a long period. They were in any case surrounded by a very large area of common, which could be used by the farmers, and in which they later cleared block fields to increase the area of arable land. The *Waldhufen* in Zotzenbach became therefore an island in the middle of a sea of block fields. Nitz sees the reason for the small size of the *Waldhufen* firstly in the emphasis on a pastoral

[54] Niemeier, G., 'Frühformen der Waldhufen', *Petermanns Geog. Mitteilungen*, Vol. 93, 1949, pp. 16-18
[55] Krüger, *op. cit.*, pp. 34-35
[56] Nitz, *op. cit.*, pp. 95-99

economy requiring a small area of private arable land only, and secondly in the holding in common of the forest and waste, in which all could graze their animals. This had been taken over from the traditions of the old settlements in the Rhine valley at the foot of the Odenwald.

Zotzenbach is only one of a number of settlements with short *Waldhufen,* which occur in the relatively favourable Weschnitz basin. It appears that Lorsch introduced the form in this early area of colonization and later developed it further in other areas. The similarity between Zotzenbach and the settlements in West-falia discussed above is quite striking. Whether there was any connection between the founding of similar settlement forms in the various regions of western Germany or whether they represent completely isolated occurrences is something which we cannot yet make a judgement on. It is, however, possible that these early forms were produced by Frankish state colonization, which would explain the founding of similar forms in areas remote from each other at about the same period.

It is somewhat easier to trace within western Germany the development of the linear settlement with *Waldhufen* from this early stage through to a form more similar to the ' ideal ' form described above. In the Odenwald, Nitz considers that it was the demand to increase the area of arable land which led to the lengthening and widening of the *Waldhufen.* Lorsch began to plan settlements with somewhat larger *Waldhufen,* but this did not mean the extinction of the common woodland. In many settle-ments, however, these short strips were lengthened so that even-tually the common woodland disappeared and the *Waldhufen* ran from valley top to valley top. The lengthening process was an irregular one, although the permission of the local lord would certainly have been required. This explains why in the Odenwald there are many linear settlements which were laid out at about the same time but in which the length of the Waldhufen and the extent of the common woodland are very variable. Engel suggests the same development for the Ohrnwald. Early forms with short *Waldhufen* can be seen on the edges of the Ohrnwald, whereas in the centre the *Hufen* extend far back towards the tops of the valleys[57]. Obviously, says Engel, the settlements on the edge of the Ohrnwald are far older planned forms than those in the centre. In the latter settlements, the width of the strips is very constant at 125 metres, indicative of planning, but the length varies greatly suggest-ing private clearance after the initial foundation of the settlements.

[57] Engel, A., *op. cit.,* p. 80 ff.

In those areas of western Germany in which linear settlements with *Waldhufen* occur, it is rare for the fully developed forms, typical of the eastern colonization, to be represented. In Westfalia only very small linear settlements with short strips occur. In the lower Rhine these earliest forms occur, together with some small villages which have far longer strips. In the eastern Odenwald forms occur approximating to the eastern colonial forms, but the full length of the strips was not planned from the start but developed over the years through their occasional extension by private individuals. In the northern Black Forest there are also some areas of well developed *Waldhufen*, but again these were probably produced slowly and not founded as classic *Waldhufen*.

A major problem is whether there is a connection between the linear settlements with *Waldhufen* in the west and the planned forms in the east. A map of the distribution of *Waldhufendörfer* shows a completely blank area between the settlements in the Spessart and the Ohrnwald (the most easterly areas with these forms in western Germany) and the most westerly areas of the eastern colonization in the Thuringian Forest and the Frankenwald. There are three possible ways in which the *Waldhufen* may have developed in the east. There may have been a direct connection between those areas in the west, in which the *Waldhufen* was already known, and the eastern areas. If this is so it is most likely to have been through the colonization of Franconians and there is some evidence that settlers from Franconia transferred the *Waldhufendorf* from the west to the Erzgebirge[58]. Secondly, it is possible that forms similar to the *Waldhufen* were imported by Dutch settlers. It is certain that the Dutch penetrated into Thuringia and Saxony and it is also known that they had experience of the *Marschhufendörfer* of the North Sea coast. There is, however, no proof that they introduced this new form of settlement into the inland areas which they settled in the east[59]. Thirdly, it is conceivable that the *Waldhufendorf* arose in the east independently of outside influences. It is known that there were forms in the Fichtelgebirge which were in some ways similar to the fully developed *Waldhufen* before the full development was achieved. There may have been a transformation in these local forms when applied to new areas of colonization resulting in the appearance of the true *Waldhufendorf*[60].

The great expansion and the uniformity of the fully developed

[58] Krüger, *op. cit.*, pp. 39-40
[59] *ibid.*, pp. 40-42
[60] *ibid.*, p. 44 ff.

Waldhufendorf depended upon the adoption of a set areal measurement and the development of the necessary survey techniques. The unit adopted was the *fränkische Hufe*, which had a normal area of 24.2 ha, though occasionally being 27.5 ha[61]. Generally the *Waldhufen* laid out in the area of eastern colonization after the start of the twelfth century were one *fränkische Hufe* in size. But the adoption of this measurement not only meant that all the strips had the same size; they also had the same dimensions. It is clear that the *Waldhufen* were surveyed in a uniform way, so that each had a length of 270 *Ruten* and a width of 4 *Seile*. With a *Rute* of 8.64 metres, the length of the *Waldhufe* was constant at around 2,330 metres. The *Seil*, the chain with which measurements were made, was equal to 3 *Ruten* or around 26 metres. The width of the *Waldhufen* was therefore approximately 104 metres.

The first recorded reference to this unit of measurement dates from between 1156 and 1162, when the Markgraf of Meissen had land cleared and settled in Saxony[62]. It probably developed in the course of the eastwards colonization of the Erzgebirge, from where it spread right across to Galicia. The measurement seems to have been adopted generally when the *Waldhufendorf* as a planned form developed, and it forced a high degree of uniformity on the *Waldhufendörfer* which were subsequently founded. The *fränkische Hufe* seems to have developed from older measurements. It is exactly half the area of the older *Königshufe* and it is almost exactly the same size as the early *Standeshufe*, which measured 24.86 ha[63]. The details of length and breadth measurements outlined above also appear to have connections with earlier traditional measurements. Finally it appears that the *fränkische Hufe* of approximately 24 ha became accepted in many areas as an acceptable area for a family farm.

With the adoption of this common unit of measurement and the spread of settlement across the forests of Saxony, Silesia and Galicia, a vast number of *Waldhufendörfer* were founded all very similar to that shown in figure 11. This classic form of *Waldhufendorf* was developed with both a single row of farms and a double row; in the first case the strips of land on both valley sides were owned by the one farm, which then stood in the middle of its land, in the second case the farm consisted of a strip, which included only one side of the valley and the farm was then at one

[61] *ibid.*, pp. 106-19
[62] Krüger, *op. cit.*, p. 117
[63] *ibid.*, pp. 110-17

end of the strip. In those areas colonized at a late stage, especially in the south of (present-day) Poland, variations to this general form occur, which Krüger describes as forms of decay[64].

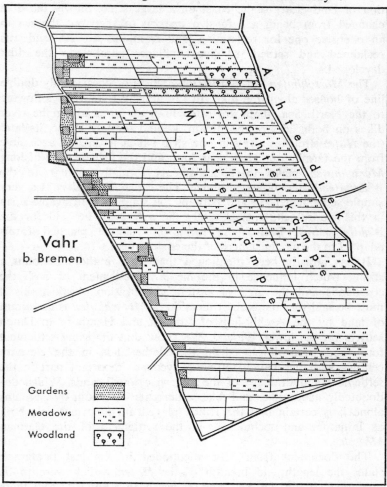

Fig. 12. Marschhufendorf Vahr, near Bremen (topographical map 1 : 50,000)

Very similar settlement forms to the *Waldhufendorf* developed along the North Sea coast and along the major river valleys of Germany. The *Marschhufendorf* (fig. 12) developed in the Netherlands before it reached northern Germany, and it may well have

[64] Krüger, R., *op. cit.*, p. 75

been brought to Germany by Dutch settlers. The development of this form depended on the construction of dikes which allowed, for the first time, settlement at ground level, and also the cultivation of land close to the coast on a large scale. Slowly the dike changed from being a defensive weapon to keep out the sea to an offensive one for reclaiming land from the sea. As land was reclaimed and settled, so linear villages parallel to the dike developed.

The *Marschhufendorf* consists of a single or occasionally double line of houses along the dike. In the marshy river valleys flowing to the North Sea, there are often lines of farms along the river dikes on both sides of the stream. Behind the farmhouse, its land (the *Hufe*) stretches away in one strip which is directly accessible from the farmhouse. The linear form and the field pattern of long *Marschhufen* make these settlements formally similar to the *Waldhufendörfer* discussed above. The *Marschhufendorf* is a very simple settlement form and perhaps the simplest conceivable form in this natural situation. Exactly the same can be said for the *Waldhufendorf*. Both these forms are simple planned forms adapted to the circumstances of the environment.

It has already been mentioned that some authors discount a strong Dutch influence in the medieval settlement of both the coastlands and the area of eastern colonization. Against this it must be said that the earliest mention of *Marschhufen* is in a grant of land by the Archbishop of Bremen and Hamburg to Dutch settlers on the lower Weser[65]. We know that the same settlement form had been developed in the Netherlands in the eleventh century and that Dutch settlers played an important part in the settlement and drainage of the eastern colonial lands. Whilst undoubtedly many dikes and dike settlements were built by Germans alone it is certain that the Dutch played an important role both as initiators and technicians in the settlement of the German *Marsch*.

The document from 1106 mentioned in the last paragraph states the length and breadth of the *Hufen*, which were to be measured out on the new land. It has been estimated from these measurements that the area of the *Hufen* must have been around 48 ha[66]. Fliedner considers that this area was the norm in the *Marschhufen* laid out around Bremen and the lower Weser[67]. Apparently, however, there were no constant measurements of

[65] Helbig and Weinrich, *op. cit.*, pp. 42-45
[66] Helbig and Weinrich, *op. cit.*, p. 43
[67] Reported in Krüger, *op. cit.*, p. 63

length and breadth, which were in practice very variable. As
Krüger comments, the maintenance of a constant area but
variable dimensions requires a degree of skill in surveying, which
would be quite astounding for the twelfth century[68]. The field
pattern associated with these dike villages will not have been so
regular as that associated with the fully developed *Waldhufendorf*,
where uniform measurements and systems of measurement were
the rule.

The likelihood that the *Waldhufendorf* developed from the
Marschhufendorf has often been discussed. This theory was put
forward by Huppertz and supported by Müller-Wille, but if we
accept that the settlement forms in the Münsterland and in the
Odenwald, described by Niemeier and Nitz respectively, are ninth
century forerunners of the *Waldhufendorf*, then this theory is no
longer tenable[69]. On the contrary, it is chronologically possible
then for the *Marschhufendorf* to have been a development from
the *Waldhufendorf*. Fliedner sees the Bremen *Marschhufendörfer*
as the full development of earlier forms to be found in the
Netherlands and established considerably before 1106. There may
therefore be a difference of less than a century in the date of the
earliest forms of *Waldhufendorf* and *Marschhufendorf*. All that
can be said is that there is no clear indication of any direct transfer of one of these forms to the areas in which the other form was
established, though it is rather unlikely that the *Marschhufendorf*
is the forerunner of the *Waldhufendorf*.

In the early *Waldhufendörfer* of the Odenwald, the settlers were
allowed to extend their *Hufen* at will into the forest. The later
colonial *Waldhufen* were fixed at 24 ha and the strips could not
generally be enlarged at the expense of the forest. Fliedner considers that the latter was also true of the *Marschhufen* in the
Bremen area. The 48 ha if a basis for all the *Marschhufen* was
obviously a sufficient area for providing for a family and the
system would not allow for any free enlargement of strips. However, in East Friesland and Oldenburg the common law of *Anschuss*
(*Aufstrecksrecht, Opstroekrecht*) seems to have applied to some
early *Marschhufendörfer*[70]. This law allows the farmer to extend

[68] *ibid.*, p. 63
[69] Huppertz, B., *Räume und Schichten bäuerlicher Kulturformen in
Deutschland.*, Bonn 1939, p. 142
Müller-Wille, W., ' Die Hagenhufendörfer in Schaumburg-Lippe ', *Peter-
manns Geog. Mitt.*, Vol. 90, p. 246
[70] Müller, G., ' Das Aufstrecksrecht und seine Nachwirkungen bis zur
Gegenwart ', dissertation in the Rechts-und Staatswiss. Fak. of the
University of Münster, 1950 (unpublished)

his strip into the waste until he meets another farmer's land or an administrative boundary. The results of the working of this law can be seen along the west bank of the lower Weser. In Moorriem for instance the ownership parcels have reached a length of 8 kilometres (plate 2)[71]. This area was settled in the early eleventh century, at which time the houses of Moorriem were located behind the Weser dike close to the river. The strips were extended westwards towards the old *Marsch* and eventually into the peat-bog area beyond. At some time, the settlement was moved from the dike inland to the edge of the *Marsch* and the peat-bog, retaining the linear form. There may have been some administrative pressure on the farmers to move, although it seems likely that the continual extension of the strips under the law of *Anschuss* may have forced them to relocate their farmhouses closer to the centre of the strips. It could be that these settlements were early examples of *Marschhufen* and that later this form was regularized by establishing a uniform size (48 ha according to Fliedner) as in the *Waldhufendörfer* of eastern Germany.

It has been seen that the *Waldhufendorf* is distributed through the late-settled upland areas of eastern and central Germany. The *Marschhufendorf* occurs along the lower Ems, occasionally on the coast of East Friesland, along the lower Weser, and up the *Elbe* as far as the Lenzer Wische. Very similar forms are also to be found along the Baltic coast, where marshy land has been reclaimed. Just north-west of Rostock for instance the settlements of Börgerende and Rethwisch could be classed as *Marschhufendörfer*. Similar settlements occur even further eastwards on the coast between Stettin and Danzig.

Another type of *Hufendorf*, similar in most ways to the *Wald-* and *Marschhufendörfer*, is the *Hagenhufendorf*. These settlements are spread out across northern Germany from Westfalia through Lower Saxony, Brandenburg, Mecklenburg to Pommern. It is only in Lower Saxony, in the former Duchy of Schaumburg-Lippe, where a large concentration of these settlements occurs, however, (some 25 in all)[72]. These *Hagen* or *Häger* settlements were founded in the period from the eleventh to the thirteenth centuries often by unimportant feudal lords, who still

[71] Mayhew, A., ' Zur Strukturellen Reform der Landwirtschaft in der Bundesrepublik Deutschland erläutert an der Flurbereinigung in der Gemeinde Moorriem/Wesermarsch ', *Westfälische Geog. Studien*, Vol. 22, 1970
[72] Blohm, R., ' Die Hagenhufendörfer in Schaumburg-Lippe ', *Veröff. d. Prov. Inst. f. Landesplanung u. niedersächs. Landes-und Volksforschung*, Hannover—Gottingen, Series AII, Vol. 10, 1943

had small areas of forest or waste, which could be used for settlement and therefore yield some profit. The unique quality of the settlements lies neither in their form nor in the field pattern but in the rights which were granted by the lord to the settlers. *Hagen* settlements may be small formless hamlets, large nucleated *Haufendörfer* or linear villages. The fields can be divided into blocks, can be in the form of a *Gewannflur* or in that of a *Hufenflur* as in the *Waldhufendorf*. While there appears to be no standard size or form to these settlements, there was certainly one form which was most common and this has often been referred to as the *Hagenhufendorf*. Here the settlement is linear and the land parcels of each farm run back from the farmhouse to the edge of the forest. Blohm makes a distinction between the *Waldhufendorf* and the *Hagenhufendorf* in that the latter has a single row of farmhouses, which is not placed centrally in the *Hufen*, so that about two-thirds of the strip is on one side of the house and one third on the other. Whereas in many *Waldhufendörfer* the stream, the village street and the row of farmhouses closely parallel each other, here in the *Hagenhufendörfer* of Schaumburg-Lippe the settlement and the village street were built some distance from the stream.

Whether the differences between these two colonial settlement forms are really significant or whether the *Hagenhufendorf* is merely a regional variation of the *Waldhufendorf*, it is the *Hägerrecht* (the law granted to the *Hagen* settlements) which really distinguishes them. The colonists in *Hagen* settlements formed settler cooperatives, the head of which was usually called the *Hagenmeister* or *Hachmeister*. Among the rights usually given to the individual colonists was that of inheritance without payment of dues and of freedom from feudal services. The majority of the colonies laid out in the twelfth or thirteenth centuries with these *Hagen* rights carry the suffix -*hagen* in their names, and it is certainly through the place-name rather than the settlement form that one can distinguish the *Hagen* settlements.

REGULAR STREET VILLAGES

The linear *Hufen* settlements which have been discussed so far cover a large area in eastern Germany. They are really, however, confined there to the upland areas in the south, for the *Marschhufendörfer* and *Hagen* settlements are a mere sprinkling across the North German Lowland. The greater part of the new settlements established by the Germans during the eastern colonization were simple street villages (*Strassendörfer*) or green villages

(*Angerdörfer*). It has already been pointed out that, as the colonization penetrated further east, so the settlement forms became more regular. The Teutonic Order during the colonization of East Prussia established large, regular *Strassendörfer* with planned *Gewannfluren* (fig. 13). A vast area was settled with the

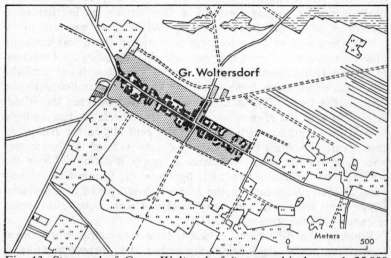

Fig. 13. Strassendorf Gross Woltersdorf (topographical map 1:25,000 Gransee)

same forms and a degree of uniformity was achieved as nowhere else in Germany. The *Strassendorf* and the *Angerdorf* are the characteristic settlement forms of the whole area of the eastern colonization, with the exception of those areas where the *Hufensiedlungen* are dominant. In some areas other forms are also important (e.g. the *Rundling* along the middle Elbe and the small hamlets of Mecklenburg) but only rarely do these other forms become the dominant forms.

The *Strassendorf* is quite simply as the name suggests a settlement along a road. In the planned settlements of eastern Germany, the farmhouses were placed close to each other on both sides of the road (fig. 13), so that a very dense settlement resulted. The majority of these villages were associated with a *Gewannflur,* for the Germans introduced the three-field system to the Slav lands in the east. This meant that the farmhouses in the settlement could be placed far closer together than in the *Hufen* settlements, for the frontage did not have to be the width of a *Hufe* as in the latter. It is certain that in some cases the looser structure of the

Waldhufendorf was turned into the dense settlement form of the *Strassendorf*, through the division of the frontage. In cases like this it is obviously quite difficult to make a distinction between the settlement forms, which are almost identical; the only differences lie in the field pattern. It is also fairly certain that some *Strassendörfer* developed slowly as a secondary settlement form from small hamlets or even *Einzelhöfe*. But the vast majority of these settlements are medieval planned forms in eastern Germany.

As with the *Waldhufendorf* it has been tempting to look to the origins of the planned *Strassendorf* in the settlement forms which existed in western Germany at the start of the eastern colonization. Some planned street villages have been found but the connection with the eastern planned forms cannot be proved. Nitz has found *Strassendörfer* laid out by the Carolingian emperor in the Rhine Rift Valley. These are dated at least as early as the ninth century and therefore considerably pre-date the eastern colonization[73]. The same author points to the *Strassendörfer* established at the end of the thirteenth century by the Bishop of Speyer in the same area[74]. Other planned *Strassendörfer* placed in the first millennium have been identified in the Rhön foreland and in East Friesland. Undoubtedly more examples of medieval planned forms will be brought to light in western Germany, but at the moment they are very scattered and totally insignificant compared with the vast distribution of such forms in the east.

There are grounds for considering the *Strassendörfer* in the east as original creations. It cannot be established with any certainty that the west German *Strassendorf* was a cultural export to the east German lands, although this is possible. But the small number of *Strassendörfer* in western Germany compared to the vast number in the east and their extreme regularity makes it very likely that the decisive stages in the development of the planned *Strassendorf* were acted out in the course of the eastwards colonization. The *Strassendorf* can be considered to be the simplest form of settlement that could have been developed where an open-field system of farming was involved. The leaders of the eastern colonization were interested principally in making money out of the new settlements and they therefore founded

---

[73] Nitz, H. J., ' Regelmässige Langstreifenfluren und fränkische Staatskolonisation ', *Geog. Rundschau*, 13, 1962, pp. 350-5
[74] Nitz, H. J., ' Entwicklung und Ausbreitung planmässiger Siedlungsformen bei der mittelalterlichen Erschliessung des Odenwaldes, des nördlichen Schwarzenwaldes und der badischen Hardt-Ebene ', In *Heidelberg und die Rhein-Neckar Lande*, Heidelberg, 1963, pp. 210-35

rationally arranged villages, given the imposition of the intensive (at that period) three-field system.

An apparently quite similar form to the *Strassendorf* is the *Angerdorf* or green village, which occurs together with the *Strassendorf* throughout eastern Germany and in some areas is the dominant form (fig. 14). Here the road which forms the axis

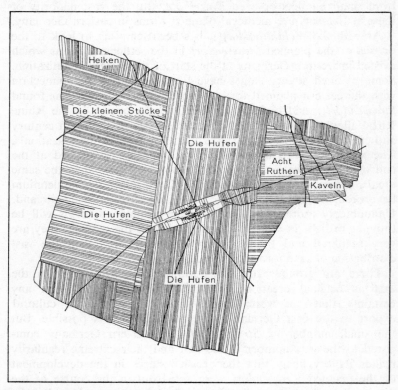

Fig. 14. The colonial Angerdorf Schönfeld (after Krenzlin)

of the settlement is split into two arms which join up again at the far end of the village. The houses are arranged along the outside of the two arms and in the centre there is a green on which there are often wells and ponds for watering cattle, the church and occasionally other public buildings. Sometimes later on, squatters were allowed to build on the edge of the *Anger*. The size and shape of the green varies somewhat though throughout the eastern parts of Germany they were generally similar to that shown in fig. 14. The land of the colonial *Angerdorf* was generally held in open fields, though in some cases part of the landholding was in a *Hufen* behind the farmhouse.

An important question in the analysis of eastern settlement forms has been the relationship between the *Angerdorf* and the *Strassendorf*. August states clearly that the *Angerdorf* is to be seen simply as a modification of the *Strassendorf*. Both forms are developments during the eastern colonization, both are associated with a planned *Gewannflur* and they are both primary planned forms, which have not developed from other forms over time[75]. Schröder on the other hand implies a distinction, at least formally, for he deals with the *Strassendorf* as a linear form and the *Angerdorf* as a green village[76]. Engels considers the *Angerdorf* also separately as the third stage in the development of the green village[77]. The first stage is the old hamlets, often with small greens to be found in north-west Germany, for instance the *Drubbel*. From this form the circular villages or *Rundlinge* along the German-Slav border developed as a planned form of the German colonization. Finally quite suddenly the *Angerdorf* developed from the *Rundling* as a major form of the large-scale colonization of the east. The development is both an increase in the degree of planning and also in the size and shape of the green, which in the fully developed *Anger* reaches a considerable size. This is merely a working hypothesis, backed at the moment by very little evidence. The same applies to the attempts by Thorpe to establish relationships between green villages throughout the whole of Europe and to point out an old ' green ' tradition[78]. What cannot be denied is that the *Strassendorf* and the *Angerdorf* exist side by side in eastern Germany and were often founded at about the same time.

There is a strong concentration of *Angerdörfer* in the area around the mouth of the Oder river. Further east it is the *Strassendorf* which becomes the dominant form. In neither area does the non-dominant form disappear altogether. Engel points to the very rapid introduction of the *Angerdorf* into the area of the lower Oder[79]. According to him no villages eastwards to a line

[75] August, O. and Schlüter, O., *Atlas des Saale- und Mittleren Elbegebiets*, part 2, 1958, pp. 66-68
[76] Schröder, K. H. and Schwarz, G., ' Die ländlichen Siedlungsformen in Mitteleuropa ', *Forsch. z. dtsch. Landeskunde*, Vol. 175, 1969, pp. 62-81
[77] Engel, F., ' Erläuterungen zur historischen Siedlungsformenkarte Mecklenburgs und Pommerns ', *Ztsch. f. Ostforschung*, 1953, pp. 208-30
[78] Thorpe, H., ' The green village as a distinctive form of settlement on the North European Plain ', *Bulletin de la Société Belge d'Études Géographiques*, Vol. 30, 1961, pp. 5-134
[79] Engel, F., *op. cit.*, 1953, pp. 224-5

F

south from Wismar were laid out with an *Anger*. The form was therefore unknown to the Germans until around 1200. Then suddenly eastwards from this line after 1216 the *Angerdorf* rapidly became the favourite colonial form. There is no real explanation for this sudden introduction but it could be put down to the very rapid acceptance by settlement planners of a newly developed more rational form. But eastwards the *Angerdorf* dies out in areas of later colonization. While Engel sees this simply as a reduction in the intensity of settlement, Mortensen considers it indicative of a change in the system of farming[80]. During the period in which the majority of the *Angerdörfer* were laid out, there was a strong emphasis on a pastoral economy. In the large-scale colonization of the east it was grain production which was most important, however. The green therefore lost its importance as an area on which cattle could be grazed and settlements were planned as *Strassendörfer*. From central Pommern eastwards then the dominant settlement form became the *Strassendorf*. Mortensen is therefore saying that the *Strassendorf* is a development from the *Angerdorf*. Other authors have taken a diametrically opposed view and consider the *Strassendorf* to pre-date the *Angerdorf*[81].

As with all other settlement forms of the east, the *Angerdorf* is also found in western Germany. There are a large number of settlements with a central green in the north-west, as has been shown earlier, but these *Drubbel* are generally small and quite irregular in layout. The *Fortadörfer* of Fehmarn and eastern Schleswig have also already been discussed. These are planned settlements but are characterized by their small size and by the rectangular shape of the green. For south Germany Jäger has written that planned settlements are present in surprisingly great numbers[82]. He points to *Angerdörfer* with planned *Gewannfluren* on the Fränkischen Alb around Eichstätt. There are further examples of planned *Angerdörfer* in the Frankenwald in the far north of Bavaria, in the Bayerischen Wald, and in the Fichtelgebirge[83]. However, few of these forms, even the medieval planned forms have the regularity of the east German

[80] Mortensen, H., 'Probleme der mittelalterlichen deutschen Kulturlandschaft', *Ber. z. dtsch. Landeskunde*, Vol. 20, 1958, p. 103

[81] Schröder and Schwarz, *op. cit.*, p. 77

[82] Jäger, H., 'Probleme und Stand der Flurformenforschung in Süddeutschland', *Ber. z. dtsch. Landeskunde*, Vol. 20, 1958, p. 153

[83] Topographischer Atlas Bayern. München, 1968, maps 63, 70, 71
Fehn, K., 'Entstehung und Entwicklung der mittelschwäbischen Angerdörfer des 14 Jahrhunderts', *Mitteilungen der Geographischen Gesellschaft*, München, Vol. 48, 1963, pp. 50-51

Angerdörfer. Some of the green villages in western Germany certainly pre-date the colonial forms of the east and may be a stage in the development of the latter.

A particularly interesting group of regular planned *Angerdörfer* occur in an area 20 or 30 kilometres west of Augsburg in Central Swabia[84]. In and around the Zusam valley the forest was cleared and several settlements founded between 1300 and 1350. The founders were relatively unimportant local lords, monasteries and burghers who employed planners (called the *Reutmeister*) to plan the settlements and attract the settlers. All the settlements were based on the *Angerdorf* and they appear to conform to strict controls on size of settlement, land division and size of *Anger*. The size of the settlement depended upon the area available, but only two village sizes were used, one with 12 and the other with 21 farms. These were arranged along a green, which was generally about 50 metres wide. These settlements were planned to have both *Hufen*, running behind the farmhouses and land in open fields. The *Hufen* were however truncated by the village fence (*Etter*), which cut the settlement off from the fields. The *Etter* was a typical feature of the older settlements of southern Germany, especially of the *Haufendörfer*, and effectively enclosed all the buildings of the village and restricted growth on the open fields beyond. The fields had approximately a constant width of around 45 metres. The individual farm was to be 25.5 hectares and any land left over after the division remained in the possession of the lord. Where not enough land was available the lord tried to buy what was needed from his neighbour. The farms rarely reached this size for the clearing of the forest went slowly and then came to a halt before the planned area of clearance had been achieved. The high degree of planning in these few settlements reminds one of the eastern colonization and indeed the middle Swabian *Angerdörfer* are the most clearly regular and planned settlements of this type in western Germany. The date of their foundation places them after the main period of *Angerdorf* planning in the east. It is therefore very tempting to see these as feedbacks in the development of the planned *Angerdorf* or if not then simply as the application of an idea developed in the east to the few remaining uncleared areas in the west.

The discussion of the settlement forms which were used in the settlement of the waste and of the east German lands has pointed to some apparent relationships between these forms and earlier Germanic forms, but it has not been possible to provide clear

[84] Fehn, *op. cit.*, pp. 33-58

proof that these relationships actually existed. It is also not possible to state categorically that any forms developed in the colonization of the waste in western Germany were used in the east, though this would seem likely. In a few cases it does seem that forms which were fully developed in the east were used in the late colonization of the waste in western Germany. What is clear, however, is that at the end of the period of high medieval colonization there was a major contrast between the almost exclusively planned settlements in the area east of the Elbe and Saale and the large areas of older and less obviously planned settlements in the west. True large areas in the west had also been settled for the first time between the ninth and thirteenth centuries, but throughout the lowlands in the west the older settlements were growing fast in an unplanned manner throughout the middle ages. The planned forms in the west were also generally smaller and less regular than those in the east. Between the extremes of planned and unplanned settlements, were those of the area along the middle Elbe, the small hamlets and *Rundlinge*, which, though planned forms produced by the German colonization, are small and irregular by comparison with the later regular forms of the east. Therefore it was at this time that one of the basic distinctions between the pattern and forms of settlement in east and west Germany was produced.

Farming in the high middle ages

In the broad treatment of settlement form in the previous section of this chapter, mention was made unsystematically to the agricultural economy in various parts of Germany. The high medieval period witnessed a steady intensification in farming, new demand patterns arose and as shown above the agricultural area increased very considerably.

During the high middle ages there were improvements in the system of farming, in the selection of seed and stock, and in farm implements. One of the first references to the three-field system of farming dates from 763, when a document of the monastery at St Gallen clearly refers to a rotation of fallow, winter sowing and summer sowing. Starting possibly on monastic lands or the land of territorial lords, the three-field system spread throughout Germany and, as has already been mentioned was adopted in many colonized eastern areas. This system meant a considerable intensification of farming over previous systems. Increased production of foodstuffs from the same area of land, together with the production from the new areas which had been cleared, meant that it was not only possible to feed the increasing population but also to produce a surplus for sale.

The three-field system was the dominant form of open-field agriculture at the end of the period of economic expansion in the fourteenth century. In the more fertile plains of Germany farming in most of the villages was run on this system. It was not, however, the only system of open-field agriculture which was practised. The infield-outfield system on the *Esch* in north-west Germany has already been described. From here settlers seem to have introduced the system into Mecklenburg. The *Esch* (i.e. the infield) was a very small area of land, which had to be manured each year to produce regular crops. On the *Esch* rye was grown year after year, often with no rotation with other crops at all (the *ewige Roggenbau* of the Weser-Ems Raum). The *Esch* demanded a large area of outfield and a large herd of sheep for the production of the manure required. Most of settlements in the north-west also had areas of meadow on which a few cattle could be grazed. This infield-outfield system was therefore an intensive user of a small area of land, but for the whole parish it was a far less intensive user of the land than the three-field system.

The two-field system was also common in some parts of Germany, but it is not necessarily a forerunner of the improved three-field system, as has been suggested. In some parts it does not appear until the early modern period. Abel points to the coincidence of those areas in which a very intensive form of agriculture was possible from an early period and the two-field system (winter sowing – fallow – summer sowing – fallow)[85]. He suggests that so much capital and labour had to be put into the intensive forms of cultivation, that only a minimum of effort could be put into the open fields; hence the dominance of the extensive two-field system. Four-field systems have been considered by Krenzlin as characteristic of parts of Mecklenburg and Pommern, though she considers them to be a development from the infield-outfield system rather than from the three-field system[86]. Nevertheless the areal importance of these four and more field systems is relatively insignificant in comparison to the three types already dealt with.

But of course not the whole of Germany had open fields. In some of the more infertile and barren parts, farming progressed

---

[85] Abel, W., *Die Geschichte der deutschen Landwirtschaft vom frühen Mittelalter bis zum 19 Jahrhundert*, Stuttgart, 1967, p. 87
[86] Abel, W., *op. cit.*, p. 87

barely at all during the high medieval period. Abel cites contemporary accounts which contrast the high ground of the Eifel with the fertile Rheingau area. On the Eifel around 1300 farming systems were still primitive. By annual burning, scrub was cleared from an area every six, eight or ten years and grain was sown for just one year. In the Rheingau on the other hand, there were very heavy grain crops and the fruit trees gave a bountiful harvest. The same land was often used for grain crops as well as vines and many sorts of fruit tree, including apples and nuts, cherries and pears[87]. Between these extremes there were many other systems. Many of the upland areas had only slightly more intensive systems than that described for the Eifel. The cultivation of grain on outfields after many years of fallow was very common, but frequently was combined with the exploitation of the woodland, which was cleared to make way for the grain crop. Numerous examples throughout Germany could be given to illustrate the combination of extensive grain cropping with a woodland economy. One area where the woodlands were used to particularly good effect was the Siegerland, where the demand for bark for tanning and charcoal for the iron industry led to high returns on the clearing of the woodland.

Many areas had an economy based on improved pasture as well as arable. The *Egarten* of southern Germany were areas used for some years as meadow or pasture and then broken up for arable cultivation. In Westfalia the *Vöhden* were used in a similar way; the land went over into private use during the arable years, but was used in common when put to pasture. It is noticeable that during the high middle-ages with the growth in trade in agricultural goods, a regional specialization set in in pastoral products. East Friesland had developed a very specialized pastoral economy certainly as early as the Carolingian period. Somewhat later in the Alps and other uplands in the south a second region of pastoral farming developed. In both these areas the pastures were improved and kept in good condition. Pastoralism dominated the scene in some areas to the extent that if the trade in dairy products and meat in exchange for grain was disturbed, the people suffered near famine conditions.

The prosperity of many areas in Germany in the high middle ages was not derived from the cultivation of grain or the keeping of cattle, but from the intensive cultivation of high-value crops. In some villages it was permitted to grow these crops on the fallow

[87] Abel, W., *op. cit.*, p. 82

field of the open-field system. This practice may have begun towards the beginning of the thirteenth century and a century later we have written records of its existence. It may, however, have been considerably later that the cultivation of the whole fallow field became commonplace. Where the fallow field was not available, crops such as beans, flax, hops, vegetables, fruit and hemp had to be grown on private land outside the open fields. It is well known that there were large areas of ' gardens ' in the high middle ages and that the gardens often covered two or three hectares. These areas were often located close to the settlement; they were fenced off and intensively cultivated. In areas with very favourable natural conditions these gardens certainly contributed considerably to the peasant's income.

Perhaps the most important of these special crops grown quite commonly by the end of the high middle ages was the vine. While there is considerable written and archaeological evidence for the existence of vineyards along the Rhine and Mosel in Roman times, there is little proof that they survived the disturbed period of the great folk movements. The first mention of the vine after this period appears in the legal codes of the Germanic tribes at the beginning of the sixth century. The Lex Salica punishes the murderer of a vintner twice as heavily as the murderer of a farm labourer and the Lex Burgundiorum also sets out to protect vineyards. At the end of the sixth century, Gregory of Tours mentions vineyards in Alsace and for the first half of the seventh century there is reference to the granting of the wine tax by King Siegbert to the Bishop of Speyer[88]. For the Upper Rhine area, Winkelmann has produced a table showing the increase in places with vineyards from the seventh century until the end of the ninth century. This increase from 17 in the seventh to 333 in the ninth century may, however, reflect simply the improvement in documentation during this period[89]. Undoubtedly some expansion did take place during this period and by 800 there were vineyards along the Upper Rhine, the Mosel, the Lahn, the Main and the Upper Danube between Regensburg and Passau[90].

Between 800 and the end of the middle ages, however, there was a very rapid expansion of the vine throughout Germany. It is interesting that this expansion continued beyond the high middle ages through the period of settlement decay in the fifteenth

[88] Winkelmann, R., ' Die Entwicklung des oberrheinischen Weinbaus ', *Marburger Geographischer Schriften*, Vol. 16, 1960, page 21
[89] Winkelmann, *op. cit.*, p. 26
[90] Abel, W., *op. cit.*, p. 127

century, reaching a maximum extent in the sixteenth century. By the end of the fourteenth century not only had the area under the vine in south-western Germany expanded very considerably, but it was also being grown in northern Germany in Westfalia, along the Weser and even north of Hamburg and in East Prussia. It had spread with the occupation of the waste and the colonization of the east. Hillsides covered with forest were cleared and vines planted in its place, while existing vineyards were cultivated more intensively and with more care than ever before. Undoubtedly it was the territorial lords, the bishops and the monastic authorities who were the greatest vintners of the early middle ages. They generally cultivated their vineyards through the labour of their own serfs. Later in the high middle ages however many of these great wine makers went over to a share-cropping system, in which their tenants on the vine slopes worked the vineyards and received part of the crop. The Cistercians were only cultivating about one tenth of their vineyards directly through their granges during the high and late middle ages; the remaining nine-tenths being cultivated by tenants. Undoubtedly the individual peasant farmer in the regions with vineyards became more and more involved in growing the vine privately during the later middle ages and the monopoly of the secular and clerical rulers disappeared.

The vine has always been a far more important crop in the economy of rural areas where it is grown than the area which it covers suggests. It demanded from the peasant a very high investment in labour but it also gave him a very great financial reward from a very small area of land. In southern Germany in favourable natural circumstances farmers specialized almost exclusively in the cultivation of the vine and wine making. These skilled workers were invited to the colonial areas of East Prussia by the Teutonic Order to found vineyards and a wine trade there. The degree of specialization, which was found in many of the wine areas, points to a major difference between the vine and other crops grown at the time. Wine was a commercial product which brought high money returns to the producer. Most of the other crops grown served largely to feed the producer's family and perhaps only relatively little was left over for sale. Duby points clearly to the commercial nature of the medieval wine trade, which he states '. . . injected life into the rural economy by stimulating a new and important demand for cereal supplies and by animating currents of exchange between wine and grain countries '[91]. The

[91] Duby, G., *Rural economy and country life in the medieval West.* Translation from the French by C. Postan, 1968, p. 141

Cologne merchants exported Rhine wines at this time to England and the Low Countries for instance and in Germany itself there was a great trade in wine between town and country. The best wines remained in the private vineyards of the great nobles who received very high prices for the product, but the small peasant benefited too, though his wine was of lower sale value. A traveller through the most favoured parts of the Rhinelands in the middle of the thirteenth century may well have had a similar experience to that of a French traveller through Auxerre, south-east of Paris, who remarked that ' these people sow nothing, reap nothing and gather nothing into their barns. They only need to send their wine to Paris on the nearby river which goes straight there. The sale of wine in this city brings them in a good profit which pays entirely for their food and clothing '[92].

The cultivation of the vine and of the other special crops described above was fostered by the change in the pattern of demand which took place during the high middle ages. In the early middle ages the demand for agricultural produce was very small. Almost the whole population had a very direct connection with farming and there were few large towns in which a non-farming population had to be fed. But slowly through the Carolingian period and the Saxon Empire the number of towns grew and therefore the demand for foodstuffs increased. Gradually a monetary system developed in which townspeople bought farm produce at regular markets and the farm population was able to buy town produced goods. With the disintegration of the Empire and the creation of a large number of *de facto* independent states, the number of town foundations increased enormously. In the east, a very large number of planned towns were founded, often at the same time as the villages which were to supply them with foodstuffs. Whilst some of these towns never grew much above the size of a village, and many of them remained the homes of farmers rather than traders, the growth of existing towns and the founding of many quite successful ones led to an increase in demand for food products. This rise in demand had very far reaching effects on the village and the whole agricultural system.

Whilst very great trading centres grew up like Lübeck, Hamburg, Bremen and Leipzig, engaging in long distance trade, each town was deeply involved in trading with the rural areas immediately outside its walls. Around the towns rings of different crops or of the same crop under different systems of agriculture developed, in a similar way to that postulated by von Thünen in

[92] Duby, *op. cit.*, p. 140

the nineteenth century. Immediately around the town there soon developed a ring of intensive free cultivation of garden crops. Beyond this inner ring other crops, all grown under less intensive systems, were produced. Demand was of course not the only factor influencing the location of agricultural production and especially with those crops which are very demanding on the environmental conditions the simple pattern of rings around the towns was distorted. Nevertheless, the effects of a new pattern of demand were felt throughout the high middle ages.

The increase in demand was certainly a major factor in the increase in corn prices which took place during the thirteenth and early fourteenth centuries[93]. The price increases must have affected other arable crops, and some certainly to a greater degree. This was a considerable spur to the colonization of new land. As a result, poorer or less accessible land was cleared and cultivated. There is evidence that demand kept ahead of supply during the thirteenth century, so that prices were continually rising. In this situation even land which was considered marginal or sub-marginal a century later was being made to yield a good return. Frequently the seed/yield ratio was far lower on these poorer soils and they were rapidly exhausted because of inadequate manuring. The high prices being paid for agricultural produce also encouraged the fragmentation of the land. It was possible for a father to divide his land equally between his sons, and for each new farm still to make a handsome profit. Evidence has already been brought for the division of the open fields into very small parcels in the fourteenth century[94]. Agricultural prosperity undoubtedly encouraged the adoption of a system of partible inheritance (*Realteilung*) and therefore the creation of small farms with fragmented landholding. When the depression hit farming both these trends from the boom period were going to lead to disaster. Those who were cultivating marginal land in the new situation and those dependent on income from the sale of farm produce were to be badly hit by the new circumstances, for indeed, the slump in agriculture came.

[93] Abel, W., *op. cit.*, p. 128
[94] See pp. 26-7

3 The late medieval agricultural depression

Some authors have doubted whether an economic depression of great magnitude and of considerable duration ever took place in the late middle ages. The work of Abel and others in Germany has put the fact of a late medieval depression beyond doubt, however. Their work in Germany is supported by massive evidence from other European countries, where similar price movements and population changes took place at approximately the same time. Falling prices for agricultural products, rising prices for some craft products, rapidly rising real wages, settlement desertion and the expansion of forest and waste are the characteristics of the late medieval period throughout Europe between c. 1350 and 1500.

Population movements

Medieval population statistics are difficult to obtain and must be treated carefully. There would, however, appear to be sufficient evidence to suggest a steady rise in population up to the beginning of the thirteenth century and a fall in population from the the middle of that century until the beginning of the sixteenth. The decline in population affected town and country alike, although the towns benefited from a strong rural-urban migration. It is much easier to establish population decline in the medieval town than in the countryside, where records are found less frequently.

The decline in rural population was a result both of a surplus of deaths over births, and a high rate of out-migration. It is, however, difficult to distinguish between the two causes in the available statistics. It is possible in a large number of cases to prove loss of population for villages, through a comparison of the number of farms occupied in the mid-fourteenth and mid-fifteenth centuries. The movement from the countryside to the town is easily proved from the lists of immigrants, which exist for a large number of towns. The proof for a high death rate in the countryside is far more difficult. Many contemporary sources speak very generally in terms of high death rate in town and country alike. Abel quotes a Thuringian Chronicler for the year 1438 who wrote:

> . . . the people died of hunger, and in villages, and on the streets they fell dead and lay there for a long time before being buried . . . and because the dead were left unburied for such a long time, the air was poisoned . . . and a great plague broke out and a terrible wave of deaths, which claimed more victims than the previous period of starvation . . . so that some villages and many small towns died out and not a human being was to to be found in them[1].

In Holstein and in Saxony mass graves of this period have been found in rural areas, the dead coming presumably from the surrounding deserted settlements[2].

The medieval town depended on migrants from the countryside to sustain growth or at least stable numbers. This was true not only for the late middle ages but also for the whole period from the eleventh century. Two major periods of settlement desertion and rural-urban migration must be treated separately. That period with which we are concerned here, the late medieval period, was a time of falling population and very general out-migration from rural areas, both from those close to the town and those in more remote areas. The other period is that from the eleventh to the fourteenth centuries which has been described already as one of increasing population and settlement expansion. During these centuries of development and expansion, however, many villages close to the rapidly growing towns were deserted as the villagers moved into the towns and the towns for their part swallowed up the former lands of the villages. The desertion of these settlements was not a sign of economic decline or high death rate, but rather one of boom conditions in which the rate of urbanization was particularly rapid.

During the late medieval period, however, the newcomers in the towns came from further afield and in large numbers. In Danzig between 1370 and 1379, there was an annual average of

---

[1] Abel, W., *Die Wüstungen des ausgehenden Mittelalters*, Stuttgart, 1955, p. 81-82
[2] Abel, W., *op. cit.*, 1955, p. 78

immigrant registrations of 192, in Hamburg between 1401 and 1420 an annual average of 107 and in Frankfurt-on-Main 48 between the years 1430 and 1500[3]. This movement to the towns does not seem to have led to any great increase in their size. Many of them reached a zenith in their development during the middle of the fourteenth century and did not achieve the same population totals again for another two centuries[4]. Cologne had approximately 35,000 inhabitants in the mid-fourteenth century, from which time the population fell considerably. By 1574, over two centuries later, the population had reached only 37,000. The population of Worms and Speyer fell by more than one half in the fourteenth and fifteenth centuries. If the late medieval period was one in which there was simply a redistribution of population between town and country in a situation of general economic prosperity, as some German researchers have suggested, then one would expect the towns to have grown rapidly. Most of the evidence suggests that urban populations fell in spite of the positive balance of migration.

The desertion of settlement

The population movements suggested above led to a radical change in the settlement pattern of the German countryside. While it is very difficult to produce reliable quantitative material on population changes and totals, the facts of settlement desertion are spread so obviously both in the field and in written records, that they can hardly be challenged. Throughout Germany, and especially in the later settled upland areas, traces of arable terraces in woodlands, the occasional ruins of old churches standing alone in the fields, the presence of an old village pond with perhaps a lime tree far from present-day farms give testimony to the former existence of settlements.

The number of settlements which did completely disappear in the late medieval period form in some areas a very high proportion of the total number of settlements which existed beforehand. It is obviously difficult to compile comprehensive lists of cases of settlement desertion. It is clear that no trace will be found of some villages, which have disappeared, so that the final total will probably underestimate the real position. On the other hand, some cases will be counted, which are either not cases of settlement desertion at all or which occurred at a time other than the

[3] Abel, W., *op. cit.*, 1955, p. 33
[4] *ibid.*, p. 33

late middle ages. Some settlements may have changed their names, so that their sudden disappearance from the written sources does not mean that they were deserted. In some other cases two settlements coalesced, the final large new village taking the name of only one of its component settlements, whilst the name of the other disappeared from the map. It has already been shown above that some cases of settlement desertion took place during the previous period of the high middle ages through the process of rapid urbanization. In some instances it may be difficult to separate these from others which occurred later in the fourteenth and fifteenth centuries. Neverthless it is probably right to assume that the majority of quantitative statements on the number of settlement desertions in the late medieval period underestimate the true magnitude of the changes. This is especially so where the pattern of settlement in the high medieval period was not one of nucleated villages but a more dispersed one with isolated farms. It is relatively easy to trace villages which have disappeared; on the other hand, it is far more difficult to trace the disappearance of isolated dwellings.

A rough idea of the magnitude of village desertions is given by measuring those villages lost against the total of villages lost plus those which survived. The loss of settlements measured this way is frequently extremely high. Alone on the topographical map, scale 1:50,000, of part of the Eichsfeld near Duderstadt, which covers an area of approximately 500 square kilometres, there are 78 deserted settlements out of 138 which existed before the desertion – this gives a desertion quotient of 56 per cent[5]. The southern Eichsfeld would seem to have suffered a similar loss of population. The map of Schlüter and August of part of Bezirk Erfurt north and west of Mühlhausen shows a loss of 200 out of 360 villages, that is 55 per cent[6]. Müller in 1911 gave a figure of 59 per cent for the whole of the Eichsfeld[7]. The same figure is given by Jäger for the area adjoining the Eichsfeld to the north[8].

In another area close to the Eichsfeld, but physically and historically very different from it, the proportion of deserted settlements rises to 83 per cent[9]. This is the area between the Elbe,

[5] Jäger, H., *Historisch–landeskundliche Exkursionkarte von Niedersachsen, Blatt Duderstadt, Erläuterungsheft,* Hildesheim, 1964, p. 15
[6] Schlüter, O. and August, O., *Atlas des Saale– und mittleren Elbegebietes,* Part 2, 1961, pp. 103-4
[7] Quoted in: Abel, W., *op. cit.,* 1955, p. 6
[8] Jäger, H., 'Zur Methodik der genetischen Kulturlandschaftsforschung', *Ber. z. Dt. Landeskde.,* Vol. 30, 1963, p. 187
[9] Quoted in: Abel, W., *op. cit.,* 1955, p. 7

Saale, Sülze and Bode, just south of Magdeburg. Here only 33 of the 179 settlements which existed in the eleventh century survive. The 146 places had all disappeared by the middle of the sixteenth century. Though this is an extreme example, quite large areas would appear to have a settlement desertion quotient of between 50 per cent and 80 per cent. In the High Rhön between 50 per cent and 60 per cent of settlements were lost and in the Seulings-wald this was around 70 per cent[10].

All these areas appear to have had a nucleated settlement pattern before the desertion of settlement. In north-western Germany, on the other hand, a very much lower desertion quotient has been derived in an area with a far less nucleated pattern of settlement. Abel suggests that desertion was negligible there, with below 10 per cent of the settlements lost[11]. This may be roughly accurate; on the other hand, he probably overlooks the desertion of many small hamlets and isolated farms. Again there appears to be some justification for maintaining that the losses of villages in the areas of older, early medieval Germanic settlements are less than in those of high medieval colonization. In the Leine valley, on the loess around Hildesheim, on the fertile *Gäue* of Württemberg and in the Rhine Rift few of the older Germanic settlements were lost. However, a far higher proportion of the younger settlements in the surrounding areas were lost. Whilst the old settlements of the Leine Valley near Göttingen survived, many of those in the Göttinger Wald and in the northern Eichsfeld disappeared. Nearly all those places which disappeared had names which ended in *-rode, -hagen* and *-feld,* suggesting a foundation date in the twelfth or thirteenth centuries. In the southern Eichsfeld of the 157 settle-ments founded between 800 and 1300 which disappeared in the late medieval period, no less than 66 per cent had names ending in *-rode*[12].

It would appear from the above discussion that the degree of settlement desertion was greatest in those areas with a nucleated settlement pattern at the start of the fourteenth century (and these were generally the areas with a considerable dependance on grain crops in the open fields), and in regions colonized late in the high medieval period. Abel has drawn together much of the available evidence in a map of settlement desertion reproduced here as

[10] Jäger, H., ' Entwicklungsperioden agrarer Siedlungsgebiete im mittleren Westdeutschland seit der frühen 13 Jahrhundert ', *Würzburger Geog. Arb.,* Vol. 6, 1958, pp. 65-71
[11] Abel, W., *Die Geschichte der deutschen Landwirtschaft,* 1967, p. 111
[12] Schlüter, O. and August, O., *op. cit.,* part 2., 1961, p. 103

fig. 15. The whole of north-west Germany can be seen to have lost less than 20 per cent of its settlements and the same applies to the Bavarian plateau. On the other hand, in an area on and between the Upper Weser and middle Elbe and in Württemberg

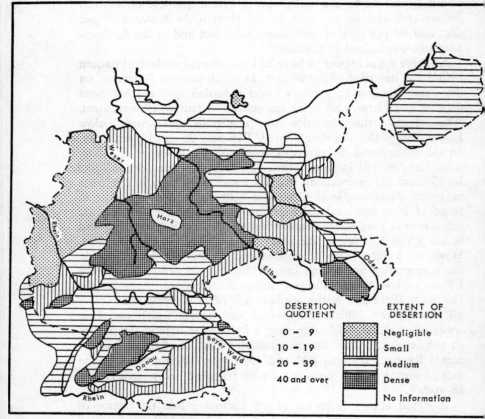

Fig. 15. The desertion quotient in Germany. A measure of village desertion in late-medieval Europe (after Abel)

over 40 per cent of the settlements were lost. This map may give a general idea of the distribution, but it makes no claim for exactness. It may well reflect the amount of research applied to different areas of Germany and it certainly reflects differences in the ease of finding desertions.

But of course a large number of settlements survived! It would not be right if the process of settlement desertion was seen entirely in terms of those settlements which were lost completely.

It has long been realized that any attempt to judge the true impact and extent of population decrease and migration must take note of the partial desertions, in which, though never completely deserted, some of the farms were left unoccupied for a long period. That a large number of villages lost population is testified to both by records of population before and during the late middle ages, and by the numerous complaints of landlords that their revenues were falling, partly because a large number of their farms were not occupied and could not be let. The main difference of course between these shrunken villages and the complete desertions is that whereas the majority of the latter were lost for ever, most of the former grew again in the early modern period.

Abel has collected a considerable amount of evidence for population loss in settlements which did not completely disappear[13]. In the Amt Wittenberg on the Elbe in 1474 there were 94 *Hufen* left uncultivated out of a total of 963 in 30 villages. The village of Holloben in Saxony paid in taxes in the years 1394 and 1395, 30 *Scheffel* of rye, 54 *Scheffel* of oats and 33 *Groschen* (coins). The population had fallen so much by 1421 that the landlord only received 5 *Scheffel* of rye, 9 *Scheffel* of oats and 5 *Groschen*. While not all the decrease in revenue is due to population decline, this was the major factor. In the Ohrnwald in 1437 one farmer in Beltersrot farmed alone what previously had been five separate farms. The farmers had moved away or died and no new tenants could be found[14]. In the Seulingswald the village of Schenkolz had only one dwelling in 1585, Lampertsfeld had only two and Wüstefeld only nine[15]. Some of these shrunken settlements may have been completely deserted for a short while but then reinhabited later. Temporary desertions are very common features. In the Gersfelder Rhön for instance, there were 26 temporary desertions of settlement whereas only 18 settlements were lost permanently[16]. In the former Amt Aerzen near Hameln, 45 per cent of all settlements were totally deserted during the late middle ages and subsequently resettled[17]. The loss of population and of settlements in the late middle ages was therefore considerably

[13] Abel, W., *op. cit.*, 1955
[14] Engel, A., ' Die Siedlungsformen im Ohrnwald ', *Tübinger Geog. Studien*, Vol. 16, 1964, p. 19
[15] Jäger, H., 'Entwicklungsperioden agrarer Siedlungsgebiete im mittleren Westdeutschland seit dem frühen 13. Jahrhundert', *Würzburger Geog. Arbeiten*, Vol. 6, 1958, pp. 65-67
[16] Jäger, *op. cit.*, pp. 68-70
[17] Marten, H. R., ' Die Entwicklung der Kulturlandschaft im alten Amt Aerzen des Landkreises Hameln-Pyrmont ', *Göttinger Geog. Abh.*, Vol. 53, 1969, pp. 54-56

higher than a simple desertion quotient worked out on the number of settlements deserted permanently would suggest.

The decline in the cultivated area

With a rapid decline in the rural population leading to a large scale abandonment of farms, agricultural land was bound to go out of cultivation. This loss of farmland is testified by the arable terraces frequently found under woodland. These are especially common in the late-settled uplands of central Germany. On the other hand, large areas which were left uncultivated for much of the later medieval period, were subsequently reclaimed for farming as the demand for agricultural land and produce increased again in the succeeding centuries. Not all the deserted arable land went totally out of agricultural use. Some of it was used as pasture or for rough grazing, through which the ridge and furrow of the medieval arable fields were preserved.

The scale of the settlement desertion was so great, that not all the land could be cultivated by the remaining villagers. In many cases complete villages were deserted not through short range migration to neighbouring settlements but through long range migration to the towns, and through the death of the inhabitants. The scale of the desertion can be seen for the eastern colonial area in the figure of 6,000 deserted *Hufen* out of a total of 32,000 in control of the Teutonic Order. This was in 1419. Just 20 years later 80 per cent were deserted in the administrative area of Schwetz on the Weichsel[18]. According to a contemporary source, in the middle of the fifteenth century only 3,013 of the original 21,000 villages in the land of the Teutonic Order remained inhabited and about the same time over 1,000 churches were counted in ruins[19]. All round the deserted villages the forest was creeping back to take over again from corn and pasture. This pattern of events is suggested too in the results of several pollen analyses, such as that at the Roten Moor in the Rhön[20]. The percentage of grain pollen increases to a peak around A.D. 1200, from which date there is a steep and continuous fall to a nadir between 1400 and 1450. From 1500 there is a rapid increase in the percentage of grain pollen, as the cultivated area grew again. The pollen diagram of the Roten Moor shows the rapid expansion

[18] Abel, W., *op. cit.*, 1955, p. 29
[19] Abel, W., *op. cit.*, 1967, p. 118
[20] Overbeck, F. and Griez, I., ' Mooruntersuchungen zur Rekurrenzflächenfrage und Siedlungsgeschichte in der Rhön ', *Flora*, 1954

of the wooded area during the late medieval period, an expansion in which birch, hazel and beech were the main contributors.

The landlords were the group who had most to lose when land went out of cultivation, for it meant a loss of income to them. The extent of this problem can be judged from the numerous orders which were published preventing migration or at least making it very difficult. In the fourteenth century it became far more common for the lords to levy fines on those leaving their farms. It even became common for the lords to insist that farmers who wished to leave their farms should find a suitable replacement before they left. In a period where men and not land were in short supply this could mean that the farmer remained tied to his plot. It became more difficult for fleeing peasants to find refuge in other communities, even in the towns. More and more pressure was put on the towns to return the peasants to their home villages.

At the same time of course land became very cheap. Whereas land rents had been very high at the end of the high medieval period, they began to fall in the fourteenth and stayed at very low levels during the fifteenth century. There was a great deal of land available and farmers could afford to underbid landlords for the rent of the land. Sitting tenants could often succeed in getting their rents reduced, in spite of general opposition from the landlords. The situation became so difficult for the lords that they often offered several years free of taxes as an encouragement to settlers. As a result, in spite of falling prices for grain, many farmers took on more land. For this reason the average size of farms increased in area. This meant that less land went out of cultivation than might be expected from the bare figures for desertion.

Where the remaining inhabitants of a shrunken village moved to a larger settlement nearby leaving their home village completely deserted, they were not relieved of their rights and duties with respect of their old farmland. Very often the land remained in cultivation, rights to the common lands were maintained and the villagers continued paying dues to the lord. Very often the group of migrants retained their identity in their adopted village, building their houses together in one quarter and even electing their own administrative officers, apart from the inhabitants of the adopted village. This is another reason why the area of land which went out of cultivation was less than might be thought. The late medieval period was, in terms of agrarian structure, a time at which farms were growing in size, though as Engel has pointed out, this does not mean that the field size was necessarily growing[21].

Changes in land use during the late middle ages

It has already been suggested that the area of woodland increased at the expense of the cultivated land. This was especially true in the hilly areas of central Germany, the Rhön, the Weserbergland, the Harz, the Thuringian Forest and the Seulingswald for instance. Jäger has calculated that in the Seulingswald, the wooded area increased by about 27 per cent of the total area during the late medieval period[22]. However, there were changes in the relative and absolute importance of the main types of agricultural land use as well. Not only was arable land replaced by woodland, it was also turned over to pasture.

The decline in the arable area is strongly suggested by the results of pollen analyses, such as that at the Roten Moor mentioned previously. This evidence is confirmed by many written sources, which point to the conversion of arable both to woodland and to pasture. A document from 1487 points out that the land of the village of Mildenhöft in the Altmark, which was deserted in 1444, was being used as pasture by the population of the neighbouring village of Zienau[23]. In Swabia the Zimmerische Chronicle recorded that the lands of many villages, which had been destroyed by war or by plague, were used as pasture[24]. Sometimes it was the landlords who turned over large areas to sheep ranches, evicting what remained of the local population. This was not nearly as common as it appears to have been in England, but was neverthless significant locally. In south-west Germany for instance a number of the larger monasteries, such as Bebenhausen near Tübingen, kept very large herds of sheep on their estates.

The decline of the arable acreage is not surprising. The demand for grain in the late medieval period was inelastic over the greater part of its price range. There was little chance of increasing the demand for grain except through an increase in the population. An increase in prosperity had little effect. With the declining population of the fourteenth and fifteenth centuries, the demand for grain fell and its market price started a slide downwards, a slide which was not to end before the first half of the sixteenth century. At the same time, the price of labour was increasing rapidly, whilst the products of urban craft industries were either

[21] Engel, A., *op. cit.*, 1964, p. 97
[22] Jäger, *op. cit.*, 1958, p. 67
[23] Abel, W., *op. cit.*, 1955, p. 44
[24] *ibid.*, p. 44

becoming absolutely more expensive or at least relatively so. Some contemporary sources suggest that it did not pay at all to grow grain for the market and so land was just left idle. Farmers were unwilling to take land even as a gift, because the cost of cultivating it was greater than the return from the crop.

On the other hand, the demand for animal products was more elastic than for grain, then, as it is now. Whilst the price of animal products appears to have fallen, at least during the second half of the fifteenth century, the fall was not nearly so great as that of grain. From late medieval records it appears that the consumption of meat was very large even by present-day standards. This applies to both town and country, and right through the social classes. Regulations governing the meals to be given to servants in the town or to the feudal peasant farmers in the country show that in most cases two meat meals a day were the rule and that a pound of meat was not an unusual amount to be devoured at one meal. In many of the towns of late medieval Germany the average meat consumption was as high as three or four pounds of meat per head per day. In spite of a general decline of population during this period and the slump in arable farming, the craftsmen in the town and the agricultural workers in the country remained quite prosperous, for they received high prices for their craft products or for their labour. Their demand for grain changed little in spite of the falling prices, but the money saved on grain purchases (except in famine years) together with the increase in their real income could be partly spent on animal products. The demand for these products therefore fell at a far slower rate than that for grain. At the same time the costs of production for the farmer of these animal products was generally far less than those of grain. There was every encouragement therefore for the farmer in the late medieval period to change from arable production to pastoral farming, where the farmer was producing partly or largely for the market.

So great was the demand for meat that a major trade in cattle throughout Germany grew up, bringing animals from East Friesland south into Westfalia and on a larger scale from the east, and especially from Hungary, to the south and west of Germany. Extremely large markets were held in some of the most important medieval towns such as Cologne and Nürnberg, whilst elsewhere along the route there were recognised resting places, such as the Geist in Münster, described by Müller-Wille[25]. The Geist is the

[25] Müller-Wille, W., ' Blöcke, Streifen und Hufen ', *Berichte zur deutschen Landeskunde*, Vol. 29, 1962, p. 304

southern part of a dry sandy ridge running roughly north-south through Münster. In the fifteenth century the old and complex field pattern of narrow strips was abolished through the creation of a block-field pattern. Farms were also moved to make way for cattle pasture. Around 100 hectares were used for this purpose, a testimony to the size of the trade, which was run partly by two local monasteries, Überwasser in the town and St Moritz to the east of it.

Whilst forest, rough grazing or pasture were taking over from arable land, the vine, together with some other specialized crops, was still expanding the outer limits of its growth area, and the vintners remained prosperous. During the late medieval period there was a rapid expansion of vineyards in East Prussia, which was stimulated and supported by the Teutonic Knights. Vintners from southern Germany and even from Italy were invited to come to Prussia to lay out new vineyards for the Order. Expansion also took place across the North German Lowland, into Schleswig-Holstein and Silesia. But although the northward expansion of vineyards seems today something quite exceptional, the expansion within the established vineyard regions of south-west Germany is just as significant.

Winkelmann, working in the Upper Rhine area, sets the maximum extent of vineyards for that region in the first half of the sixteenth century, though other writers have suggested an earlier date[26]. It is during the early part of the sixteenth century that the number of settlements with vineyards reaches a maximum, though there is little knowledge of the area of vineyards in each settlement. By 1500 they had climbed up the slopes of the hills on either side of the Rhine, taking the place of woodland. So great was the expansion that at the end of the fifteenth century and at the beginning of the sixteenth, numerous restrictions were placed on the creation of new vineyards by town councils and the nobility, worried about the decline in the arable area. For Württemberg, Schröder sees the first few years of the seventeenth century, up to the start of the Thirty Years' War, as the period with the maximum extent of vineyards[27]. He claims for the Taubergrund that the decline of viticulture did not begin until the end of the eighteenth century. While it is undoubtedly true that in some of the most favoured areas and in areas which

[26] Winkelmann, R., ' Die Entwicklung des oberrheinischen Weinbaus ', *Marburger Geog. Schriften*, Vol. 16, 1960, pp. 30-33
[27] Schröder, K. H., ' Weinbau und Siedlung in Württemberg ', *Forschungen zur dtsch. Landeskunde*, Vol. 73, 1953, p. 63

escaped the Thirty Years' War relatively unharmed there was no break in viticulture during the sixteenth century, there would appear to be sufficient evidence to show that there was a retreat from the margin of cultivation in the early part of this century. The retreat in northern Germany probably started earlier than this. Nevertheless we can identify the late medieval period as one during which the area of vineyards was increasing and towards the end of which it perhaps reached a maximum.

It was not only the vine which was a profitable plant to grow during this period of agricultural crisis. Fruit of all varieties was in great demand in the towns, as was wine. In fact the profitability of the two products often benefited the same areas, where the vine and the fruit tree grew together. This applies especially to the Upper Rhine and Württemberg. Other areas specialized in crops less demanding on the climate but still of considerable commercial value. Hops grew to be a major crop by the end of this period when there were hop gardens the length and breadth of Germany. Flax was another plant of considerable value as were the various plants used in dyeing. Market garden crops too could be found around any of the medieval towns, serving the urban market and using the town sewage for manure. Fresh vegetables of all sorts were produced together with fresh milk in some instances. Throughout Germany therefore, islands of prosperity and even development were found in an ocean of decay and desolation.

The importance of these commercial crops is seen in the history of the settlements which during the late middle ages had some part in this trade. Strong evidence shows that villages with a stake in the wine industry were far less affected by population decline and desertion than villages dependent upon the arable fields[28]. There is even evidence which suggests that new settlements were established during the late middle ages for the purpose of engaging in the wine trade[29]. In the Neckar basin, where in 1500 there were rather more parishes with viticulture than without, only one village with viticulture was deserted to every two without[30]. In areas with a high density of towns (and a high demand for wine) and good natural conditions for viticulture, the desertion of settlement may have been even less severe.

The wine villages were frequently walled during the late medieval period, partly at least to protect the wine supply of the

[28] Schröder, *op. cit.*, pp. 100-8
[29] *ibid.*, pp. 83-88
[30] *ibid.*, pp. 103-4

towns and monasteries, which consumed huge quantities. There is a close correlation between the number of walled villages in the highly urbanized areas of Württemberg in the late medieval period and the number of villages with a highly developed viticulture[31]. A further effect of viticulture on the settlements of south-western Germany at this time was the fragmentation of the land parcels. Elsewhere in Germany land was going out of cultivation, farms were growing in size and in some places there was a consolidation of land parcels taking place. In those areas with viticulture, the population was not declining at the same rate, if at all. The wine trade was prosperous and looked like staying so. Therefore the individual farmer felt no great incentive to attempt to enlarge his vineyard and consolidation was difficult. With such a labour intensive branch of farming an increase in size also meant the need to hire more labour at a time when labour was rare and expensive. The large ecclesiastical landowners on the other hand did go some way towards land consolidation and the enlargement of their holdings.

So in a situation with general agrarian depression, widespread desertion of settlement and loss of cultivated land to forest and rough grazing, those areas with highly specialized farming presented a stark contrast. They were prosperous regions, still expanding farming and cultivating new land. They had, in some cases at least, a rising population and their villages were not decaying but if anything growing and improving. These were the entirely market-orientated regions and significantly they were located mainly where there was a high density of towns. In south German towns, such as Esslingen and Tübingen, some of the great medieval wine cellars of the ecclesiastical rulers have been preserved to testify to the value which was put on wine during this period. But the other crops which have been mentioned from fruit to fresh vegetables helped many an area to survive the economic crisis in agriculture more or less unscathed.

The causes of settlement desertion

As we have seen, some authors have disputed the view that the desertion of some villages and the shrinking of others was a sign of population decline and agricultural depression. They argue that villages lost population through migration to the rapidly growing towns and to the larger and more prosperous villages near to the town. In other words the late-medieval period was one of rapid

[31] *ibid.*, pp. 88-93

economic development and population growth and the desertion of some settlements is an indication of the degree of urbanization and agglomeration. The evidence of very considerable settlement desertion as well as the loss of arable land, together with evidence that, in spite of great cultural and architectural achievement, the towns also lost population seem to refute this theory. The movement of prices during the period also does not seem to support the urbanization theory.

Abel identifies the reasons for the desertion of settlement under two headings: firstly, the causes of the decline of population and secondly, the causes of population movements[32]. Without the decline of population, the desertion of settlement could indeed simply have been a result of agglomeration, whilst without population movements the decline of population might simply have led to a reduction in size of all settlements but a desertion of none.

THE LOSS OF POPULATION

Not only did population in the countryside decline during the late medieval period, but the total population of Germany also fell. Whilst countrymen flooded into the towns, the towns could at best manage to maintain their population steady. At worst they lost a large proportion of the population and did not regain their early fourteenth century numbers until the sixteenth century. Population movements explain only relative changes between town and country and we must look to changes in birth and death rates to explain absolute changes in population in late medieval Germany.

We know relatively little about the birth rate at this time. There are indications in contemporary literature that perhaps there was a decline in birth rate. For instance, around the middle of the fifteenth century, it was noted that few of the Burgher families of Vienna managed to exist for more than a few generations before dying out. This was attributed to the low birth rate. The birth rate was certainly still high compared to modern rates but even a small fall if sustained would have been quite enough to turn a growing population into a declining one. Abel suggests as a possible order of magnitude a fall from about 42 live births per thousand in the high middle ages to 39 per thousand in the late medieval period[33]. The scarcity of information on this topic makes it difficult to state categorically that a falling birth rate played a

---

[32] Without doubt the best discussion of the causes of settlement desertion is to be found in Wilhelm Abel's book *Die Wüstungen des ausgehenden Mittelalters.*

[33] Abel, W., *op. cit.*, 1955, p. 85

part in the decline of population in the fourteenth and fifteenth centuries. That there was an increasing death rate is, however, beyond dispute.

In the past too much emphasis was sometimes put on the epidemics of the late medieval period as an explanation of settlement desertion. One must be careful on the other hand not to underestimate their importance. The significance attached by some authors to destruction during wars and feuds was also undoubtedly too great, though again they no doubt contributed to a high death rate in some areas. The south-west German wars between the town-leagues in the last quarter of the fourteenth century certainly took a heavy toll of population and settlements in Swabia. There were numerous other smaller wars during the late medieval period, which again locally led to the disappearance of settlements. It is unlikely, however, that these local conflicts could have produced the very large and very general falls in population registered not only throughout central Europe but also in Britain, Scandinavia and other countries of Europe. The devastations of war almost certainly led to famine, which left the population weaker in its resistance to epidemics.

Death on a large scale was recorded for the early years of the fourteenth century. The worst years were those from 1309 to 1318 when famine throughout Europe caused the desertion of many farms and even complete settlements. This was, however, nothing in comparison to what was to come. Between 1348 and 1350 the Bubonic Plague raced through Germany, decimating the population. In Bremen it is estimated that between 60 per cent and 70 per cent of the town's population died through this first epidemic[34]. In many towns large pits had to be dug to bury the dead, as no room was left in the graveyards (for instance in Vienna and Osnabrück). A contemporary source for Vienna mentions 40,000 dead being buried in one complex of pits, and, although this is probably exaggerated, the report suggests that very large numbers of bodies were buried. More precise evidence is given for selective groups of tradesmen in some towns. For instance in Hamburg 35 per cent of the 34 master bakers died during the first epidemic, while 76 per cent of the members of the town council died.

These figures relate only to the first epidemic at the midcentury. Abel lists the later epidemics, which also killed large numbers of townsmen[35]. In the years 1356 and 1357 bubonic

[34] Abel, W., *op. cit.*, 1955, p. 77
[35] *ibid.*, pp. 79-83

plague again swept the whole of Germany. In 1364-5 the plague returned following a famine. Plague devastated the population locally in many parts of Germany between 1369 and 1379 but it was only in 1380 that the whole of Germany was affected again. We hear then from Vienna again of the burial of 15,000 people. Epidemics were recorded from one part of the country or another throughout the remainder of the fourteenth century and into the fifteenth. In 1438 the whole of Germany was again affected by an epidemic which killed thousands of people. Further outbreaks are recorded throughout the fifteenth century. During the 150 years from *c* 1350 until 1500 disease had taken a great toll of life in the German towns. Even the incoming rural migrants could not prevent widespread falls in population. For the countryside there is little written evidence of the affects of the plague but it must be assumed that it made some inroads into the rural population too. One might think that the most remote settlements would escape the plague sooner than the towns and the larger accessible villages. Yet it was often just these small remote younger settlements which were deserted. The reasons for their desertion are obviously connected with population movements rather than simply birth or death rates.

SETTLEMENT DESERTION AND MIGRATION

In the later stages of expansion during the high medieval period, the frontier of settlement had been pushed onto land which was far from ideal for settlement and for agriculture. The dry sandy areas of the Lüneburg Heath and the Fläming had been cultivated, the drought-ridden *Börde* around Magdeburg had also been occupied. The higher slopes of the Alps and Central Uplands of Germany had been settled and the poor soil cultivated. In short settlement and cultivation had been pushed onto land which was marginal at this time. Come a depression in agriculture or a slight deterioration in the climate, then these areas were going to be hit very hard economically.

The expansion onto marginal land was undoubtedly a major factor in the desertion of a large number of settlements in the late medieval period. The great loss of settlements on the Magdeburger Börde has already been mentioned above, and on the Fläming only four of the 30 settlements founded in the high medieval period survived. In both cases drought was the major problem, for settlement and cultivation had lowered the water table. The same was true of much of the *Geest* in north-west Germany, where the soil was also rapidly exhausted by cultivation. In the contemporary sources we can read of more spectacular cases, in which villages were lost in avalanches, rock falls, floods and sand storms. We must not, however, forget the main course of settlement desertion, where the population declined in numbers through gradual out-migration until finally the remnant of the original population moved to another larger settlement in better conditions, leaving the original village totally deserted.

In support of this theory is the fact that in general a higher proportion of the young settlements founded in the thirteenth or fourteenth centuries were deserted than the older more established settlements of an earlier period. Some evidence for this has already been presented. The younger villages were generally those founded in the least attractive areas for settlement and agriculture. They were therefore the first to go. This can be clearly seen from the relative frequency with which younger and older place-names appear in the lists of settlements which were deserted. Always it is names ending in *-rode, -hausen, -heim, -hagen* and the like which disappeared from the map in the greatest number. These were the typical suffixes attached to the forest clearance villages of the high middle ages.

But of course settlements in what would appear to be an excellent position to survive also disappeared. These cases cannot be explained by a bad selection of village site or by poor soil or by excessive slope or difficult micro-climate. Here it was the crisis in agriculture alone or perhaps in conjunction with local factors, such as the type of landlord, which was important. The very high loss of later settlements located in positions which were not ideal in terms of agriculture and settlement is also explained only in conjunction with the crisis in agriculture. The depression of grain prices combined with the high wages of hired labour led to a selective weeding out of settlements so that only those located in more favourable positions survived.

Basic to any discussion of the effect of the agricultural depression on settlement desertion is the degree to which farmers were tied to the market. If farmers traded very little of their produce at the market but were interested primarily in satisfying their domestic needs, then a depression in the price of grain would not have affected them very much. Some author have indeed maintained that the majority of the peasant farmers of the late medieval period were not part of a market economy. In fact, most farmers were producing for the market far earlier. The rapid growth in the number and size of towns, which took place between 1200 and 1400, would not have been possible without an increase in the amount of food coming into the town markets. This period witnessed an expansion in town-country trade, which affected villages further from the towns. Not only was the purchase of food vital for the existence of the medieval town, the sale of surplus produce was essential for the well-being of the majority of farmers. Abel suggests that the medieval farmer was not interested in accumulating monetary wealth as the farmer or businessman in a well developed capitalist economy is[36]. He did, however, find money something essential to cover the costs of running a farm at this time.

One of the most important monetary demands on the peasant farmer came from the landlord, the Church and local state officials such as the *Vogt*. This was for the payment of interest on loans and the payment of taxes. By this time the rendering of dues in kind and labour had been widely replaced by payments in money. The farmer was therefore forced to sell a part of his produce to be able to meet these demands. The size of the money payments which were made by the farmers varied very considerably from area to area. In Prussia the amount was very modest, being in general about 8 per cent of the harvest, though as Abel points out even here considerably higher demands were made of farms farming good soils[37]. In Werder near Potsdam, for instance, the lord took 10 Prussian Mark for each farm unit (*Hufe*), the equivalent of 5,000 kilos of rye. This would have been about one-half of the total income of a grain farm under a three-field system. In Werder, however, there was an intensive pastoral farming system from which the lords could exact more than the normal level of dues. In contrast to the low dues of the areas under the Teutonic Order, many parts of western Germany contributed a far larger part of their gross income to lord and Church. Near Lübeck farmers paid around 30 per cent of their gross incomes in the mid-fifteenth century, while in Bavaria towards the end of the fifteenth century the percentage varied widely between 10 and 34 per cent. Where these dues were paid entirely in money, as they frequently were, the farmer was forced to market a considerable crop.

The need for money did not, however, end there. Very frequently labour had to be paid in money as well. Where the labour requirements of the farm or estate could not be covered by the family or by feudal labour service, then workers had to be hired. The cost of labour rose fast during the late medieval period

[36] Abel, W., *op. cit.*, 1955, p. 128
[37] *ibid.*, p. 124

and so labour costs became a growing part of farm expenditure. There were already organized labour gangs which went around Germany hiring themselves out to do specific jobs and then moving on, so great was the demand for outside labour.

These two demands for money from the farmer were by far the most important ones. But still other smaller demands were made of him to pay for goods and materials purchased in the towns. Town craftsmen had to be paid in money and again this could only be acquired through the market. The towns were already forcing a monetary system on the rural population and town and country were becoming more and more dependent upon each other. The problem for the peasant was that his money income came largely from the sale of grain, so that he depended on a high price for this product to meet all the money demands made of him.

The nobility were integrated far more into the capitalist economy, of course, than the small peasant farmers. They depended heavily on hired labour and on town craftsmen, both of which had to be paid in money. Abel cites, as an example of the expenses of a nobleman in late medieval Saxony, the costs of the Knight Hans von Honsperg in Clöden around 1474[38]. His total expenses amounted to 158½ Schock of new Groschen, which we shall call 158½ units for convenience. Of these costs, 62½ units were spent on wages – 39 per cent. This covers wages for both skilled craftsmen from outside the estate (potters, coopers, wheelwrights, for instance,) and estate and household workers. The next most important cost on income was clothing, which came to 44 units or 28 per cent. This appears to be an incredibly high proportion for mere clothing – it represents some 41,700 kilos of rye or in Abel's calculations about 16,000 DM or over £1,400 in modern terms (for the year 1954). Yet for the late medieval period this was not a great deal for a noble family to spend. In some towns there were even regulations passed setting out the maximum amount which could be spent on clothes and jewellery. That for Regensburg limited the family to a grain equivalent of 100,000 kilos of rye!

Of the three remaining costs at Clöden food was the most important with 27 units or 17 per cent of total costs. The knightly household did not live from bread alone but spent large sums on hops, spices, honey, fish, figs, raisins, almonds, rice and sub-tropical fruits. The two remaining items were for the inventory (saddles, ropes, carts and the like) 13 units or 8 per cent, and for cattle 12 units or 8 per cent. The last item, cattle, could have been

[38] Abel, W., *op. cit.*, 1955, p. 147

divided between the other items, inventory and food, for it includes both carcasses and live cattle.

These expenses were covered by an income which was derived almost entirely from agriculture. The income was made up partly from the sale of produce from the land directly cultivated by the lord or monastery and partly from the payments of taxes, dues, interest and fines from the peasants. The proportion from each of these two sources varied very considerably from lord to lord, but, of course, any economic depression in agriculture would mean declines in income from both sources.

The depression in grain prices hit both peasant and lord alike therefore. Undoubtedly the price indexes of crucial significance are those for grain and labour costs. It is impossible to gain any overall view of prices for grain and labour throughout Germany, but some indication of absolute and relative movements can be obtained for a few towns such as Braunschweig, Göttingen, and Frankfurt/Main. In Göttingen the price of rye fell from 5 RM per 100 kilos in 1400 to less than 2½ RM per 100 kilos throughout the second half of the fifteenth century[39]. It did not start to rise again until well into the following century. On the other hand, the payment of an unskilled worker for chopping a certain quantity of wood rose from just over 9 kilos of rye equivalent in 1400 to a maximum of almost 15 kilos in 1460, after which it fell back to just under 8 kilos in the first years of the sixteenth century. Of course, the most startling increases were seen in the wages of unskilled workers as one would expect in this economic climate, yet the skilled craftsmen also registered quite impressive wage rises. Neither farmers nor the nobility could prevent either falls in grain prices or rises in wages, although they attempted both. Ordinances were passed to restrict wage rises but they had little effect because of the competition in the labour market. Both farmer and lord achieved little more than pages of written protest.

The effect of these relative price movements on farmers of the time varied considerably according to the size of the farm and the degree to which the farmer depended on sales of grain to maintain his standard of living. The great bulk of middle-sized farms in Germany probably sold just enough of their produce at the market to pay for taxes and dues of all types to the landlord and Church, for a little hired labour and for a few products of the urban craftsman. This farmer was forced to sell a greater proportion of his crop as the price fell. The need to realize enough

[39] Abel, W., *op. cit.*, 1955, pp. 96-97 These prices are 10 year running averages.

to pay the lord together with losses which came about through devaluation of the currency meant that there was less and less of the crop left to feed the farmer and his household.

At the two extremes there were the large farms in the North Sea coastal areas and the small cottagers throughout Germany. The former sold a large proportion of produce and were hit extremely hard by the fall in prices. Yet the turnover was still quite considerable so that they were able to stay in business and await better times, without ever approaching the bread line. The small farmers may even have benefited from the situation. They produced very little for sale and they were underemployed on their own small plots. They therefore suffered little from the fall in grain prices and they could sell their labour for very high wages. They were also able to take over land, which was coming onto the market as a result of death or desertion at very cheap rents. They were also in the best position to leave the village when the situation became extremely desperate, for there was often little the lord could do to prevent them leaving.

For the lord or for the monastery or for one of the Orders of Knights the battle to maintain their standards of living was an extremely difficult one to fight. Their income from the sale of their own produce fell, while the wages of their workers rose. But their total income derived from dues and taxes also fell because the farmers were unable to pay. When they did pay it was often in coins devalued by a half or more. Many lords held land which had been deserted by the occupiers and had gone out of cultivation. They received, of course, no income from deserted holdings. It was extremely difficult to find new occupants at the same rates of dues and taxes. Whereas competition between employers for labour pushed wage rates up, so that between occupants for deserted holdings pushed rents down. The landlords were forced to grant free years to new tenants and then low rents in the following years. So that even when new tenants could be found the income derived from them was small. The granting of low rents and privileges to new tenants led of course to a general lowering of rents on all farms. Rents fell by as much as two-thirds. But even with falling money payments, many farmers found it difficult to pay. The lord could do little to force the farmer to pay and so he was generally forced to accept even less than the agreed amount. The lords tried in various ways to prevent these losses of income. The attempts to prevent farmers leaving their farms have already been described. In most cases these attempts failed or did little to remedy the situation. For some lords the only way out was to turn to robbery. The rise of the robber baron in the late medieval period is a symptom of the financial crisis in which the nobility found itself.

It was this crisis in agriculture, caused largely by the decline in population, which was behind the desertion of vast numbers of settlements. There was some voluntary adjustment of supply to the new demand situation (the change from arable to pastoral farming), but the adjustment came largely through a falling price and a fall in production, through the desertion of settlement and the loss of their fields.

Effects on the surviving settlements

So far emphasis has been placed on the deserted villages and fields and the reasons for their desertion. It is perhaps even more important to understand the changes which took place in the surviving settlements.

The theory that the desertion of settlement was merely the result of settlement concentration has been rejected, for it does not admit that there was a decrease in the size of the population and that it was accompanied by economic depression in agriculture. However, this is not to say that the concentration of the population in fewer and more favourable settlements did not take place. It did and it was a very significant movement for the development of settlement pattern, village form and field pattern. At the end of the period of depression and population decline, the number of settlements over large parts of Germany had declined considerably. People left in decaying villages had moved to those settlements which proved more resistant to decline, and so these resistant settlements declined only slightly or not at all.

With renewed population increase in the sixteenth century and a consequent rise in the demand for land, these surviving villages grew rapidly, while pressure on the land often led to division of fields into smaller parcels. In those areas most severely affected by settlement desertion, the settlement pattern which evolved in the sixteenth century was often totally different from that which had existed at the end of the high medieval period of economic expansion. A fairly dense spread of hamlets was replaced by a far less dense cover of larger villages. In other words the sixteenth century was a period during which in many German regions the *Haufendorf* developed for the first time. This will be dealt with at greater length, however, in the next chapter.

Numerous examples can be found to demonstrate the effects

H

of this process, but perhaps one of the most spectacular cases is that of the Sintfeld in eastern Westfalia (fig. 16). Here a pattern of small hamlets was replaced by one of a few large settlements, which approach the size of small towns. There is no obvious line of development here between many of the hamlets and the larger settlements, for especially in the southern part of the Sintfeld the loss of population and the destruction of settlements had been so great, that a completely new settlement pattern was developed, planned by the local rulers[40].

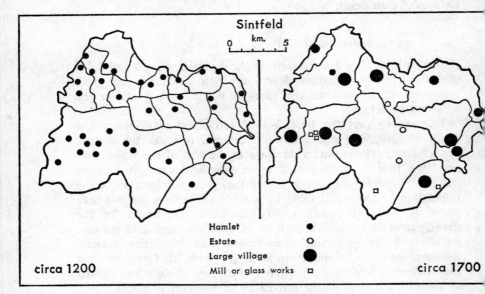

Fig. 16. Settlement desertion in the Sintfeld

In those cases where farmers from a deserted village moved into one which survived, the new group were often clearly distinguished by the position of their farm buildings in the settlement and by the obvious disadvantages, which they suffered compared to the established farmers. Obviously it was normal that they were forced to settle on the edge of existing villages and this often meant the houses were built in unfavourable surroundings. The new farms also had no land directly adjoining the farmhouse but were forced to accept blocks far away from the settlement. Sometimes they went on cultivating their old fields near the deserted settlement. Very often they were also unable to

[40] Schäfer, P., 'Die wirtschaftsgeographische Struktur des Sintfeldes', *Spieker*, Vol. 13, 1964, pp. 22-27

get any part of meadows close to the village, or at best they held less than the old established farmers. Nevertheless the increase in population due to migration certainly led to a division of land, especially in those fields close to the settlement, even though the new farmers often received only small parcels. This was, therefore, another stimulus to the creation of the *Gewannflur*, the complexity of which increased with further division due to the rise in population in the sixteenth century.

The release of large areas of farmland through the desertion of farming settlements led partly to an increase in the amount of waste land, but also partly to an increase in the average size of farm. The farmers who took over the land often used it very extensively, concentrating their labour on their existing fields close to the farm. At the most extensive the land was afforested, the woodland being used for grazing. In the east, as we shall see later, much of the land came into the hands of local rulers, who created for themselves large estates, which were often cultivated very extensively. Working in south Germany, Grees has pointed to three main forms of extensive land use practised on the deserted fields: pasture, (*Weide*): meadow, initially cut just once a year, (*Mähder*); and a rotation of arable cultivation with a long period of pastoral use, (*Egartenwirtschaft*)[41].

Quite large areas were given over to the extensive pasturing of cattle. Grees mentions that the Albuch, on the eastern Swabian Alb, which today has a fairly dense forest cover, was kept free of woodland in the fifteenth and sixteenth centuries through the grazing of cattle. During the same period specialized cattle farms (*Schweighöfe*) were founded in parts of Württemberg. Perhaps more widespread was the growth of large-scale, extensive sheep grazing. Throughout the Swabian Alb specialized sheep stations were founded by local rulers, by town councils and by monasteries, some of the herds having over a thousand head of sheep. But even the small farmers were able to increase the size of their flocks as pasture on the land of deserted settlements became available. It is probable also that the famous wandering herds of sheep on the Alb developed at this time.

The *Mähder* extended over very large areas of the Alb. They were unmanured meadows, originally cut once a year, though later sometimes twice. Grees mentions that the town of Ulm managed to buy 200 *Tagwerk* (60 ha) of *Mähder* land in the

[41] Grees, H., 'Die Auswirkungen von Wüstungsvorgängen auf die überdauernder Siedlungen', *Erdkundliches Wissen*, Vol. 18, pp. 50-66

40 years from 1529[42]. The third form of land use, the *Egartenwirtschaft*, was also very widespread on the Alb. It was, of course, outside the regulated open-field system and the *Egarten* lay physically beyond the limit of the three open fields. Not all the land which became available through settlement desertion was used in the extensive manners mentioned above. Large areas were also incorporated into the open fields of the growing settlements and in some cases formed even fourth, fifth or sixth fields. It is also true that this phase of extensive use did not continue everywhere far into the sixteenth century. With the growth of population and therefore of the demand for land, so the arable fields were pushed further and further out at the expense of the extensively used areas.

The size of farms therefore, increased at first quite considerably. This affected all sections of the community; the lord's estate, the established farmer's holding, the cottager's smallholding and the common land all increased in size. Grees has noted that the land transfer took place in several different legal forms, which were of some consequence, in the later development of land holding. It was quite common for one farm, which had been left by its tenant, to be made over to another tenant in the same district. This was very frequent where both the land of the farmer and the land of the vacant farm belonged to the same landowner. It was not uncommon for more than two units to be joined together in this way. Many of the landowners, however, were unwilling to grant land with such permanency, for they hoped for an upturn in the economy and the chance to find new occupiers for their vacant farms, and therefore the chance to charge full rents again. So they let their vacant farms as *Feldlehen*, which were completely separate from the farms held by farmers by right. Although the lord could take back the *Feldlehen* at will, they held certain advantages for the farmers. They could, for instance, be divided freely, whereas permission for this was often refused on the inherited farms held by right. Land was also granted in small fields rather than as complete farm holdings. Parcels of land were sometimes granted to farmers for a constant annual payment, but also some parcels went over into the ownership of the farmer himself. Finally this period saw the extension of the common land on a considerable scale. Most of the deserted fields lay on the boundary of the parish areas of the surviving villages and it was quite natural therefore that the parishes should be expanded and the waste land added to the commons.

[42] Grees, *op. cit.*, pp. 58-65

Through the late medieval depression therefore, the settlement pattern, the field pattern, the pattern of land use and the forms of landholding all underwent a transformation. When the population began to increase again in the sixteenth century, the expansion was contained within a new settlement pattern. No longer was there a dense pattern of small settlements, farming small parish areas. There was now, over much of Germany, a new pattern of larger villages, with enormously large areas of land at their disposal. The expansion took place within these villages and there was no return to the settlement pattern which had developed in the high medieval period. Of course there were some regions which did not conform to this pattern. In the north-west for instance the degree of settlement desertion was far lower, so that the degree of settlement consolidation was much less. The small *Drubbel* did not grow in size to any great extent therefore, for the expansion in the sixteenth century was accommodated within the existing settlement pattern. In Westfalia and East Friesland the farmers were more free of lordly control and had a far greater control themselves over any land which was given up. Here too, however, the sixteenth century brought increased pressure on the land and changes in the pattern of settlement.

4   The growth of settlement and the development of agriculture in the Early Modern Period

The period from the early sixteenth century to the end of the eighteenth century witnessed positive development and growth followed by a century of depression. The sixteenth century brought a recovery in population from the low levels of the late medieval depression, a spread of settlement and rises in the prices of agricultural products. The beginning of the seventeenth century was marked by the appearance of serious economic problems but its main characteristic is the devastation of the Thirty Years' War and the subsequent depression, lasting almost to the end of the century. Prices recovered at least in some parts of Germany, and the system and techniques of agriculture improved rapidly during the succeeding hundred years. The expansion of settlement depended largely on the initiative of local rulers and businessmen from the towns as it had in the high medieval period. During the early modern period, one line of rulers in Germany, the Hohenzollerns of Brandenburg-Prussia, guided their state with clear purpose towards greatness. A succession of great *Kurfürsten* and kings carried out a policy of agricultural development, reclamation and settlement, with the aim of providing a high tax revenue for the state. At the same time many of the smaller states in Germany were also intent on putting their land to the best use, through the settlement of colonists on wasteland and the improvement of agriculture.

Growth of the economy

THE SIXTEENTH CENTURY

The sixteenth century saw price movements, which were entirely to the benefit of the farmers and estate owners. The prices of agricultural products, notably of grain crops, rose far more rapidly than those of other goods and wages. The price rise was very general covering all regions and all goods and services. It was, however, the turn of the townspeople to lament, as the price of foodstuffs rose much faster than the prices of the goods produced in the towns. Abel has assessed the average rise in the price of rye in Germany between 1516 and 1596 to have been 196 per cent. The inflation continued until the 1730s, by which time rye was costing almost five times as much as in 1516[1]. The real wages of the worker fell considerably during this period. For the farmer and especially for the estate owner this meant rising real incomes. There was a considerable incentive to increase output, either by expanding the area under crops or by making technical improvements to increase yields.

With falling real wages, the worker had to adjust his pattern of spending to meet his day-to-day needs. Those goods with a high income elasticity tended to be dropped from his shopping basket, while the products with low income elasticity continued to be bought. The effect of varying income elasticities is seen in the price increases of agricultural products, grain prices rising faster than those of animal products. As a result, the arable area expanded at the expense of the pastoral area, while reclaimed land was put to arable as far as was possible.

The farmer benefited greatly from the rising prices and falling real wages. During the sixteenth century farmers in many parts of Germany built up large fortunes for themselves. They built new farmhouses and fitted them out as well as was possible at the time, often using imported materials. Prosperity amongst farmers was general but was especially marked in the areas of large arable farms in the north and east. The large estate owners were, however, even better off, for not only did they have the profit from their own farm produce, but also the rent income from their farms occupied by tenants. There are many records of farmers protesting at the very high rents which they were having to pay, but on the other hand records exist of complaints by estate owners that rents were not keeping up with profits in farming. The extremely high income of many lords in the sixteenth century is reflected in their luxurious style of life and their many large and extravagant palaces. Some of the nobility also engaged in trading agricultural produce. Others branched out into the craft industries as entrepreneurs. The fortunes which formed the basis of these trading and industrial operations were earned in agriculture.

The price rises of agricultural products continued until the end of the sixteenth century. The first falls in the price of rye

[1] Abel, W., *Agrarkrisen und Agrarkonjunktur*, Berlin, 1966, Appendix 2

appeared in most markets only in the first years of the seventeenth century. By this time the promise of great profits through agriculture had led to the reclamation of waste land, and therefore the extension of the farmed area. Farming was intensified to some extent with improved techniques and implements and a farming literature began to appear treating important technical problems of the day. The sixteenth century came to a close therefore in continuing prosperity after nearly a hundred years of growth and development in farming.

THE SEVENTEENTH-CENTURY DEPRESSION

Even before the Thirty Years' War started in 1618 there were signs of serious economic problems. Soon after the turn of the century and in some areas just before, corn prices began to fall and some large landowners and businessmen, whose prosperity was based on high grain prices, found it impossible to pay off their debts and were forced to sell their property. Soon after 1605, when extremely low prices were recorded, prices for agricultural produce rose again and indeed, in northern Germany and in Holland reclamation of land got under way on a large scale. In most parts of Germany, however, any great rise in prosperity was prevented by the outbreak of war. There were very sharp price variations throughout the war. A part of the price rises was due to the debasing of coinage, but this did not account for the famine years of 1624-5 and 1637-8 when the price of grain soared to many times its previous height. These were exceptional levels, the average rye price lying during the war only slightly above the low level of 1605.

The Thirty Years' War devastated the greater part of Germany. Especially in periods of famine whole regions were plundered by troops looking for food. Villages were destroyed and deserted. Land went out of cultivation and the population declined. The high death rate was a result of famine and plague, and only to a far smaller extent of military action. It took a considerable time for these areas to regain the population and the arable land, which they lost during the war. In the very few areas which were largely untouched by the war, there was a measure of prosperity during those years with high grain prices. In East Friesland new colonies were founded in the 1630s, while in Schleswig-Holstein land was being reclaimed from the sea and large new farmhouses being built at the same time. But these were only a small part of Germany and for most of the country the war brought poverty, devastation, hunger and death.

Estimates of the decline of population in Germany during the Thirty Years' War, though varying considerably, suggest that it may have been as great as a third. In some badly devastated areas it was far higher. Although a high rate of population increase after the war made good these losses in a few decades, the losses were bound to have a serious effect on consumption and therefore on the price of agricultural products. In the years after the war the price of agricultural products fell below their lowest levels during the war. The last half of the seventeenth century was marked by a long and severe depression, during which wages and prices of craft products fell far less severely than those of corn and animal products. Again farmers and landowners were severely hit by falling incomes and again, therefore, agricultural improvement and land reclamation and settlement also suffered. It must be remembered that this depression occurred throughout Europe, so that the Thirty Years' War was not the only reason for it. The recovery in agricultural prosperity did not come until the beginning of the eighteenth century and even then it was a very slow process.

THE GOLDEN CENTURY OF FARMING

The eighteenth century was a period of relative prosperity and rapid advance in farming. Agriculture became fashionable. It was considered the most important form of business and a subject for scientific enquiry, it was practised by the royalty of Europe, and was discussed by the aristocracy at many a social gathering. Farming societies, generally founded by powerful landowners, flourished, and agricultural literature proliferated in this century of technical progress and of farm expansion. Wasteland and marsh were again reclaimed on a large scale, after the little progress that had been made during the previous depression years. In Prussia, Frederick the Great (Friedrich II) settled over 300,000 colonists on reclaimed land, much of which lay in the *Urstromtäler* of the Elbe and Oder.

For the prices of agricultural products, the eighteenth century started with little promise. These had risen from the depths of the depression in the 1660s but were still low compared to those in the first half of the seventeenth century, falling yet lower in the first decade of the eighteenth. From about 1710, however, there seems to have been an upward trend, which continued to the end of the century, with only a slight flattening out in mid-century. Wages and the products of town-based crafts increased only slowly, if at all. Farming again became very profitable therefore rent incomes increased rapidly to the joy of the landowners and real wages fell for the landless labourers. High profits, both from the sale of produce and from rents, gave a stimulus to expansion and intensification in farming. On the other hand low wages led to hunger, and in famine years, to death for the labourers and small peasant farmers. Many were forced to take on jobs away from home (in northern Germany for instance, many thousands sought work each year in Holland – the *Hollandgängerei*), but when these sources of employment dried up, they were left with the choice between emigration and starvation. In the early nineteenth century large numbers of peasants and labourers chose the former.

The demand for agricultural produce in the eighteenth century was stimulated by a rapidly rising population. Abel estimates that the population of Germany rose from ten millions in 1650 to eighteen millions in 1740[2]. In the following 60 years the population of Brandenburg-Prussia more than doubled within the area of the state in 1740. Part of this growth was taking place in the towns, so that their demand for farm produce grew throughout the century. But abroad too both population and demand were rising, and this stimulated agriculture in the export-orientated regions of eastern Germany. England was the most important customer for the great estates of the east, but the Netherlands and Scandinavia also bought grain from this region. Not only grain was exported, however. Both northern and southern Germany supplied animals and dairy produce to England and France. With such an unprecedented boom in agriculture in the eighteenth century, the famous judgement of Frederick the Great is understandable: ' Of all the arts farming is the greatest; without it there would be no business-men, no poets and no philosophers. Only that which is produced from the soil is true wealth '.

Change and growth in rural settlements

It was during this period that profound differences developed in the settlement pattern and the organization of farming between the old settled areas of west Germany and the newly colonized lands of the east. Even within west Germany distinctions were sharpened in terms of the agrarian structure between north and south. The form of both the settlements and of the field patterns changed quite radically in this period between the end of the late medieval

[2] Abel, W., *Die Geschichte der deutschen Landwirtschaft*, Stuttgart, 1967, p. 274

depression and the enclosure of the common land. On the one hand the settlements grew through infilling; on the other the agricultural land was very severely fragmented in those areas with *gavelkind*.

KÖTTER AND SELDNER AND THE GROWTH OF EXISTING SETTLEMENTS

Between the sixteenth and the eighteenth centuries, many small settlements grew to quite large *Haufendörfer*. This expansion took place in both areas with partible inheritance and those with undivided inheritance. Where partible inheritance was common, the growth was largely due to the division of holdings and the erection of new houses for the ever-growing number of farmers. When farmhouses had been divided as many times as was possible, new houses had to be built. However, this is not the whole explanation. Some of the expansion was due to new classes of settler, called *Seldner* in southern Germany and *Kötter* in the north[3]. This new class was often landless and without capital. They squatted on whatever land they could find, but were occasionally granted small plots by the established farmers. Generally they had to sell their own labour or engage in a handicraft to make a living. It was not in the areas of partible inheritance, however, that the *Seldner* or *Kötter* made the greatest impact, for there was little land here which they could settle. In areas with a system of undivided inheritance, where there were large areas of common land, this new class was able to settle more easily. Complete colonies of *Kötter* settled in an unplanned fashion on the common land in spite of the opposition of the established farmers. In the villages too, the gaps between the old farmhouses were infilled with small *Kötter* houses and new streets were added at the periphery of the settlements. In this way many of the small villages in areas with undivided inheritance took on the character of *Haufendörfer*.

It has already been mentioned that *Erbkötter* were recorded as early as the twelfth century in northern Germany[4]. At this time land was plentiful and the *Erbkötter* often received generous grants of land. By the sixteenth century the more enterprising of them had expanded their holdings and had gained a certain amount of social acceptance from the established farmers, so that any difference in wealth or status between the two groups had

---

[3] The designation of this group varies considerably from area to area. Apart from the most common terms *Kötter* and *Seldner*, one also meets *Kätner, Kossäten, Warfsleute, Körbler, Gärtner* and others. These terms may mean completely different things in different regions, so that one must be extremely careful in their interpretation.

[4] See page 41

disappeared or became insignificant. However the *Kötter* were not very common in the medieval period. The great growth in their numbers occurred in the early modern period. By then land was not so plentiful and the established farmers were more careful in making land grants. Many of the *Kötter* received no land at all officially, but simply took a small part of the commons as squatters. The end of the *Kötter* settlement came with the division of the commons, after which time there was no more land available for squatters. From this time on, the new settler requiring land could only get it through working for an established farmer who would allow him to cultivate a small area of land as part payment for his labour.

We can distinguish therefore, three main types of *Kötter*, who in turn formed one of the three main groups in rural society in the early modern period.

1 The earliest *Kötter*, the *Erb-* or *Pferdekötter*, have already been discussed.

2 The *Markkötter* and the *Brinksitzer* developed mainly in the sixteenth but also in the seventeenth century, with far less land and fewer rights than the *Erbkötter*. They were sometimes settled against the will of the established farmers by the local lord to increase his income.

3 The *Anbauer* and the *Heuerleute* were settled with the great increase in population in the eighteenth century. The *Anbauer* received a very small area of land indeed and were compelled to live largely from selling their labour or engaging in a craft. The *Heuerleute* were not true *Kötter*, in that they could only lease land from their employer.

A similar threefold division could be made for the *Seldner* of south-western Germany. Grees identifies just these three groups in eastern Swabia[5]. As with the *Kötter* in northern Germany, the *Seldner* of the eighteenth century received very little land and Grees prefers to call them *Häusler*. Within the village, the true *Kötter* and *Seldner* occupied a social position between the old established farmers and paid labourers. There was some movement between these three groups and as already mentioned it was not uncommon for the *Erbkötter* to be recorded as old established farmers in the early modern period. It became progressively more difficult for the *Kötter* to move up the social scale as land became

[5] Grees, H., 'Das Seldnertum im östlichen Schwaben und sein Einfluss auf die Entwicklung der ländlichen Siedlungen', *Ber. z. dt. Landeskunde*, Vol. 29, 1962, pp. 104-50

scarcer. The *Anbauer* or the *Heuerling* of the eighteenth century rarely managed to move up the social ladder at all.

Distribution of the Kötter. As has been suggested, *Kötter* are recorded in the early modern period in both northern and southern Germany, as well as in the eastern areas of colonization. The intensity of settlement varies considerably, however, as the result in part of the different policies of local rulers. This is to be clearly seen in the contrast between some conservative ecclesiastical territories in southern Germany and neighbouring territories of imperial knights. Wirth has drawn attention to the contrasts between the strict control of settlement exercised by the ecclesiastical authorities in Bamberg and the encouragement of settlement by landless classes in the territories of the knights[6]. Whilst it is clear that the policy of the rulers of the various small independent political units was of crucial significance to the destiny of *Kötter* settlement, it is also clear that these policies varied from one part of the state territory to another. Grees mentions that the Seldner were not settled in the Allgäu possessions of the Bishop of Augsburg but were settled in large numbers on the land of the same bishop outside the Allgäu[7].

This latter example suggests that perhaps the *Kötter* or *Seldner* were absent from those areas with an almost exclusively pastoral character. There are also relatively few settlers of this group in the North Sea marshes. However, here the commons were divided at a very early period and so the scope for cottager settlement was restricted. There is no conclusive evidence on this relationship. There is even less evidence to connect the *Kötter* settlement with any particular physical region. Grees again points out that while missing from the Allgäu, there is quite dense *Seldner* settlement in other parts of the Alps[8].

Undoubtedly the inheritance system is of great significance in the explanation of the distribution of these classes. In those areas with partible inheritance (*Realteilung*) the children of farmers were generally found land through the division of properties on the death of the father. On the other hand in the areas where farms were inherited intact by one heir (*Anerbenrecht*), the non-inheriting children frequently settled as *Kötter* or *Seldner*. In consequence, the *Seldner* and *Kötter* are found throughout the

[6] Heinritz, G., Teller, H., and Wirth, E., ' Wirtschafts- und sozialgeographische Auswirkungen reichsritterschaftlicher Peuplierungspolitik in Franken ', *Ber. z. dt. Landeskunde*, Vol. 41, 1968, pp. 45-72
[7] Grees, H., *op. cit.*, p. 111
[8] *idem*

areas with non-partible inheritance systems.

The significance of Kötter settlement. The settlement of these new classes was significant in three main ways:

(a) through their cultivation of large areas of previously unused land;

(b) through the changes which they brought to the settlement and field pattern; and

(c) through their specialization on certain craft products and the consequent effect on the local economy.

Ritter considers it likely that in those areas with a large *Kötter* population, this group accounted for one third of the total clearances[9]. There is no doubt that they were very active in this field. Throughout the commons of the Weser-Ems Raum, large areas of heath or peat bog were reclaimed and settled by *Kötter*. With the great population growth of the eighteenth century, the pressure on the land from the *Kötter* became greater and they pushed further and further into the *Mark*[10]. The old established farmers tried in many cases to prevent the settlement but only rarely were they able to do so completely[11].

The changes the *Kötter* brought to the settlement form and field pattern were quite radical. In those areas where there was a pattern of small hamlets and *Einzelhöfe* (such as in much of the Weser-Ems Raum) the coming of the *Kötter* led to a spread of low density settlement over a wide area. At the same time the hamlets were infilled to become small nucleated villages. On the other hand, in south Germany dense *Haufendörfer* developed with the settlement of the *Seldner*. Grees draws a distinction between ' open ' villages in which *Seldner* settlement was permitted or even encouraged, and the closed villages where often the *Seldner* were not allowed to build and were forced to live as tenants in existing buildings[12]. The former often developed into large *Haufendörfer*, often with a strong industrial base, whereas the latter remained

[9] Ritter, G., ' Die Nachsiedlerschichten im nordwestdeutschen Raum und ihre Bedeutung für die Kulturlandschaftsentwicklung ', *Ber. z. deutschen Landeskunde*, vol. 41, 1968, pp. 96-97

[10] Brunken, O., *Das alte Amt Wildeshausen*, Oldenburg, 1938, pp. 53-68 Baasen, C., *Das Oldenburger Ammerland*, Oldenburg, 1927, pp. 147-59

[11] See above, p. 14

[12] Grees, H., ' Das Kleinbauerntum in Ostschwaben und sein Einfluss auf die Entwicklung von Siedlung und Wirtschaft ', *L'Habitat et les paysages ruraux d'Europe. Les congrès et colloques de l'université de Liège*, Vol. 58, 1971, pp. 179-203

smaller and often still show today a purely agricultural economy. In general in these southern areas new settlement was concentrated in the area of the old village so that *Streusiedlung* was not typical.

Grees makes the important distinction between *Seldner* settlement of only local significance and that with regional importance[13]. In the first case the *Seldner* often initially settled on land in the village belonging to an established farmer, for whom he worked a certain number of days each year. Later this relationship generally became less clear, but it led to the infilling of the settlement and the marginal extension of the built-up area of the village. The cottagers who settled in the eighteenth century (the *Heuerlinge* in the north, the *Häusler* in the south) were also dependent on the granting of land by the established farmers for their houses and in return worked anything up to 200 days or even more for the farmers[14]. They again tended to infill the settlements in an irregular way.

On the other hand, there were the *Seldner* with regional importance. It is very common to find heavy concentrations of *Seldner* in certain villages, which provided central functions for the surrounding region. This is especially common in areas with a low density of towns, where the *Seldner* performed many of the functions which in the towns were performed by craftsmen and traders. Here the *Seldner* were often settled initially in the late medieval period, just before the period of settlement desertion. Further settlement took place with the renewed expansion of population in the sixteenth century. In contrast to the settlements where the *Seldner* were only of local significance, here they were often on both sides of a road leading out of the village, thereby changing the form of the village quite considerably. An example of this phenomenon is the village of Westerstetten near Ulm in south Germany (fig. 17). Here the original core of the settlement can be seen around the Maierhof and the Widumhof. This core has been infilled by *Seldner* to form a small nucleated village. Onto this village has been added the *Seldengasse*, the row of *Seldner* houses leading up to the Obere Wiesen. Most of these settlers were engaged in a craft and serviced the surrounding area.

In terms of the field pattern, the *Kötter* and *Seldner* often added an area of small enclosures to the open fields of the old settlements. These are the *Kämpe* of north Germany, which were dis-

[13] Grees, *op. cit.*, 1963, pp. 137-47
[14] Brägelmann, P., *Inwieweit kann das Heuerlingswesen einen Beitrag zur Gesundung der landwirtschaftlichen Arbeitsverfassung leisten?* Münster. 1958, pp. 30-38

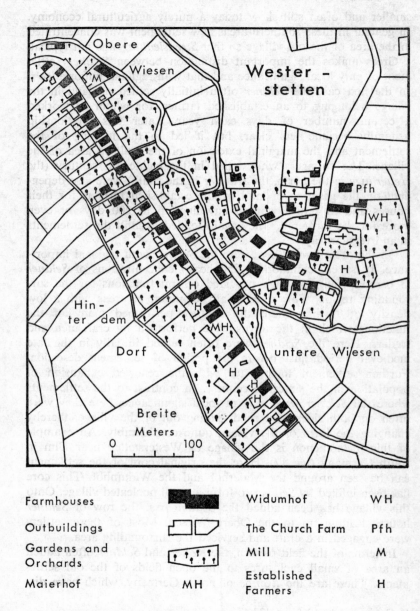

Fig. 17. The Seldner in Westerstetten, Swabia (after Grees)

tributed about the commons. In some areas completely new settlements of *Kötter* were founded by the landowners, the fields of which were totally enclosed. Baasen calls these the *Alte Kampsiedlungen*[15]. The *Heuerlinge* and *Häusler* of the eighteenth and early nineteenth centuries frequently only received very small gardens or were allowed to cultivate small areas of land loaned to them by the farmer for whom they worked. In these cases the field-pattern obviously changed very little.

Of great significance was the contribution of the *Seldner* and *Kötter* to the local economy through their production of manufactured goods for sale. Almost all the *Kötter* were forced to have another occupation besides farming to support their families. Sometimes they were exclusively concerned with a craft and had little if any contact with agriculture. Their importance for trade and industry was early recognized by many rulers, who encouraged their settlement. The population policy of the imperial knights in Franconia has already been mentioned. Wirth, Heinritz and Heller have pointed to the effects of this policy on the present-day economic structure[16]. The early characteristics of these settlements as craft and trading centres can still be seen today. It is these *Seldner* settlements which have industry, and which provide a large number of the commuters to the nearby large towns. In contrast the old settlements on church lands remain primarily farming communities.

In north Germany too the *Kötter* and especially the *Heuerlinge* engaged in crafts, and then walked many hundreds of miles hawking their products deep into Holland and even into Russia. They formed the bulk of the labour force in the textile industry. Ritter quotes figures for this industry[17]. In the Amt Westerstede in Oldenburg around 1800, there were 142 farmers, 387 *Kötter*, 162 *Brinksitzer* and 567 *Einlieger* (similar in status to the *Heuerlinge*), that is these cottager groups made up almost 90 per cent of the population of the area. Amt Westerstede in the winter season 1792-3 had 1,600 spinners. The village of Zetel in the neighbouring Amt Bockhorn, with a similar social structure, had a total of 373 looms in 1797. Many of the cottagers, who could not earn sufficient money through farming and the textile industry, were forced to spend the summer digging peat in the peat bogs of the eastern Netherlands to supplement their incomes (the famous *Hollandgängerei*). The *Kötter* specialized locally in other

---

[15] Baasen, *op. cit.*, pp. 147-59
[16] Heinritz, Heller, and Wirth, *op. cit.*, pp. 45-72
[17] Ritter, *op. cit.*, pp. 100-1

I

branches of industry – in the Siegerland and Sauerland in the metal industries, around Delmenhorst in the cork industry and in Oldenburg in the tobacco trade.

The settlement of these various groups especially from the early sixteenth century until the period of the enclosures is then of considerable importance for the growth of settlement and the development of the economy. Settlements expanded, new house forms developed and the economy of whole regions changed. To these groups, often neglected in the literature which concentrates on the old established farming population, can be traced back many of the variations in the social and employment characteristics of present-day rural settlements.

INHERITANCE SYSTEMS

The effect of inheritance systems on settlement and field patterns and upon the local economy has often been described and used to explain various features of settlement growth or economic development. There are, however, few systematic studies of inheritance forms, their distribution and their effects. One notable study is that by Röhm, which was carried out in south-west Germany in the Land Baden-Württemberg[18]. This study emphasizes the complexity of the subject and the danger of assuming that inheritance systems are something fixed for all people at all times.

The reasons for the development of different inheritance systems are extremely complex and most theories can be contradicted by evidence from one part of Germany or another. Those theories which are based upon physical geography and ethnic origins fail most empirical tests. The distribution of partible inheritance systems in Baden-Württemberg corresponds closely to the areas of early medieval Germanic settlement, while those settled in the later medieval period generally have a system of undivided inheritance. This can be explained in that the colonization of the later middle ages took place under strong feudal control and that the nobility generally prohibited partible inheritance. On the other hand, in the older settlements the farmers managed to preserve more freedom for themselves and were able to retain partible inheritance[19]. It is postulated that the oldest Germanic settlements (the *Etterdörfer*) were originally located at a considerable distance from each other so that land was freely available. A system of partible inheritance was possible in these circumstances, without

---

[18] Röhm, H., 'Die Vererbung des landwirtschaftlichen Grundeigentums in Baden-Württemburg', *Forschungen zur dt. Landeskunde*, Vol. 102, 1957
[19] Röhm *op. cit.*, pp. 66-96

causing any shortage of land. As land became less plentiful, the system was not changed. The land in strips on the open-fields could be easily divided, while in some cases daughter settlements were founded some distance from the old settlement to relieve the population pressure. Frequently these old villages were located in the more fertile areas, so that a fall in the land area of each holding was not necessarily reflected immediately in a fall in the produce of the farm. In the later colonized lands, however, the entrepreneurs considered that any reduction in the size of holdings would lead to a bankruptcy of farming on the generally poorer soils and a consequent fall in tax revenues. They therefore insisted on a system of undivided inheritance. This theory certainly would produce a distribution of systems in Baden-Württemberg similar to the one mapped by Röhm in 1953. This, however, is not proof of the validity of the theory!

For Germany as a whole, a modern map of inheritance patterns shows a northern and eastern block and a southern one (corresponding roughly to the present Land Bayern) in which undivided inheritance systems are dominant and a central and south-western block in the Länder Baden-Württemberg, Hessen and Rheinland-Pfalz where partible inheritance systems are most common (fig. 18). This distribution has been fairly stable throughout the early modern period and up to very recently. As Röhm remarks it is amazing how firmly the farming population defended the legal framework over hundreds of years[20]. This threefold division of the country is reflected in similar distributional maps of farm size, degree of fragmentation, numbers of full-time farms and settlement forms[21]. In all cases the effects of the partible inheritance system mark off the south-west of Germany from the majority of other areas.

Obviously other factors than simply the date of the earliest German settlement are needed to explain this macro-distribution. A map prepared by Röhm on the basis of a questionnaire throughout the parishes of the Federal Republic shows numerous interesting anomalies in this general distribution[22]. There is for instance the case of the coastal marshes in Lower Saxony and Schleswig-Holstein and the sand-dune East Friesian Islands. In 1960 Röhm recorded generally mixed inheritance systems here, though on the

[20] Röhm, *op. cit.*, p. 85
[21] Mayhew, A., 'Structural reform and the future of West German agriculture', *Geographical Review*, Vol. 40, 1970, pp. 54-68
[22] Röhm, H., 'Die Vererbung des landwirtschaftlichen Grundeigentums in der Bundesrepublik Deutschland, 1959-61', in *Atlas der deutschen Agrarlandschaft*, zweite Lieferung, Wiesbaden, 1965

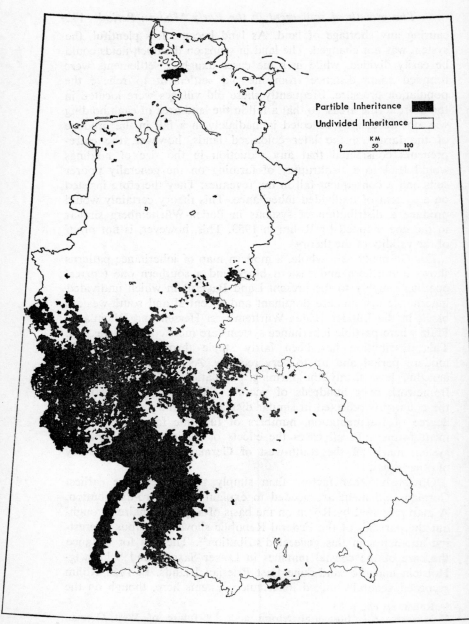

Partible Inheritance ▓

Undivided Inheritance ☐

K M
0   50   100

Fig. 18. The distribution of inheritance forms in Germany
(after H. Röhm)

islands of Langeroog and Spiekeroog partible inheritance, unchanged in form, was found. In the Eichsfeld around Duderstadt,
today on the East German frontier, there is again an island of
partible inheritance. This is explained largely through political
division – the Eichsfeld remained under the control of the Bishop
of Mainz, whilst the surrounding areas were in Hannoverian hands.

Yet in spite of this little changing general distribution, there has
always been considerable local variation in the ways in which
these systems have been practised. Röhm remarks on the
' elasticity ' of interpretation of the legal system[23]. Even in the
areas with ' strict ' prohibition of partible inheritance, land was
divided and in areas with partible inheritance sons were occasionally paid their inheritance in cash instead of land. It has been
especially common close to the major industrial centres for land
to be equally divided between heirs for there was always the
opportunity of supplementing the income from a small, fragmented
farm by employment in industry. In very poor areas it has
frequently happened that there has been land division, where one
would expect undivided inheritance. It was often impossible for
the farmer to save money in which to pay off the non-inheriting
sons, and yet he wanted to give all his heirs something. Therefore
the farm was divided. Such flexibility was common in all communities, in spite of the general inflexibility of the systems over time.

The significance of inheritance forms for settlement and economy.
The great significance of inheritance systems can be seen in
present-day farm structure distributions. They exert a great
influence on the form and density of settlements, the fragmentation
of the land and the structure of the economy. In areas with
partible inheritance one frequently meets the ' type ' examples of
Haufendörfer. In the old settlements of the south-west building
was generally confined within the limits of the *Etter,* the division
between the built-up area and the open fields. The division of
inheritance brought with it the division of not only the fields but
also often the farmyard. When the available building sites in the
village had been used up, the division of existing buildings began
and so the totally chaotic settlement form developed that we know
today.

In the areas with undivided inheritance there was less pressure
on the building land within the village although, as was noted, it
is in these areas that the greatest number of cottagers settled.
Nevertheless in many areas the cottagers expanded the village

[23] Röhm, *op. cit.,* 1957, p. 85

outwards, not greatly increasing the density of settlement. Alternatively in the north, they settled across the extensive commons, without changing the character of the small nucleated settlements to the same degree as those in south-western Germany. In many cases the great old Lower German farmhouses of the established farmers continued to dominate the settlements in the north, whereas in those areas with partible inheritance, the physical evidence of differences in social class became less as buildings were divided and the settlement constantly increased in density. In the fields the existence of partible inheritance also made itself felt. Before the consolidation of the land after World War II in the parish of Bornich overlooking the Rhine gorge and including the Lorelei rock, there were 169 farms, all of which were under 10 ha in size, and whose land was divided into 21,768 parcels, or on average 129 parcels per farm[24]. This example could be replicated hundreds of times for the areas with partible inheritance.

This high degree of fragmentation combined with the reduction in the size of farms obviously did not leave the economic structure of the village unaffected. As farms became smaller, farmers were forced to supplement their farm incomes. So it was a characteristic of many of these villages to have an array of crafts well beyond what one would expect to find in a farming village. At a later period full-time farming ceased entirely in many of these settlements and the landowners commuted to jobs in the local towns. Today in the Westerwald, east of the Rhine Gorge, there are vast areas of land which have gone out of cultivation, where no full-time farmers remain and where the former farming population now earn their living by commuting to local centres of industry.

The degree of division of parcels was greatest in those periods when the population increase was greatest. The early modern period therefore, the late sixteenth century and again the eighteenth and early nineteenth centuries witnessed much division. During the late medieval period and during and after the Thirty Years' War it is to be assumed that the fragmentation continued at a lesser rate.

Whilst the early modern period saw fragmentation of the land and concentration of the settlements, in the areas with partible inheritance, in the eastern parts of Germany and in some of the western areas with undivided inheritance, the opposite was happening, that is, the consolidation of land in the hands of a few

---

[24] 'Forschungsstelle für bäuerliche Familienwirtschaft', *Förderung bäuerlicher Selbsthilfe bei der Verbesserung der Agrarstruktur*, Vol. 6, 1962, p. 120

owners with the creation of the East German 'Gutshof' or estate.

The rise of the Gutsbetrieb in the east

The northern parts of the area of medieval eastern colonization were characterized throughout the nineteenth and early twentieth centuries by large estates. These were especially common in Vorpommern between Stettin and Stralsund and in Mecklenburg. Eastern Holstein, Brandenburg, Pommern and East Prussia also had many large estates. On the other hand, in Saxony and in the hilly parts of Silesia they were uncommon and where they did exist, far smaller.

This distribution gives important clues to the reasons why the large estates developed. It will be noticed that the limit of the distribution in the west runs through Holstein. More exactly it is a line running roughly through the towns of Flensburg, Schleswig, Segeberg and Hamburg[25]. The division is formed south of Hamburg by the Elbe as a rough approximation. This is of course the eastern border of the Empire before the colonization of the eastern lands began in the high middle ages. The estates are therefore associated with colonial areas and are far less common in the old settled parts of west Germany. As will be shown this is a question of the legal framework. In the old Germanic areas of the west, the rights of farmers were firmly anchored in the legal codes. It was extremely difficult for any lord to dispossess farmers, who, in spite of the size of their taxes and contributions to the state and the landholder, were nevertheless essentially free men. In the areas of colonization the legal situation was quite different. The rights of the colonists were not common rights dating from far back into the early medieval period. They were at most inscribed in documents which even at the end of the Middle Ages were of relatively recent origin. Indeed it proved easy for the estate owners to introduce measures which in turn tied the colonists to the land and then gradually made them servants of the lord.

The other main coincidence of the distribution of estates is that with the area of grain cultivation for export in the period up to the nineteenth century. Indeed, it is in those areas where it was possible both to grow grain and get it easily to the coast for export that most of the estates developed. The greatest concentration was on those most fertile parts of the terminal and ground

[25] Kuhn, W., *Die deutsche Ostsiedlung in der Neuzeit*, Köln, 1955, Band I, pp. 158-9

moraine of the last ice advance (*Weichsel*) which lay close to the Baltic or a navigable river. Inland from Danzig and Stettin, the two major grain ports, estates prospered with the growth of the grain trade. Further from the coast and in the hillier areas of Saxony and Silesia neither the grain trade nor the development of estates proceeded very far.

The estates in the east had a variety of origins. One starting point was the farm given to the *Lokator* who planned and laid out new settlements for the territorial lords. In time these *Lokatoren* were often able to gain control of their local areas as the power of the territorial lords waned. Where the German knights had expelled the Slav nobility and taken over their land, their arable farms were another basis for the later development of large estates. Elsewhere the Slav nobility often managed to keep their land (in parts of Mecklenburg, Pommern and Silesia) and again estates developed. Abel mentions also the lands of the territorial lords and of the church as other potential origins for estates[26]. These holdings were often relatively small by later standards – the important thing was their position in the law. The owners of these properties were often entrusted with local judicial powers and were in a position to lay claim to land when it became vacant.

The development of the feudal estate in the east reached its zenith in the period from the mid-fifteenth until the end of the eighteenth century. Yet we must look back into the late medieval period for its origins. The colonists of the high middle ages were free farmers, free to appeal to their territorial lord against any attempt by local rulers to curb their freedom. The local lords worked their own land with hired labour, which at the height of the colonization was fairly plentiful. Their farms were in any case small, often not much larger than those of the farmers, and rarely over 100 ha. Only in East Prussia did the territorial lord take a direct interest in cultivation. Here the Order of Teutonic Knights farmed in estates of many hundred hectares. The largest, around the Marienburg near Danzig, was probably about 1,400 ha[27]. In the fourteenth and fifteenth centuries with the break-up of the political system, the territorial lords sold most of their rights and privileges to local rulers who were now not only the policemen but also the judges – and there was no longer any right of appeal to a higher court. Whereas previously the local lords could not demand labour service from the farmers,

[26] Abel, W., *op. cit.*, 1967, pp. 159-60
[27] Kuhn, W., *op. cit.*, Vol. 1, p. 143

they now had the rights formerly reserved to the territorial lord, which allowed the latter to call on the farmers for service in various circumstances. During the period of settlement desertion and later during and after the Thirty Years' War, the local rulers made much use of this new power.

The grain trade also started back in the high medieval period. The demand from the Flanders towns in the late thirteenth century was met in part by the exports from the east German territories. The grain came in general from the grain taxes imposed on farmers and from the occasional surpluses that occurred on the lords' own farms. Only in East Prussia on the estates of the Teutonic Order was there a real export-orientated agriculture in the late thirteenth and fourteenth centuries. It was the extremely rapid rise in the price of grain, starting in the first quarter of the sixteenth century and lasting through to the first few years of the seventeenth century, which provided the stimulus for an export-orientated extensive grain economy.

In spite of the changes in the legal position of the local rulers and the farmers in the fourteenth century, there was little change in the way of life of the colonists and little restriction of their freedom. It was the period of settlement desertion in the fifteenth century when the flow of settlers dried up and a flight from the land began that the colonists first noticed the changes. In the fifteenth and sixteenth centuries their freedom was lost, sometimes slowly, in Poland extremely rapidly. The desertion of settlement meant that the rents and dues upon which the local rulers were dependent fell drastically. Frequently the lords had only small holdings which were worked primarily to supply the needs of their households. The period of settlement desertion led to attempts both to tie farmers to their land and later to increase the area of land farmed by the lord for the export trade. Despite these efforts many local lords were made bankrupt during the period and forced to sell their land to new ruling families, who often came from the towns.

Probably most of the colonists had received their land originally on the understanding that they had to find a settler willing to take over the farm if they wanted to leave. In the period of active colonization in the thirteenth and fourteenth centuries this agreement was not important for there were always newcomers willing to take over deserted farms. As the wave of settlers turned into a mass exodus from the land in the fifteenth century, the rulers reactivated this almost forgotten legislation in order to keep their subjects on the land and maintain their revenues. In East Prussia a general edict was issued in 1420 reaffirming the duty of each farmer to provide a substitute in the case of his leaving the land[28]. In 1436 an extradition treaty was signed with Poland for the return of farmers who had left the land without permission. In 1445 it was made compulsory for each farmer who left his farm to have the written permisssion of his lord, but in 1508 the Prussian nobility demanded the return of farmers from the town of Königsberg, even though they had legally left the land. Finally in 1526 the first act of the newly created Duchy of Prussia was to affirm the prohibition of migration on the whole male population. Similar ordinances were made in the other eastern colonial areas. And so one basic freedom was lost.

The effects of the loss of population on wages was of course to raise the real wage considerably. With wages rising and incomes falling, the rulers in the east tried to obtain cheap labour and retain it through legal restrictions on movement. Labour was in many cases found in the form of migrant workers from Poland but there was also a source in the families of the farmers. In various parts of the north-east legislation was passed, under which the children of farmers had to offer their labour to the local lord and, if he offered a normal wage, they had to take up his offer. Later the paid labourers were forced to work on the estates on terms determined by the lords. The landowners were also obviously interested in controlling the labour market and to this end maximum wage agreements were made throughout the area of the eastern colonization in the fifteenth and sixteenth centuries.

The land which went out of cultivation due to the loss of settlement was generally claimed by the local rulers and eventually fell into their hands. Abel quotes figures produced by Korth for the Mittelmark (the heart of Brandenburg) which show that of the land of the large estates of that area in 1800, 27.7 per cent had been derived from the late medieval settlement desertion[29]. At first some of the land was given over to sheep rearing and much lay idle. Later, however, towards the end of the fifteenth and especially in the sixteenth century the waste land in the north-east at any rate was given over to grain.

The full development of the estate economy came in the sixteenth century when, especially during the period after 1550, we see the large scale enlargement of the estates and the development of a system of compulsory labour, which was forced on the

---

[28] Kuhn, W., *op. cit.*, p. 148. What follows is largely based on Kuhn's work, which is thoroughly recommended to all those particularly interested in the development of settlement in the east.

[29] Abel, W., *op. cit.*, 1967, p. 160

formerly free farmers by the lords. It was the great rise in the price of grain following recovery from the depression of the late medieval period that stimulated expansion of farming and new settlement throughout Germany in the sixteenth century[30]. Whereas elsewhere his expansion was carried by the farmers, in the north-east it was produced by the estate owners at the expense of the farmers. In the fifteenth century the grain export trade had slipped from the control of the Teutonic Order to that of the local rulers, but it remained of limited importance. In 1492 the leading grain port, Danzig, exported only 10,509 *Last* (about 25,000 tons)[31]. Fifty years later in the mid-sixteenth century the average export from Danzig was yearly 50,000 to 85,000 *Last* (120,000 to 205,000 tons), and in record years exceeded 100,000 *Last* (245,000 tons). It was not only in the far east around Danzig that grain became the most important export crop. Stettin developed once the river Warthe had been made navigable and Kiel became important as the port for the Holstein estates. Hamburg also gained a part of the trade from Holstein and the lower Elbe valley. So the cultivation of grain for export spread throughout north-east Germany.

Besides markets, which were assured in western Europe, the estate owners needed large areas of land and a plentiful and cheap supply of labour. The former could be obtained through the cultivation of the waste and by dispensing with their sheep runs for the planting of grain. They took over land which they had formerly held but had subsequently let out to farmers and also managed to get control of parts of the common land. At the start of the sixteenth century labour on the estates was provided largely by paid workers and only a small proportion by feudal service. As the estates grew and the intensity of cultivation increased, the estate owners tried to supplement the work force by settling land-less peasants on very small plots, so that they were forced to seek additional income from work on the estate. These *Kossäten* or *Gärtner* were quite often settled in their own villages (*Kossäten-dörfer*) near the farm buildings of the estate, so that they were close to their work. In the Mittelmark of Brandenburg, there were already 5,487 *Kossäten* in 1570 and this rose to 8,387 by 1624[32]. In spite of the increase in size of the estates and the number of workers available, such was the demand for grain and such were the profits to be made in its cultivation that these were no longer

[30] See above pp. 118-20
[31] Kuhn, W., *op. cit.*, pp. 149-52
[32] Kuhn, W., *op. cit.*, pp. 154-5

sufficient by mid-century. The estate owners needed more land and more labour and this could come now only from the farmers. Around the middle of the sixteenth century, the first signs of the infamous elimination of the free farmers (the *Bauernlegen*) appeared. Until mid-century the expansion of the estates had been largely positive, in that waste land had been broken up and cultivated, new employment opportunities created and, as Kuhn points out, new techniques introduced[33]. By consolidating their own estate land and separating it from the land of the ordinary farmers, they were able to introduce the four-field system which increased the yield of grain by an eighth. Indeed the estate owners remained the main initiators of reform and progress in agriculture in spite of their conservative position on social reform. After 1550, however, they began to destroy the structure of the farming system, taking over the farmer's land and reducing the occupiers to the status of *Kossäten* or worse. It was a renewed rise in the grain price around mid-century which was the stimulus to expansion. The free farmers were forced to sell to the lords under a variety of threats. The legal code allowed the lord to take over the land, where it could be proved that the occupier was a bad farmer or was disobedient. Throughout those areas in which grain could be grown and shipped to western Europe, the number of farmers began to fall from 1550. The decline in the last half of the century varies widely, generally being highest in the Polish areas. Figures quoted by Abel from the source mentioned above (Korth) for the composition of land in estate hands in 1880, suggest that 18.7 per cent was derived from the *Bauernlegen*[34].

The *Bauernlegen* meant changes in both the settlement form and the field pattern. It was recommended by agriculturalists at the end of the sixteenth century that the area of arable on the estate should ideally be as large as that of all the farmers put together. This meant it was possible for the lords to lay out very large fields and use efficient methods. The three arable fields on which the lord also formerly held his land, were now broken up and a completely new system emerged, with the lord's land consolidated. The settlement pattern changed as the estate buildings (the *Gutshof*) came to dominate the settlement and the farmer's houses decayed and disappeared to be replaced by houses thought adequate for estate workers.

The degree to which the settlement pattern did change varied very much. In the example of Warlitz in western Mecklenburg

[33] *ibid*, p. 155
[34] Abel, W., *op. cit.*, 1967, p. 160

(fig. 19) the estate buildings have simply been constructed beside the old village, which has been little changed, its original form being a *Rundling*. Sometimes the village was totally changed and

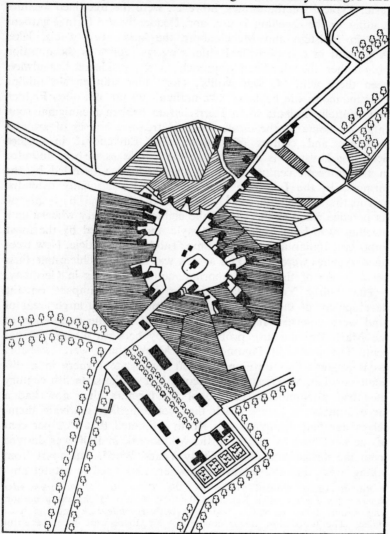

Fig. 19. The Gutsdorf Warlitz in Mecklenburg (after Benthien)

a completely new settlement form was determined by the lord. Very frequently the old village had rows of houses of estate workers joined onto it (the *Katenzeilen*). The estate buildings themselves also varied between the very grand and little better than those of a large farmer. The art of laying out estates progressed through to the nineteenth century, reflecting changes in taste. Typical for the estates, however, were the tree-lined avenues leading to the dwelling house, and frequently the formal gardens and in Holstein and Mecklenburg the landscaped glacial lake. A peasant in one of Fritz Reuter's essays replies to the question of whether the tree-lined approach to the residence has always been there with ' O wat woll's', Herr, hier stünnen süs schöne Plummenböm; die hebbens' äwe aufhau't un uns dei ollen Fichten ahn Wötteln inplant; so 'n Herrschaften hebben mennigmal sonn Infäll '[35]. Some of the estates became treasure houses of art and sculpture and centres of culture. Gut Emkendorf in eastern Schleswig-Holstein is a good example[36]. This estate was founded in the fifteenth century on land that had been deserted by the farmers. In the following centuries it was continually extended and in the seventeenth century had about 5,000 ha. The height of its prestige came at the end of the eighteenth century when a new dwelling was built in Louis XVI style and decorated by the most important Italian artists of the time, Taddei and Pellicia. New tree-lined avenues were made and a park was laid out. This estate then became one of the most important cultural centres in Germany.

The Thirty Years' War had an important impact on the development of the estates. The population fell and large areas of land were deserted. It has been estimated that the population of the Mark Brandenburg probably fell by between 40 and 60 per cent. The losses in Pommern and Mecklenburg were probably even greater. This development left the estate owners in a difficult position. Whereas in the second half of the sixteenth century they had attempted to get rid of the farmers, they now had a large number of farms which they could neither cultivate themselves nor find occupants for. Korth estimated that 18.2 per cent of the land held by estates in the Mittelmark in 1800 was derived from the devastation of the Thirty Years' War[37]. But apart from taking areas into the estates the owners also tried to attract any-

[35] Reuter Fritz. Quoted from his *Die Feier des Geburtstages der Regierenden Frau Gräfin*. Reuter is the best known Mecklenburg author, who wrote about his native region in both *Hochdeutsch* and the local dialect. The translation is 'Of course not sir, there were nice, beautiful plum trees here before; they pulled them up and planted these old firs with no roots; these people sometimes have such ideas '.

[36] Degn, C. and Muuss, U., *Topographischer Atlas, Schleswig-Holstein*, Neumünster, 1966, p. 87, and *Luftbild Atlas, Schleswig-Holstein I*, Neumünster, 1965, p. 51

[37] see Abel, W., *op. cit.*, 1967, p. 160

one, irrespective of character, wealth or intelligence, to settle. To encourage new settlers they invested large sums in buildings, stock and machines. In many parts they did not, however, make the farms over to the new farmers, but let them on a one-life lease so that the heir had no right to inherit the farm. This sort of lease enabled the lords in the eighteenth century to take over more land easily by refusing to renew leases on farms.

At the same time the regulations on worker migration were tightened up to make sure that those already on the estates did not leave. The term ' *Leibeigenschaft* ' was used to describe the legal relationship between the peasant and the estate owner. The meaning given to this term varied from region to region sometimes meaning the total lack of freedom of the person and the total physical and spiritual dependence on the lord and again some-times simply the old situation of material dependence through land ownership[38]. This legal development spread throughout the north-east in the first half of the seventeenth century. It left a totally feudal situation throughout the region, which was to last unchanged until the start of the nineteenth century. The individual had decision-making rights only in the smallest details of life, he had no chance to show initiative or through his own talent to rise above his ' station ' in life. The full development of the system in the nineteenth century meant the total enslavement of the rural population.

With the development of new and more efficient methods of agriculture in the eighteenth century, the estate owners had an incentive again to enlarge their estates. A new ' *Bauernlegen* ' began although on a more restricted scale. However, regionally it was of great importance. In Mecklenburg and Vorpommern it led to the total eradication of a free peasantry, the destruction of almost all the villages and creation in their place of estate villages (*Gutsweiler*), dominated by the estate buildings, which were sur-rounded by the small cottages of the estate workers. With the high earnings from the grain trade and a compliant peasantry behind them, the nobility in the east could concentrate their talents on politics and the army. They could play their part in building a bigger and better Prussia.

The growth of existing settlements and renewed colonization

THE PERIOD BEFORE THE THIRTY YEARS' WAR
Recovery from the great depression of the late middle ages was

[38] Kuhn, W., *op. cit.*, pp. 163-5

at first slow and then in the sixteenth century there was a period of very rapid economic and population growth.

The increase in the number of *Kötter* or *Seldner* throughout Germany has already been discussed, as well as the growth of the estates with the corn trade in the east. Quantitative data has been given by many different authors, to show the growth of population during this period. In the Rhine Valley between Karlsruhe and Speyer, the population increased on average by about a quarter between 1464 and 1530[39]. In the village of Rheinsheim the number of households rose from 62 in 1464 to 72 in 1530, and close by in Oberhausen from 65 to 83 in the same period. Between 1530 and 1618 (the eve of the Thirty Years' War), however, the population on average doubled – in Rheinsheim there was an increase from 72 to 160 households and in Oberhausen from 83 to 150[40]. Saalfeld gives the growth in the number of farms in the Leine loess plain near Gandersheim in eastern Lower Saxony between 1524 and 1620 as 37.5 per cent and for the area around Evessen between 1540 and 1619 as 22.9 per cent[41]. Abel estimates for the whole of Germany that the population fell from 14 million in 1340 to around 10 million in 1470 and then rose to reach 14 million again in 1560[42]. He estimates that by the start of the Thirty Years' War the population may have risen to 16-17 million.

It is clear that the sixteenth century was a period of rising population and, as we have noted before, rising prices for farm produce. Nevertheless many of the settlements deserted in the late middle ages were never reoccupied, the growing population being accommodated in fewer but larger settlements. This meant that in many areas the villages grew into large *Haufendörfer*, which were separated from each other by many miles of arable fields and commons. Born mentions that in the Schwalm region in northern Hessen, villagers deserted declining settlements and moved to larger villages, where indeed they sometimes received special rights and could preserve their collective identity[43]. The land of the deserted villages was then joined to that of the remaining settlement. Initially too, the size of the farm probably increased very

[39] Musall, H., 'Die Entwicklung der Kulturlandschaft der Rheinniederung zwischen Karlsruhe und Speyer vom Ende des 16. bis zum Ende des 19, Jahrhunderts', *Heidelberger Geog. Arb.*, Vol. 22, 1969, pp. 65-66

[40] *ibid.*

[41] Saalfeld, D., *Bauernwirtschaft und Gutsbetrieb in der vorindustriellen Zeit*, Stuttgart, 1960, p. 33

[42] Abel, W., *op. cit.*, 1967, p. 152

[43] Born, M., 'Wandlung und Beharrung ländlicher Siedlung und bäuerlicher Wirtschaft', *Marburger Geog. Schriften, 14*, 1961, pp. 17-18

2 Moorriem–settlement along the Moor-Marsch border in Oldenburg. Aerial photograph by Hansa Luftbild GmbH, Münster/Westph. W. Germany; released – Regierungspräsident Münster/Westph. No. PK 344 dated 4.7.1957

1 Fen-colonies in the East Friesland Moor. Aerial photography by Hansa Luftbild GmbH, Münster/Westph. W. Germany; released – Regierungspräsident Münster/Westph. No. PK 3 dated 17.10.1956

3 Gross Hesepe and its Esch in the Emsland. Aerial photography by Hansa Luftbild GmbH, Münster/Westph. W. Germany; released – Minister for Economic Affairs and Transport NRW No. PK 145 dated 6.7.1955

4 Wurt settlements in the Krummhörn, East Friesland. Aerial photography by Hansa Luftbild GmbH, Münster/Westph. W. Germany; released Regierungspräsident Münster, Westph. No. PK 714, dated 11.10.1957

considerably as the remaining farmers cleared bush from deserted land, but with the sixteenth century rise in population, farm size seems in some areas at least to have started to decline again. Born again for the Schwalm points to the occurrence of land fragmentation in the sixteenth century and for 1580 shows that the dominant size of farm was between 1 and 5 ha. In Ottrau and Röllshausen, both north of the town of Alsfeld, respectively 64 per cent and 70 per cent of the holdings were smaller than 5 ha[44].

As well as the expansion of existing settlements and of their fields, many new villages were founded and completely new areas colonized. On the Hohenlohe Ebene in northern Baden-Württemberg, several new settlements were founded in the sixteenth century, some being daughter settlements from existing villages in the area[45]. Saenger notes the founding of Sommerberg around 1550, Winterberg before 1563 and eight other settlements before 1570. Around Hameln on the Weser new settlements were founded in the first half of the sixteenth century at Laatzen, Multhöpen, Deitlevsen, Niederdehmke and Hilkenbreden[46]. In the Rhön there was already rapid colonization by the start of the sixteenth century[47]. Here a completely new settlement pattern arose. The large villages were deserted or reduced in size during the late medieval period, while a large number of hamlets and *Einzelhöfe* were founded in their place in the early modern period. These newly founded hamlets (Sandberg in 1544, Mosbach 1546, Sommerberg 1546 for instance) maintained a high growth rate throughout the sixteenth century.

In the North Sea marshes, with the end of the disastrous floods which had destroyed large areas of settled land in the late middle ages, the sixteenth century saw a start made in the reclamation of the polders[48]. Perhaps even more than in other parts of western Germany, commercial agriculture was of considerable importance in East Friesland. With the rise in grain prices in the sixteenth century there was a fair chance of profitable investment in

---

[44] Born, M., *op. cit.*, pp. 21-23
[45] Saenger, W., ' Die bäuerliche Kulturlandschaft der Hohenloher Ebene und ihre Entwicklung seit dem 16. Jahrundert ', *Forschungen z. dt. Landeskunde*, Vol. 101, 1957, p. 82
[46] Marten, H. R., ' Die Entwicklung der Kulturlandschaft im alten Amt Aerzen des Landkreises Hameln-Pyrmont ', *Göttinger Geog. Abh.*, Vol. 53, 1969, pp. 68-70
[47] Jäger, H., ' Entwicklungsperioden agrarer Siedlungsgebiete im mittleren Westdeutschland seit dem frühen 13. Jahrhundert ', *Würzburger Geog. Arbeiten*, Vol. 6, 1958, pp. 92-97
[48] Slicher van Bath, B. H., *The agrarian history of Western Europe, A.D. 500 to 1850*, London, 1963, pp. 200-1

K

reclamation work. In the Netherlands large-scale polder-making began around 1540 and reached a maximum rate in the first half of the seventeenth century. This activity then spread over into East Friesland where reclamation was in progress in the Harlebucht before 1570 and in the Rheiderland south of Emden (Bunder Neuland Polder) in 1605. The reclaimed land was suitable for grain cultivation and gave very high yields. The grain trade was well organized then, as also in east Germany and, as there, needed harbours for shipment. So at this time we see the development of the *Sielhäfen*, as important trading ports[49]. The *Siel* is a lock gate which is fitted into the dike, at each place where a river flows into the sea. As trade grew, harbours were founded in the protection of these locks. The *Sielhäfen* developed as small urban settlements in a rural agricultural area, the population consisting mainly of traders, sailors and craftsmen. As settlement and cultivation expanded in the *Marsch*, so the *Sielhäfen* expanded in both number and size. As more and more land was reclaimed and new dikes built, so new *Sielhäfen* had to be constructed, whilst the old harbours, which were now inland, returned to agrarian obscurity.

With investments the size of those in land reclamation and in the location of completely new settlements, the question of the part played by the rural nobility and urban entrepreneurs is obviously interesting, but difficult to answer. In the late middle ages the lords had suffered financial losses because they received fixed payments. Consequently the old feudal organization had been dissolved and the farmers persuaded that their personal freedom was a good thing. In fact freedom from personal feudal ties also meant freedom for the lords to raise taxes and rents. In the late medieval period of settlement desertion in some areas at least, the territorial lords or the state passed legislation to encourage the farmer to stay on his farm and also the settler to come in to work one of the deserted farms. This was, of course, in direct contrast to the north-east where compulsion was used to keep farmers on the land. So out of the feudal relationship between serf and lord had grown the *Meierrecht*, through which the farmer became personally free but had to pay rent on his land. In the expanding economy of the sixteenth century, the territorial lords and the state rulers were very interested in founding new settlements, attracting farmers to settle through the granting of *Meierrecht*

[49] Schultze, A., ' Die Sielhafenorte ', *Göttinger Geog. Abh.* 27/1962 and Minssen, O., *Hooksiel*, Jever, 1960

and numerous other material advantages. So existing settlements were extended in a planned fashion and new settlements founded by the territorial lords and by other landowners interested in increasing their revenues. The dispute between the local nobility and the state came in the treatment of the farmers. The state was interested in fostering a prosperous farming community and therefore restricting unreasonable demands made upon them, while the local lords were more directly interested in raising revenue now directly from the farmers. In many cases in the west the state won and carried out an agrarian protection policy, severely restricting the right of the local lords to interfere in the farmers' affairs.

A good example of a state with a protective policy for the farming community was Braunschweig[50]. Here in 1433 a law was passed to give freedom and protection to farmers in order to encourage immigration. By the sixteenth century the *Meierrecht* had become a right to use of the land which could be inherited by a child of the occupier without interference by the local lord or the state. Besides encouraging and founding new settlement, the lords and the state expanded the domain land. Many of the deserted farms were taken over and worked directly by the lords and in some instances there seem to have been some ' *Bauernlegen* ' of east German style. Nevertheless the policy of farmer protection followed by the state kept this action to a minimum. Still the area in direct cultivation by the lords increased and payments from grain sales became the major part of revenues.

Working in the north-west in the Hamme-Wumme Niederung north of Bremen, Fliedner came to the conclusion that here neither the territorial ruler nor the city of Bremen was particularly influential in the settlement development of the sixteeenth century[51]. Here too, however, large estates developed during this period. He notes for instance in Nordsiedes that of the 12 farms existing in 1350 only 4 remained at the end of the medieval period, yet no new farms were created on the deserted land because the local lord, who was originally the *Lokator* of the settlement, chose to create a large estate for himself[52]. It is, however, indeed probable that the control of the state and local rulers in the north-west was less than in many other areas of

[50] Saalfeld, D., *op. cit.*, p. 55 ff.
[51] Fliedner, D., ' Formungstendenzen und Formungsphasen in der Entwicklung der ländlichen Kulturlandschaft seit dem hohen Mittelalter besonders in Nordwestdeutschland ', *Erdkunde*, Vol. 23, 1970, pp. 102-16
[52] Fliedner, D., ' Die Kulturlandschaft der Hamme-Wumme-Niederung ', *Göttinger Geog. Abhandlungen*, Vol. 55, 1970, pp. 143-5

Germany. Especially in the *Marsch* there seems to have been a considerable degree of cooperative effort between the farmers in the colonization of land and the expansion of cultivation. In Ostfriesland near the town of Norden the farmers collectively reclaimed land from the sea in the sixteenth century. They were organized into *Deichachten,* local organizations making themselves responsible for the upkeep of the dikes and the reclamation of new land[53]. The famous farmer's republic of Dithmarschen in western Holstein also collectively organized the reclamation of land in this century. Nevertheless throughout most of Germany the hand of the ruler or of the state seems to have controlled much of the new agrarian colonization.

Greater proof of this guiding hand can be seen in settlement made for the purpose of exploiting mineral deposits or of fostering certain trades. In the Harz, for instance, the sixteenth century might be called the century of mining, for in a short period, the seven mining towns of the Harz had been founded and settlement was dotted all over the surface of the Harz plateau. The Dukes of Braunschweig were particularly interested in stimulating mining, founding four of the seven Harz towns and granting generous terms to all miners who came and settled there. They struggled too, with the town of Goslar for the control of the Rammelsberg silver deposits. In the southern Harz the town of St Andreasberg was founded by the Dukes of Honstein in 1521, who found that the privileges granted by him were not sufficient to attract miners and so more were granted in 1527 which indeed attracted a large number of settlers. In the Erzgebirge the late fifteenth and the sixteenth centuries brought intense activity again during which there was a great movement of miners between the various mining areas[54]. One of the great centres was Schneeberg with its silver mines, where the uncontrolled settlement of miners grew until the Saxon rulers took over in 1479. Most of the mining towns have an irregular, unplanned centre reflecting the initial casual settlement of miners and a later planned stage when the state or territorial power took over. Many of the mining settlements became small agricultural centres when mining eventually ceased and most miners had drifted away, so that there was some lasting effect in areas so colonized.

[53] Rack, E., 'Besiedlung und Siedlung des Altkreises Norden ', *Spieker,* Vol. 15, 1967
[54] Kuhn, W., *op. cit.,* pp. 180-205

THE THIRTY YEARS' WAR

It has been noted that the economic prospects at the start of the seventeenth century did not look promising, without the Thirty Years' War. The War led to widespread destruction and except for parts of the Weser-Ems Raum and Schleswig-Holstein an end to settlement expansion. In the north-east destruction was very severe and the effect on the development of the estates has already been discussed. Whilst destruction in the west was in many areas just as severe, the results for the settlement pattern, field pattern and social structure were rather different.

In the north and north-west the effects of the war do not seem to have been so severe. As already mentioned in Schleswig-Holstein and in the peat bogs of East Friesland new settlements were laid out and land reclaimed from the sea during this period[55]. Fliedner does not consider that the war made much difference to the settlement pattern or the structure of the economy in the area around Bremen[56]. The Duchy of Oldenburg seems to have escaped with little damage, through the clever changing of sides at the right time. Elsewhere in Germany war and the accompanying plague took a considerable toll of life and property. According to Keyser, the plague occurred in the period 1634 to 1640 throughout Germany with the exception of the north-west, though in eastern Bavaria it was a less frequent visitor than elsewhere[57]. This period of plague coincided with the highest grain price of the whole war in 1637-8, when high prices forced many to go hungry. And so we have the numerous contemporary reports telling only of destruction, devastation, hunger and death.

Born considers the war to have been a very significant period in the development of the settlement pattern, farming system and legal and social structure. He gives statistics for the Amt Schönstein of inhabited houses before, during and after the war. In the six villages cited, there were 117 houses standing in 1618. This number fell to 90 in 1634 and to only 58 in 1649[58]. However, the degree of destruction varied much from village to village. In one of those cited no houses were destroyed during the war whereas in another 80 per cent were destroyed. Though no villages were totally destroyed and deserted in the Schwalm region, Born

---

[55] See below p. 151 ff.
[56] Fliedner, D., *op. cit.*, pp. 149-50
[57] Keyser, E., ' Die Ausbreitung der Pest in den deutschen Städten ', *Abhandlungen d. Akademie f. Raumforschung u. Landesplanung*, Vol. 28, 1954
[58] Born, *op. cit.*, p. 49

shows that almost all had lost some houses, population and arable land. In this situation the surviving farmers attempted to make the best of the situation by working the better parts of the vacated land without paying rent to the lord. For his part the lord tried both to obtain the owed rents and to take as much land as he could for himself. At the end of the war a totally different pattern of landholding emerged, together with a changed relationship between farmer and landlord.

The most important results for our purposes were the widespread destruction of settlements, the fall in the population and the related economic depression after the war. Zschocke mentions that in the Rhineland the fall in population temporarily halted the fragmentation of the land through the system of partible inheritance, for now sufficient land was available for all the heirs without division of the existing parcels[59]. Indeed it was possible to do some consolidation of the strips to reestablish pre-division conditions. The rate of recovery from the war varied from region to region but the onset of economic depression in the second half of the seventeenth century slowed up recovery in most areas. Rye prices fell to a minimum around 1670 but increased slowly thereafter to the turn of the century. After a fall in the first few years of the eighteenth century, rye prices began to increase at a rate which outstripped the increase in price of all the factor inputs in farming. The golden century of agriculture had begun.

THE THIRTY YEARS' WAR TO THE ENCLOSURE MOVEMENT
This was a period of recovery and general prosperity in agriculture. Prices were rising and output was expanding. Costs were rising far more slowly than prices, so profits were booming. Agriculture was the basis of state finance and so had the support of governments. As we shall see perhaps the most dynamic expansion policy was that of the most rapidly growing state, Prussia. Colonies were laid out, new settlement forms created, farmland was produced from the most unpromising natural environments and new systems of cultivation were introduced to serve better the needs of a capitalist agriculture. Everywhere activity and expansion prevailed.

The colonies. After the Thirty Years' War there were considerable

---

[59] Zschocke, R., ' Die Entwicklung der landwirtschaftlichen Betriebs-grössen und ihre Auswirkungen auf die Kulturlandschaft ', *L'habitat et les paysags ruraux d'Europe, Les congrès et colloques de l'Université de Liège,* vol. 58, 1971, p. 425

movements of people about Germany attracted by the favourable terms offered by the states and individual landowners for settlement. As the population grew at a very rapid rate in the eighteenth century the demand for farms in the new colonies increased. The states were only too pleased to settle peasants on the land, for this was the best way of increasing income. So this period was one of colonization on a large scale.

(a) *The colonization of the North German Moor.* As already noted there was some colonization in the north even during the war. In the peat bogs of the north-west a new settlement form and a new form of reclamation spread over from the Netherlands[60]. This was the fen-colony (*Fehnkolonie*). In Groningen the first fen-colonies were founded after the secularization of church lands in 1595; the colony of Oude Pekela was settled in the years immediately after 1600[61]. In Germany the colony of Papenburg was founded in 1631 and that of Grossefehn in 1633.

As in the polders the founding of the fen-colonies took place in times of economic expansion, when the demand for peat or for corn was very high. After the early Emden colonies had been founded in the 1630s (Grossefehn 1633, Lübbertsfehn 1637, Hüllenerfehn 1639) four more private colonies were founded up to 1660 (Bockzetelerfehn, Neuefehn, Stiekelkamperfehn and Iheringsfehn). After this the depression of the second half of the seventeenth century prevented the founding of any further colonies for another 76 years. A new burst of colony foundations then took place, starting with Warsingsfehn in 1736. A further eight private colonies were founded up to 1829 when the state took over the colonization.

The fen-colony is a settlement form based on one or more canals which serve for both drainage and transport (plate 3). The main canal which was deep and wide enough to take peat barges forms the axis of settlement. On both sides of the canals, roads were constructed along which the settlers built their dwellings. The houses are generally close together and the plots belonging to the settlers are small blocks of land running back into the peat bog behind the house. The fen-colonies are therefore extremely regular linear settlements, frequently the plots are of the same size and

[60] A large number of ideas for land reclamation and settlement applied in Germany have their origins in the Netherlands. In many cases they were brought over by Dutch settlers at the invitation of German rulers.
[61] Keuning, H. J., *De Groninger Veenkolonien*, Amsterdam, 1933, pp. 61-64

the houses are spaced at a constant distance from each other.

These were settlements planned by entrepreneurs, who rented the land from the state or other landowner. Up until the founding of the colonies the *Moor* of the north-west had been almost inpenetrable and only around its edges had any peat for fuel been cut[62]. The area of *Moor* was very great and the depth of peat varied from 1m at the edges to over 10m in the best developed parts. In these circumstances it was only through the investment of large capital sums that reclamation was possible. Unfortunately in the case of the early fen-colonies the entrepreneurs sought quick profits from the peat trade and paid little attention to long-term problems.

The early fen-colonies were private developments of urban businessmen, founded to exploit the peat reserves of the *Moor*. The initial stage of settlement was dominated by the cutting and transport of the peat nearest to the canal. Colonists at this stage had only a very small area of land to cultivate. They were predominantly peat cutters and a few had become shippers. Such a large drying area was needed for the peat that even when a larger area had been cleared it could not be used for agriculture. Nevertheless while there was a good market for peat in the local towns (Emden, Leer, Aurich) the colonies and their founders prospered. As more and more land was cleared of peat so the transport to the main canal became a great burden and secondary canals were built at a right angle to it (plate 3). The *Nebenwieken* helped to dry out the peat quicker and allowed its more rapid exploitation. As more and more land became available for cultivation so these colonies changed from peat-cutting and shipping settlements to agricultural settlements with peat as a sideline. In unfortunate cases the bottom fell out of the peat market before it was all cleared and the settlers were left to try to cultivate the surface of the peat. It was then that the disadvantages of the settlements were discovered by their rapidly impoverished inhabitants.

The holdings were very small and the material under the peat was largely sand. The entrepreneurs wanted rapid exploitation and quick profits. The way to get a rapid exploitation was to settle as many colonists as possible, irrespective of how small this policy made the individual holding. The land was divided up in frontages along the canal, often only between 15 and 30 metres in width. The depth of the plot varied considerably with the density of settlement and the extent of the *Moor* area being settled.

[62] *Moor* is the German term for peat-bog. A distinction is made between *Hochmoor* – raised bog, and *Niederungsmoor* – eutrophic fen.

It was often restricted by the extension of other canal colonies. In general, however, the plots rarely exceeded 5 ha and were more often only 1 or 2 ha. In 1961 the size structure of holdings in Ostgrossefehn was as follows:

Size of Holding (ha)	Number of Holdings
0.01— 0.5	5
0.5 — 2.0	106
2.0 — 5.0	104
5.0 — 7.5	23
7.5 —10.0	11
10.0 —20.0	18
20.0 —50.0	2

(SOURCE: Census returns for Lower Saxony, 1961)

Here then in 1961 80 per cent of all holdings were under 5 ha. Similarly in Warsingsfehn 86 per cent and in Ostrhauderfehn 97 per cent of the holdings had less than 5 ha in 1961. Indeed in Ostrhauderfehn 73.4 per cent had less than 2 ha. However, the smallness of the holdings was only one part of the explanation of the poverty in the fen-colonies after the peat had been removed. The other part is the condition of the soil. Beneath the peat the colonists found sand, which was extremely difficult to cultivate and generally gave poor yields. Little could be done to improve it until much later in the nineteenth century.

So the economy of the fen-colonies changed from a peat base to one dependent on agriculture. The time taken for this transformation varied according to the local circumstances and the fluctuations of the peat market. Westerhoff estimated that in Grossefehn it took the hard working settler between 37 and 50 years to clear all the peat from his land[63]. In these circumstances the prosperity of the early fen-colonies was indeed short-lived. The poverty of these settlements was legendary. There was little employment apart from agriculture. As the excavation of the peat ceased the shipping industry suffered badly; there were no other employment opportunities and commuting was out of the question. The only possibility in the late seventeenth and early eighteenth centuries was seasonal or permanent emigration. Many of the settlers went to the Netherlands to find work in the summer and,

[63] Westerhoff, A., *Das ostfriesische-oldenburgische Hochmoorgebiet*, Emden, 1936, p. 53

when this outlet dried up in the nineteenth century, they left in large numbers for America.

The poverty of the colonies was made all the worse by the rapid growth in the population, which led to the creation of very high population densities. Bünstorf gives population data for the years 1789 to 1905 for many of the East Frisian colonies[64].

Colony	1789	1816	1833	1848	1871	1885	1905
Grossefehn	794	1268	1228	1215	1932	1994	2119
Ihlowerfehn	110	180	397	452	680	667	669
Neuefehn	294	314	373	398	366	461	432
Warsingsfehn	497	508	–	1377	1722	1891	1933

The density of settlement in these 4 colonies in 1839 was as follows: (inhabitants/sq. km.)

Grossefehn	257
Ihlowerfehn	126
Neuefehn	78
Warsingsfehn	109

Today the largest of the East Frisian colonies, Westrhauderfehn, has a population of 4,545 on an area of 1688 ha, that is a density of 264 per sq. km. The Dutch fen-colonies in Groningen and Drenthe have always had even higher densities than the German colonies, but they have also always had a far stronger economic base.

The fen-colonies did develop other sources of employment over the centuries. The most important was the shipping industry. Branching out from the shipping of peat, enterprising colonists entered both the general cargo trade using their own ships and the shipbuilding industry[65]. The shippers in the general cargo trade operated not from the cramped canals of the fen-colonies but from the coastal ports like Emden, Greetsiel and Norddeich. Their ships were generally built, however, in the yards of the fen-colonies and registered there, crews being often drawn from the colonies. This meant that a strong tradition of seafaring and shipping developed in the colonies, which is not yet dead, despite the steady decline in the industry since the mid nineteenth century. The decline of the shipping industry has left the fen-colonies again without any adequate source of employment and today a

[64] Bünstorf, J., ' Die ostfriesische Fehnsiedlung als regionaler Siedlungsform-Typus und Träger sozial-funktionaler Berufstradition ', *Göttinger Geog. Abhandlungen*, 37, 1966, pp. 58-61
[65] Bünstorf, *op. cit.*, p. 81 ff.

large proportion of those employed have to commute to the nearby towns. Only in the larger centre of Papenburg on the Ems, has a strong industrial and commercial base developed[66].

The foundation and development of Grossefehn is a well documented example of this peculiar settlement type[67]. In 1633, Emden businessmen were granted 400 Diemat (*c.* 400 ha) of *Moor* by the Duke Ulrich II of East Friesland for which they had to pay a yearly rent after the first two free years. The founders were also made to promise that the land would be cleared as rapidly as possible and the area cultivated (presumably to guarantee the Duke's income). This was an unfortunate time to found a colony. In the Thirty Years' War settlers were difficult to find and financing such a venture was something of a problem. In the end the four businessmen combined with other interested partners to found the Grossefehn Gesellschaft (Company) in 1637, which laid out plans for the settlement. The technical difficulties leading to higher costs than anticipated (the colony was developed on a slight incline) and the uncertainty of returns on invested capital led to frequent changes in the partnership. With time both the area owned by the company and the number of partners rose. In 1877 Grossefehn had an area of 1,900 *Diemat* (*c.* 1,900 ha) and the company consisted of 40 shares. A start was made on the canal, which was to be the axis of settlement in 1634 soon after the foundation. The first settlers were Dutch workers, experienced in the construction of canals. Some of these later settled permanently and were joined by settlers coming primarily from the *Geest* areas of East Friesland. The extension of settlement was very slow and new colonization ceased for quite considerable periods. But slowly through the eighteenth century the typical fen-colony form developed (fig. 20). During the last stages of expansion the first secondary canals (*Nebenwieken*) were constructed, but even so in Grossefehn the main canal is the dominant feature. This stunting of the growth of the colony in a direction at right angles to the main canal was a result of the restricted area of peat bog available for development.

The development of employment in Grossefehn is fairly typical of that throughout the fen-colonies. The first settlers were peat diggers. Some of the more successful colonists saved enough money eventually to buy a ship for the transport of peat. In 1788

[66] Rechtmann, J., ' Die neuere Entwicklung der grossen deutschen Fehnkolonien, unter besondere Berücksichtigung Papenburgs ', Unpublished dissertation, Köln, 1966

[67] Sanders, H., ' Die Besiedlung des Grossefehns ', *Neues Archiv für Niedersachsen,* 1954, 1/3, p. 48 ff.

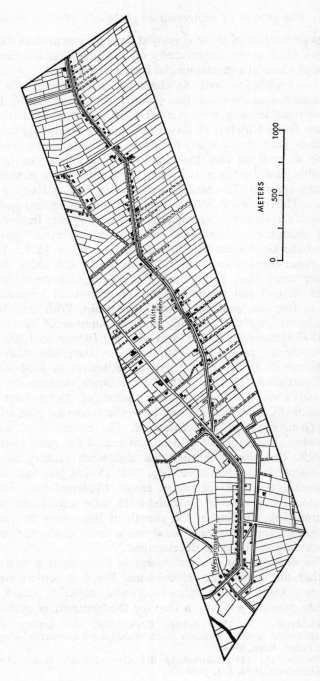

Fig. 20. The fen-colony Grossefehn (1 : 25,000 topographical map)

there were 53 peat boats in Grossefehn and by 1869 this had risen to 86. In 1869 there were also 53 sea-going vessels registered. Indeed, ten years later, this number had increased to 68, but by then the bottom had fallen out of the peat market and, with the increase in steam shipping, the end of all shipping activities in Grossefehn was imminent. A shipbuilding industry also developed and in the mid-nineteenth century five shipyards were registered here. Quite typically for this region, the poor transport connections to the markets for manufactured goods prevented the development of other forms of employment. At one time or another there were four breweries, two distilleries, five corn mills and a glass works, which opened in 1828 only to shut in 1830. Even agriculture had no chance to develop profitable vegetable cultivation as in Papenburg because of the remoteness of the colony from the market. So with the decline in the shipping industry, Grossefehn returned to agriculture and hard times. Many people left for other parts of Germany, especially the growing industrial regions, or for America. Those remaining in agriculture attempted to increase the size of their holdings by buying or renting land in the neighbouring parishes. With improved communications, large numbers of workers today can commute to other areas and so the colony has become a dormitory settlement.

The fen-colonies were, however, only one form of colonizing the *Moor*. At the end of the eighteenth century the Bishop of Münster founded several *Hochmoorkolonien* in the Bourtanger Moor. These colonies were built on the surface of the peat-bog, rather than on the underlying sands as in the fen-colonies. In 1785 the Münster authorities had come to a frontier agreement with the Dutch and were interested in securing the frontier through the establishment of settlements in the *Moor*. In 1788 eight villages were founded (Neurhede, Rütenbrock, Hebelermeer, Neuversum, Neusustrum, Hesepetwist, Rühlertwist and Lindloh)[68].

The development of two of these colonies has been recorded in detail[69]. In Neurhede, 37 settlers were allotted areas of arable and pasture in the *Moor* of about 6 ha in total. The settlers were required to build themselves homes as rapidly as possible and

---

[68] Lauenstein, J. D., 'Die Grenzscheidungskarte zwischen dem Hochstift Münster und der Republik der Vereinigten Niederlände vom 25. Oktober 1785', *Jb. d. Emsländischen Heimvatvereins*, Vol. 6, 1959, pp. 5-9
[69] Schlicht, E., 'Die Entstehung der Moorkolonie Neurhede', *Jahrbuch des Emsländischen Heimatvereins*, Vol. 6, 1959, pp. 10-23
Ottens, B., 'Hebelermeer, ein echtes Hochmoordorf', *Jahrbuch des Emsländischen Heimatvereins*, Vol. 8, pp. 124-30

because of the difficulties of establishing a new settlement in the *Moor* were given ten years free of taxes. Each settler was allowed to graze between 10 and 30 sheep on the *Moor* and to cut peat for domestic fuel. The rent which the settlers paid went two-thirds to the local farmers on the *Geest*, to whom this part of the *Moor* belonged, and one-third to the territorial lord.

Whereas in the fen-colonies the surface layer of the peat (*Bunkerde*) was mixed with the underlying sand to provide a cultivable layer of some kind, here the settlers had to cultivate the raw peat. This was generally done by burning off the surface layer and sowing buckwheat in the ashes. If there was no dry period in the spring, the burning was often unsuccessful. Even if the buckwheat was sown and started to grow, it was frequently killed by the late frosts in the *Moor*. With no good pasture very few animals could be kept. Under these conditions the 6 ha which were given to each settler were totally inadequate.

In addition to the problems of agriculture, there was that of isolation. Without roads and a long way across the *Moor* from the old settlements of the Ems valley, these villages were cut off for many weeks on end in the winter, when it was impossible to cross the *Moor*. Neurhede lay, for instance, 8 km from its church in Wesuwe, and in this region this represented a journey of several hours. Yet in spite of all these problems the population of the colonies grew; in Hebelermeer from 143 in 1821 to 378 in 1848 and 434 in 1871[70].

The incredible poverty of these settlements, in spite of improvements in the 1870s with the introduction of new methods of *Moor* cultivation, remained until after the end of World War II when at last a road network was built and agricultural improvement undertaken. The Münster colonization was typical of much of the colonization in the eighteenth century, which was carried out on very poor soil and at a very high density.

(b) *Reclamation of the polders.* Polder-making after the break during the late seventeenth century depression began again around the turn of the century. In the Weser-Ems Raum it was of two kinds; early private development by the farmers working co-operatively in East Friesland and then state development in Oldenburg under the Dukes of Oldenburg and in East Friesland after 1744 under Prussia.

In East Friesland, the farmers in the *Deichachten*, did not originally settle the polder land but divided it up and simply

[70] Ottens, *op. cit.*, p. 128

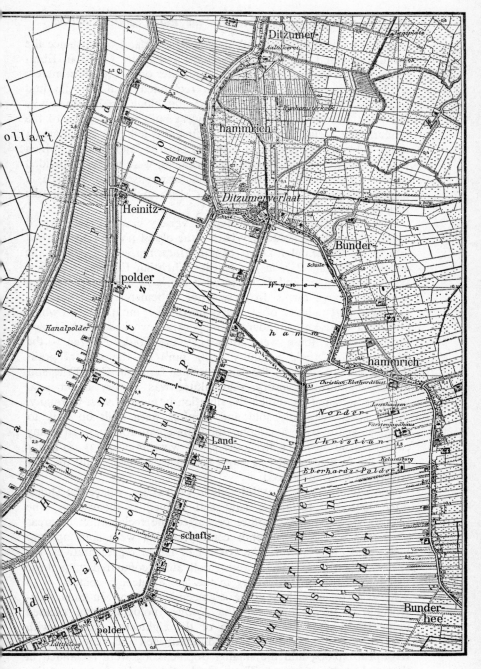

Fig. 21. The Rheiderland Polders (1 : 25,000 topographical map, 2709, Landschaftspolder)

added it to the existing farms. In the Rheiderland for instance the Bunder-Neuland, Bunder-Interessenten and Süder Christian Eberhards Polder were not settled (fig. 21). Later on, however, complete settlements were laid out on the reclaimed land. In the first settled polders the farmhouses generally clung behind the dyke but later, with growing confidence, were built in the centre of the polder. The reclaimed land was at first divided into long narrow strips between the interested farmers, but the later polders, which were reclaimed by the Prussian government, were generally divided up into large blocks surrounding the farmhouses (for instance in Landschaftspolder and on a smaller scale in Kanalpolder in the Rheiderland.

The Rheiderland shows the typical variety in social class which often occurs in the polders. Whereas the oldest polders are worked largely by the smaller farms of the *Marschhufendorf* behind the old sea-dyke (fig. 21), in the Norder Christian Eberhards Polder, Landschaftspolder and Heinitzpolder the land is divided between a few very large farms. In these latter settlements the farmhouses are large and palatial often surrounded by a moat. Their owners formed a close-knit aristocracy, who rarely worked on their own farms. Locally these were known as the *Polder-Fürsten* – the Polder Dukes, their economy being built on the sale of grain as was that of most of the larger polder farms in East Friesland in the eighteenth century. Agriculture was a very commercial business here and so, unlike the situation in most of west Germany, farms were frequently sold and empires were built up only to collapse again with a decline in commercial fortunes. In many cases rich businessmen from the towns were able to buy up farms when the farmers went bankrupt, and many of them built up very large land holdings indeed.

The situation was very different in Oldenburg, where the Dukes often kept the reclaimed land and farmed it themselves. The famous Duke Anton Günther organized the reclamation of areas of polder in the seventeenth century, which were split up into farms and given over to the control of Ducal representatives, the *Meier*. Nevertheless, these were small areas compared with those reclaimed either in Oldenburg in the late nineteenth century or in Schleswig-Holstein during the eighteenth century. In Schleswig-Holstein a great many of the *Kooge* (polders) were created immediately after the beginning of the eighteenth century, with improving grain prices. In Süderdithmarschen the very extensive Kronprinzenkoog and the smaller Sophienkoog were reclaimed in the eighteenth century. They mark the end of co-operative

5 Lower German farmhouse, Bardenfleth, Oldenburg

6 Beilstein on the Mosel. Old stone-built cellared houses in a wine village

7 The farm buildings of a recently resettled farmer in Butteldorf, Oldenburg

8 Black Forest farmhouse near Hofsgrund

reclamation by the farmers and the triumph of the state in its claim to rights of reclamation. Indeed the farmers in these two cases protested at the change in the legal position but the names of these two new polders indicate clearly how ineffective their protests were. The polder north-west of St Peter in Eiderstedt and a large part of the polder in North Friesland, north of Husum, also date from the eighteenth century.

(c) *Colonization in south Germany.* We have looked so far at significant works of reclamation and cultivation in northern Germany. But throughout Germany the states were carrying out such works, often on a smaller scale than that discussed so far, but nevertheless taken together of great significance. Rulers saw in the expansion of settlement a chance to increase their tax revenues and therefore their power, influence and general material welfare.

The settlement forms which were produced by this colonization are of course generally very regular planned forms. The street village is the most common, with the fields lying either in planned *Gewannfluren* or in the form of *Hufen* behind the farmhouses. Frequently, however, one also meets areas with dispersed settlement (*Streusiedlung*). In addition the rulers added individual new farms to existing settlements. Quite frequent too was the division of state land into small farms. On the Hohenlohe Ebene for instance, the Dukes of Hohenlohe, who followed a policy very friendly to the farmers, divided up the Tiergarten Friedrichsruhe near Öhringen in 1738 to make 10 new small farms[71]. Later in the eighteenth century they divided up other estates into smaller holdings. In Hessen the Dukes of Hessen-Nassau were extremely active in promoting new settlements and improving existing agriculture. They even pushed through some consolidation of the *Gewannflur*[72]. Throughout Germany at this time too foreigners were welcomed as settlers by the majority of the states. The beautiful little harbour on the Weser, Karlshafen, was founded in 1699 by the Landgrafen of Kassel to settle Huguenots, who created a valuable textile industry here. Extremely attractive terms for settlement were granted, including tax freedom for 25 years[73].

Perhaps the greatest of the south German development schemes of the eighteenth century was the reclamation of the Donaumoos,

---

[71] Saenger, W., *op. cit.*, p. 85
[72] Ernst, E., and Klingsporn, H., *Hessen in Karte und Luftbild*, Neumünster, 1969, pp. 88-90
[73] *ibid.*, pp. 131-3

L

an area of peat bog north of Munich[74]. After earlier half-hearted attempts to reclaim land here, real progress was made when the Kurfürst Karl Theodor became King of Bavaria in 1777. After an uncertain start work began on a large-scale in 1789. A company was set up to finance this enterprise. This was the *Donaumoos-kultursozietät* (Donaumoos cultivation society), which was founded in 1790. Most of the shares in the company were sold to the King and his immediate associates. In spite of difficulties in the creation of a cheap labour force and legal problems with the owners of the *Moos*, the company was able to make good progress in the work of drainage and road construction, so that the first colony, Karlskron in the eastern part of the *Moos,* could be founded in 1791.

The colonies were planned by the company, which had little experience of colonization and no idea of the particular problems of the Donaumoos. In many ways the history of the early colonies here is similar to that of the Münster colonies in the Bourtanger Moor. The natural problems had not been adequately solved, flooding was a regular hazard and late frosts killed the crops. The houses which the company had constructed for the settlers collapsed with great rapidity because inadequate foundations had been made. Perhaps most important were the type of settler and the density of settlement. No control was exercised over the quality of settler or over his financial situation. Only later when a new period of settlement began after 1816 was a minimum of capital a requirement for settlement. Without any financial resources many of the settlers found it impossible to survive all the problems which beset the early colonies. But the early colonies were also founded with a very high density of population. The company directed that as high a density as possible should be created, because in this way the maximum amount of tax income could be derived. In the Karlskron colony most settlers received only 3 ha, although in the second colony of Karlshuld the amount was raised to $4\frac{1}{2}$ or even 9 ha. It was also initially allowed for these small areas to be divided into smaller holdings. After the obvious failure of the first phase of colonization, the second, starting around 1816, marked an attempt to remedy some of these errors.

Against these criticisms it must be stated that the reclamation of the Donaumoos was a great enterprise by any standard. Around 19,000 ha of wasteland were reclaimed and cultivated. The colonies gave homes to thousands of landless peasants. The tax

[74] Krell, H., ' Die Besidlung des Donaumooses ', *Neuburger Kollektaneen-Blatt*, 104, 1950, pp. 5-88

income of the state was raised which helped economic development in Bavaria, though of course some ran through the pockets of the King and his associates. The atrocious poverty of the population stemmed partly from a lack of knowledge and experience and partly from the unfortunate policy of population growth at all costs. The colonization in east Germany, to which we now turn, was influenced by the same trend of political thought, but in its scope far exceeds colonization plans realized in west Germany.

(d) *Prussian colonization in the eighteenth century.* The colonization in the *Moor* and the *Marsch*, which has just been discussed, appears less significant when compared with the gigantic achievements of the Prussian government during the eighteenth century. The absolutist period in Prussian history began with the Great Kurfürst Friedrich Wilhelm, who came to power in 1640 and ended effectively with the death of Friedrich ii (Frederick the Great) in 1786. These rulers held the mercantilist belief that the economy should be directed by the state. Through economic development the tax income of the state could be raised as well as the wellbeing of its subjects. A dynamic expansion of the economy was seen as an essential counterpart of political expansion. In the eighteenth century the key to economic growth was thought to lie in agriculture, and so the rulers of Prussia invested very heavily in the improvement of the existing agriculture and in the expansion of agriculture into the waste. They personally supported the newly formed agricultural improvement societies, which were numerous in the eighteeenth century. Even under Friedrich ii, who encouraged industry and commerce and made Prussia the fourth largest industrial power of Europe, agriculture was looked upon as the main economic base of the state and was consequently given far more attention and support than other sectors.

The history of the modern Prussian nation really begins with Friedrich Wilhelm i of Brandenburg-Prussia who by his death in 1688 had overcome all the mildly democratic organizations and converted his country into a highly organized absolutist state. He introduced above all, most efficient methods of tax collection, in order to give Prussia a firm financial base. Though he was active in promoting economic expansion through new settlement at home and abroad (in West Africa for instance), it was in this consolidation of power in Prussia that his main achievement lay. Friedrich Wilhelm i of Prussia (as distinct from the Great Kurfürst), who came to power in 1713 is often called the great domestic king, for his efforts were aimed towards the strengthening of the Prussian economy. He carried on the Prussian policy of increasing rapidly both population and the area available for settlement. He invited large numbers of foreigners to come and settle in Prussia, giving them very generous terms and guarantees. For instance in 1732, 15,000 Salzburg Protestants were offered a home in Prussia. His work in reclamation and settlement included the reestablishment of German settlement in those areas of East Prussia, which had been ravaged by the plague. In 1718 he ordered the drainage of the Havelländer Luchs. After five years work 15,000 ha were reclaimed and most of it settled.

It was under Friedrich II after 1740 that the greatest works of reclamation and settlement were carried out. He was responsible for the reclamation of the bog areas of the Oder, Warthe and Netze valleys, of similar areas in East Friesland, the colonization of upland areas in Silesia and a host of other smaller projects. He is reputed to have been responsible for the creation of 900 new villages and the settlement of 300,000 colonists. Well over 100,000 ha of bog were reclaimed, 56,000 ha of it in the Oderbruch. At his death it has been estimated that one-third of the population of Prussia consisted of colonists or the descendants of recent colonists. Perhaps the best description of this work is given by Theodor Fontane in his *Wanderungen durch die Mark Brandenburg*[75]. He describes the Oderbruch before the reclamation under Friedrich II in the following way:

> Before its reclamation the Oderbruch was a wild and useless region ... crossed by an enormous number of larger and smaller arms of the Oder. Many of these streams widened out to form lakes. Twice each year the area was submerged under water, once in the spring after the snow melt in the Oderbruch and again around 24th June when water from the melting snow in the Sudeten was added to by local storms. When this happened the whole region was a vast lake, above which only the highest parts of the land protruded, and even these parts were occasionally flooded.

Friedrich I after receiving reports confirming the difficulty and great expense of reclamation decided to leave the job to his son. Friedrich II took up the challenge and converted this waste into some of the most fruitful arable land in Prussia. Fontane records

[75] Theodor Fontane is a well-known novelist and traveller who journeyed through his native Brandenburg between 1859 and the early 1880s describing what he saw in the several volumes of the *Wanderungen durch die Mark Brandenburg*.

the King's words, ' Here I have conquered a province peace-
fully '.[76]

The Prussian colonization was not merely an attempt to increase
population and the cultivated area. The projects had to promise
to show a quick return on invested capital, otherwise they were
not undertaken. Abel remarks that almost all such projects
proved to be extremely profitable to the state[77]. The return on the
capital invested in the reclamation of the Madüsee, south-east of
Stettin, in 1768 was $7\frac{1}{3}$ per cent in the mid 1770s[78]. Extremely
high returns were also shown in East Friesland in respect of
polder construction. One main reason for these high returns
during the second half of the eighteenth century was of course
that wages made up a large proportion of the costs of reclamation but were then extremely low and indeed falling. On the other
hand, the price of rye was high and rising rapidly and the price
of beef and other animal products was also high by comparison
with wages.

The settlement forms of the colonization vary in detail very
considerably, but of course they have the same high degree of
planning in common. Perhaps most of the settlement took the form
of regular villages with equally regular field patterns. Figure 22
shows the village of Tempelhof founded as a forestry settlement
in 1770[79]. Here in the uplands of Silesia the local control of the
colonization was in the hands of the state forestry officials. Most
of the settlements founded there at this time are similar, many
having 20 houses, though the field pattern varied, sometimes being
Gewannflur as in Tempelhof, sometimes consisting of large blocks
behind each house. In the Netzebruch both regular village forms,
including *Marschhufendörfer*, and regular dispersed settlement
forms appear[80]. At first sight the area does not seem to have a
particularly regular settlement pattern. However, the road network
and the regularity of the field pattern point to the hand of
Friedrich II's settlement planners. These irregular forms are often
thought of as an exception to the general pattern of colonization
in Prussia. Typical is certainly the regular street village, which
we find in the Oderbruch, the Warthebruch, in Silesia and in East

[76] Fontane, T., ' Das Oderbruch ', *Die Wanderungen durch die Mark
Brandenburg.*
[77] Abel, W., *op. cit.*, 1967, p. 294
[78] Abel, W., *op. cit.*, 1967, p. 294
[79] Kuhn, W., *Siedlungsgeschichte Oberschlesiens*, Würzburg, 1954, pp.
204-6 and Plate 50
[80] Schmitz, H. J., *Deutsche Kulturleistung im Netzegau*, Schneidemühl,
1939, p. 33

Friesland. Typical too, however, though not so spectacular, is the dispersed settlement which fills the gaps between the planned villages.

The achievements of the eighteenth century Prussian rulers went beyond this gigantic work of colonization to include the

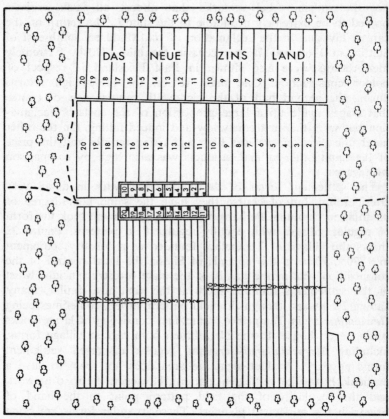

Fig. 22. Tempelhof – a planned settlement of Friedrich II in Silesia (after Kuhn)

construction of several important canals and many main roads. In the Netzebruch for instance the settlers were provided with a road network as well as finished homes. In addition Friedrich II carried out the canalization of the Netze and constructed the Bromberger Canal to join the Netze to the Weichsel[81]. He also founded industrial settlements such as the many iron works of Silesia. The

[81] Schmitz, H. J,. *op. cit.,* pp. 37-42

example thus set by the Prussian king was also followed by the Prussian nobility, who developed their own waste land for settlement in the eighteenth century, by the end of which vast areas had been settled and added to the cultivated area of Prussia. But throughout Germany during this century a very great area had been cultivated in a far less spectacular manner. It consisted of the small-scale expansion by individual farmers around their own farms and by the lesser orders of the nobility.

PRIVATE EXPANSION OF THE CULTIVATED AREA

The rise in price of agricultural products in the eighteenth century encouraged all farmers, who had the smallest interest in commercial agriculture, to expand their farms. Throughout Germany heathland was cultivated, small marshes drained, woodland cleared and deserted arable land put under the plough again. In Schleswig-Holstein and East Friesland there was still a little private polder reclamation, although most had been taken over by the state. In the peat bogs of the north-west some land had been reclaimed privately by mixing the surface layer of the peat with the underlying sands, as was done on land cultivated in the fen-colonies. But perhaps more frequently the *Moor* had simply been used by hacking over the surface layer for the planting of rye or buckwheat. The practice of burning off the surface layer of the peat and planting buckwheat in the ashes gained in popularity in the eighteenth century and led to the widespread destruction of the valuable surface layer. On the Hohenloher Ebene we hear that the farmers enlarged their holdings and the poor population of some parishes cultivated land in the commons[82]. We hear of the extension of the arable and the commons by the farming community in the area around Bremen during the same period[83]. Around Hameln the area of meadow and the size of herds increased throughout the eighteenth century[84]. Indeed evidence exists for this piecemeal expansion throughout Germany. Although it is extremely difficult to make any quantitative estimate of the reclaimed and settled area, it is certain that for Germany as a whole it was of considerable importance.

In short the early modern period after the Thirty Years' War, and especially the eighteenth century, was marked by a colonization movement of very great proportions. Much of the work was carried out privately by individual farmers, and possibly an equal

[82] Saenger, W., *op. cit.*, p. 84
[83] Fliedner, D., *op. cit.*, pp. 146-9
[84] Marten, H. R., *op. cit.*, pp. 99-100

amount of land was reclaimed in this way to that reclaimed more spectacularly by the state.

This expansion produced a host of new settlements and a large growth in the agricultural area. Both the new settlement forms and the new field patterns were in general of great regularity. Within the settlements themselves there was often considerable regularity, with houses equally spaced out, often the house forms were identical and the fields of regular and equal size. These forms came straight from the drawing board, with little amendment ' in the field '.

Many of the settlements also had poverty in common. The small size of holding combined with the unfavourable natural conditions meant that it was impossible for the average settler to produce enough to feed his family and pay his taxes. Even the realistic and agriculturally knowledgeable Friedrich II of Prussia laid out colonies in the Moor in East Friesland of only between 2 and 2½ ha. In spite of six ' free ' years no colonist could make a living from this area, in these conditions. It was the desire to settle as many people on state land for political purposes and the wish to increase the material situation of the state, and of its ruler, which led to this condition of poverty. Generalization is, however, dangerous. In the Hannoverian colonies around Bremen in the later eighteenth century, the colonists were given up to 15 ha of cultivable land, from which, given careful cultivation and the price level of the time, a reasonable living could be made[85].

After 1800, there occurred only one major event in the development of rural settlement in the German lands (excluding the events of 1945 onwards), namely the division of the commons and the enclosure movement. This important topic is examined in the final chapter.

Farming in the Early Modern Period

We shall dismiss the sixteenth and seventeenth centuries rapidly. We have seen that the sixteenth century witnessed the rapid expansion of agricultural land. We have also seen that it brought a severe rise in grain prices. An important trade in grain developed between the east German lands and the west European countries. Grain cultivation was very profitable and spread throughout those areas close to the sea or a navigable river. The seventeenth century on the contrary was a period when the prices of farm products generally declined and there was a considerable amount of

[85] Fliedner, D., *op. cit.*, pp. 83-87

devastation, although most of this had been made good by the end of the century.

We should also mention the livestock industry, for behind the wide zone of grain cultivation in northern Germany lay an important pastoral region. The beginning of the trade in cattle in the late medieval period has been already described (see above pp. 100-2), but in the sixteenth century this trade grew in scale. Abel mentions that in the course of marketing cattle from Poland and Russia, between 16,000 and 20,000 animals were often offered at one market on a single market day[86]. Apart from these regions, the main sources of cattle for sale on the German markets included Bohemia, Hungary and Rumania, as well as Friesland (East and North) and Denmark. Abel suggests that the reason for the apparent upswing in meat production was that the price of animal products did not lag very far behind that of grain in the sixteenth century. Grain could only be grown in convenient export locations, whereas cattle could be driven over hundreds of miles to market. It is probable that the sixteenth and seventeenth centuries brought no great changes in the techniques of farming, although there was undoubtedly some intensification. They brought, however, the beginnings of agricultural science and literature. Nevertheless, the advances of the sixteenth and seventeenth centuries are dwarfed by those of the eighteenth century to which we now turn.

AGRICULTURAL SYSTEMS

In the eighteenth century over most of Germany, perhaps two-thirds, open-fields and the three-field system persisted. However, it was not everywhere the same three-field system, handed down unchanged from medieval times for now the cultivation of the fallow was very common and many varied crops were grown, including peas, lentils, turnips, hemp and flax.

In the remaining third of Germany a variety of systems existed, ranging from a primitive form of infield-outfield to the most complex rotations. In the north-west and in a band cutting across northern Germany into Mecklenburg there was a one-field system, in which the infield was cultivated each year, and the outfield used for the production of manure for application on the infield. This is the system used on the *Esche* of the Weser-Ems Raum. Almost everywhere rye was the crop grown year after year on the infield, with other crops grown only at rare intervals.

Mixed in with this system, and possibly even a forerunner of

[86] Abel, W., *op. cit.*, 1967, pp. 171-80

it, was an even more primitive form of agriculture on the *Vöhden*. The *Vöhden* were cultivated and used, generally for grain crops, for five or six years and then for the same period were left uncultivated and used for pasture. They were not manured, for the farmers reserved all their manure for their private plots. In the period when the *Vöhde* was cultivated, it was divided into strips amongst the farmers and used privately. In the years when the *Vöhde* was used for pasture it was shared by all those with rights to it. It was during these years that the state of the *Vöhden* deteriorated and from which many contemporary descriptions of the appalling state of Westfalian agriculture were derived. The area characterized by this form of agriculture stretched from Westfalia into the Rhineland. A similar system was practised in the Eifel, though here grain cultivation alternated with bushes and small trees and very rough pasture.

Slightly more intensive than these systems were the two-field systems which at this time were met with mainly in the Rhine valley, especially in the lower Rhine rift valley south of Frankfurt. It has been suggested that this form of agriculture was rarely indicative of primitive farming methods, but that in fact just the opposite is true. In the region where the system occurs, there was considerable emphasis on very intensive forms of cultivation, notably viticulture and fruit growing. Viticulture expanded in especially favoured areas, despite a remarkable retreat of the vine from the less favoured areas. The high labour input which both vineyard and orchard required left so little time for grain cultivation, that only a very extensive system for grain was used. Alternatively it is suggested that the fallow year in the two-field system was no longer used for fallow, but for the cultivation of a variety of highly valuable commercial crops.

Finally there were many regions where a system was used with four or more separate fields, notably in northern Germany along the coast of Friesland and in parts of the Rhineland and Westfalia, along the Baltic coast from eastern Schleswig through to East Prussia and in Saxony. In the industrial regions of Saxony a seven-field system is recorded, with the rotation barley, wheat, rye, rye, rye, oats, fallow[87]. A seven-field system was used also in East Prussia where the rotation was frequently rye, barley, barley, oats, oats, peas, fallow[88]. In Holstein and parts of Mecklenburg a system based on complex rotations on enclosed land developed in the eighteenth century. This was the *Koppelwirtschaft*

[87] Abel, W., *op cit.*, 1967, p. 218
[88] Abel, W., *op. cit.*, 1967, p. 217

which often developed after the division of estate land and the new settlement of farmers on it[89]. Abel mentions that in some parts of Schleswig-Holstein five enclosed fields and five open fields were so used in a rotation that starting with all five enclosures under arable, after five years they were all pasture to return after another five years to crops.

LAND USE

There is little doubt that during the eighteenth century grain cultivation expanded at the expense of pasture as a result of the relative price movements of arable and pastoral products. Van Bath quotes figures for the major German towns, showing that in the second half of the eighteenth century the price of rye increased far more rapidly than those of all animal products except perhaps pork[90]. Accordingly farmers ploughed up their pasture and meadows and sowed corn. Animals were often kept merely to provide manure for the arable land; in the arable areas they were generally stall fed, which allowed for the efficient collection of the manure. At the end of the seventeenth century it is recorded that much of the polder land on the North Sea coast was turned over to arable cultivation, although the spread of arable onto the older *Marsch* was restricted by natural conditions[91]. On this enlarged arable area grain crops were most important. Rye was the main bread grain of Germany, being grown extensively throughout north Germany. It was, as we have seen, the most important crop in the north-west almost to the exclusion of all others. In Germany, in those areas of Prussia east of the Elbe and excluding Saxony, 1,142,100 tons of rye were produced in 1804, 1,013,200 tons of oats, 139,000 tons of wheat and 460,100 tons of barley[92]. In Mecklenburg-Schwerin also at this time rye was the dominant arable crop. Rye, in fact, became far more dominant in these areas as the nineteenth century progressed. In southern Germany spelt was one of the commonest grain crops in the eighteenth century, together with oats. On the Schwäbische Alb spelt was simply called corn, an indication of its position in the arable economy[93]. On the Alb oats was the crop of the summer field, while rye and barley were unimportant and

[89] Bonsen, U., *op. cit.*, pp. 219-47
[90] Slicher van Bath, B. H., *op. cit.*, pp. 221-3
[91] Rack, E., *op. cit.*,
[92] Finckenstein, Graf, H. W., *Die Entwicklung der Landwirtschaft in Preussen und Deutschland, 1800-1930*, Würzburg, 1960, Tables 1-4
[93] König, M., ' Die bäuerliche Kulturlandschaft der hohen Schwabenalb ', *Tübinger Geog. Studien*, 1958, pp. 22-23

wheat almost unknown. Much the same is reported from the Riss valley in the Alpine foreland around Biberach[94]. Here, however, rye is mentioned as a crop on the winter field while barley was the second crop after oats on the summer field. On the very fertile land around Braunschweig, wheat had become a very important crop by the eighteenth century, largely taking the place of oats[95]. The expansion of wheat could also be seen in other fertile areas, where farming was on a commercial basis, for the price of wheat exceeded that for other grain. Regionally other types of grain were important, such as the buckwheat of north Germany and the millet of the Oder, Warthe and Netze valleys in the east.

On the open fields in the eighteenth century, a large number of other crops were grown on the fallow. The cultivation of the fallow was a major advance which broke through to some parts of Germany at this time. In many areas innovators had adopted a variety of more intensive cultivation methods in the sixteenth and seventeenth centuries but these were isolated instances with no impact on the general farming system. Now in the eighteenth century the constant attempts by reformers to get the German farmer to plant clover and other valuable crops began to show results. Not surprisingly new ideas took long to reach the grass roots, for not only was communication difficult and conservatism deep seated, but also numerous legal obstacles hindered change. Ploughing the fallow prevented general rights to its use as rough pasture. Simple organizational difficulties which arose from the communal ownership of the open fields also caused problems to innovators.

Clover, though being praised in all the contemporary literature and being grown on a large scale by a few farmers, remained of small importance in most areas. Other crops cultivated on the fallow were of equal or greater importance – peas, beans, lentils, turnips, hemp, potatoes and a host of other crops. The crops grown on the fallow could frequently contribute animal fodder, needed in large amounts after the introduction of stall feeding. Being partly commercial crops they also brought more money to the individual farmer and helped to raise his standard of living. The new crops were also grown in the private fields and gardens throughout the country to which the farmer devoted most of his attention.

[94] Köhler, A., ' Die Kulturlandschaft im Bereich der Platten und Terrassen an der Riss ', *Tübinger Geog. Studien*, 1964, pp. 122 ff.
[95] Saalfeld, D., *op. cit.*, pp. 144-5

By the eighteenth century several areas of specialization had begun to appear. The essential characteristic of these regions was easy accessibility to the market. Around all the major centres of population areas specialized in the production of fresh vegetables, meat and dairy produce. The upper-Rhine–Main area, which at the end of the eighteenth century was one of the greatest concentrations of population in Germany, was also one of the most important for specialized agriculture. Some of the regions serving the large cities served also far wider markets. The orchards of Werder and the vegetable gardens of Teltow served both the neighbouring city of Berlin and areas further away. The same was true for the Altes Land near Hamburg with its extensive orchards. Away from the large centres, areas of specialism had developed where favourable natural conditions matched favourable transport access. Around Lake Constance, in the Upper Rhine Valley, along the Main and in the Palatinate, areas concentrated on commercial fruit growing. With the increasing popularity of beer, hop cultivation had developed in Franconia and Lower Bavaria. Tobacco also had beome an important cash crop in many parts of Germany but it was nowhere a monoculture.

The distribution of the vine had undergone a radical transformation by 1800. The vineyards in northern Germany were replaced frequently by orchards. The vine had been pushed back into the very favourable climatic areas of southern and western Germany, where viticulture was more highly specialized than previously; indeed in some parts of south Germany it had become the most important source of income in agriculture.

Arable cultivation covered about one-third of the total land area of Germany in 1880 and by value contributed around 55 per cent of the gross product of agriculture, rising to 72 per cent in Prussia[96]. Indeed arable farming was the most important source of earnings. Saalfeld suggests that regionally there was a decline in the ratio of arable to total agricultural land as one went from south to north and from west to east. Exceptions to this simple scheme occurred in the fertile regions of central Germany and Silesia. The highest ratios of arable to total land area in 1800 were recorded for Saxon Thuringia, central Franconia around Ansbach, the Göttingen-Einbeck area, and the Börde around Hildesheim. In these areas over half the land was in arable. The intensity of farming measured by the level of factor inputs was also highest

[96] Saalfeld, D., 'Die Produktion und Intensität der Landwirtschaft in Deutschland und angrenzenden Gebieten um 1800', *Zeitschrift für Agrargeschichte und Agrarsoziologie*, Vol. 15, 1967, pp. 137-75

in these southern and western parts of Germany and in the fertile regions mentioned above. In the eastern corn regions, farming was carried on very extensively and although grain was the major cash export crop, arable land was frequently less than one-third of the total land area.

In the eighteenth century in most areas, pastoral farming served the production of arable crops. Animals were important both for transport and for the maintenance of soil fertility. Numerous contemporary descriptions of agriculture point to the poor state of meadows and pastures and the general neglect of the quality of stock. Cattle were frequently looked upon as a necessary evil. Prices of grain feed being very high they were often underfed and, except in the towns, fattening was considered unprofitable for the same reason. In most arable areas farmers had gone over to stall-feeding, in order to turn over as much land as possible to arable and to improve the efficiency of manure collection.

Certainly the eighteenth century brought some improvements in the cultivation of the meadows and the spread of fodder crops, especially to the fallow in the more intensively farmed regions of western Germany. Yet the area of meadow was very small and much of the pasture was still communal and therefore never improved. The main reason for the neglect even of private pasture and of stock was the high prices of grain and other arable products in relation to those of pastoral products. There was little incentive to invest in pasture when the return from investment in arable farming was far higher.

It was only in those areas where natural conditions made arable cultivation very difficult that a specialist pastoral economy developed. In such areas the quality of farming was very high. It is estimated that the average slaughter animal in the old *Marsch* of East Friesland weighed at two or three times as much as the animal from the surrounding *Geest*. Apart from East Friesland the most important areas of pastoral farming were in Saxony, Schleswig-Holstein, northern East Prussia and in the mountain regions of the south. Around the major cities, pastoral specialization in dairy produce was also common. In the far east, beyond the Elbe and the Oder sheep rearing was of great importance. In 1816 there were an estimated 8.3 million head of sheep in Prussia alone. Considerable progress had been made in the production of wool with the introduction, on the initiative of the state, of the merino sheep. This stock improvement had been especially successful in Saxony, where wool was in demand from the local textile industry.

Except for these brighter patches, however, the general picture of pastoral farming in eighteenth century Germany must remain grey if not totally black.

THE FARM IN THE EIGHTEENTH CENTURY

How far did the farmers share in the general prosperity of agriculture during this century? High prices for farm products and low wages created a situation in which substantial profits could be made. The clever farmer could make high super-normal profits. During this century farmers in many regions built splendid, large farmhouses. In western Schleswig-Holstein the large *Haubarge* a house-form introduced from the Netherlands, were constructed. In Land Hadeln, not far from Bremen, unprecedented prosperity had turned ordinary farms into dwellings fit for the aristocracy[97]. On the Hohenlohe Ebene the large two-storey farmhouses which are typical today were first constructed in the second half of the eighteenth century[98].

The other side of the coin is, however, the dues and taxes which had to be paid by the farmers to the lords. These were very high throughout most of Germany. Saalfeld gives several examples of taxes and dues for the area around Braunschweig. In four villages in 1760 the farmers paid to the lord between 32.6 per cent and 52.6 per cent of the value of their harvest[99]. In addition the lord held the monopoly of certain service provision and other rights which could be turned into taxes in some cases (e.g. the right to purchase land and farm produce at low prices). In some areas the demands from the lords became so exorbitant that the farmer had barely enough produce left over to feed his family. In some areas the farmers even considered it more profitable to give up their farms and become servants[100]. The examples given above from Schleswig-Holstein, Hadeln and the Hohenlohe Ebene come from areas where both taxes and dues were reputedly low and where a commercial agriculture was well established. To these three regions we could add southern Bavaria, the Black Forest and parts of central Germany in Hessen and Thuringia.

It is extremely difficult to build up any clear generalized picture of the financial situation of Germany's farmers at this time and one is forced into giving specific examples to show how

[97] Bierwirth, L., ' Siedlung und Wirtschaft im Lande Hadeln ', *Forschungen zur deutschen Landeskunde,* Vol. 164, 1967, p. 57

[98] Saenger, W., *op. cit.,* p. 114

[99] Saalfeld, D., *op. cit.,* 1960, p. 46

[100] Abel, W., ' Die drei Epochen der deutschen Agrargeschichte', *Schriftenreihe für ländliche Sozialfragen,* Vol. 37, 1962, p. 88

variable net income throughout Germany was. The variation was due to the very different levels of dues paid in the different regions and to the degree to which farms were involved in the sale of products in the market.

For the large estates it is perhaps easier to make a more general judgement. The prices paid for estates sold in the eighteenth century, show an upward trend to the end of the century in many parts of Germany[101]. Although other factors influenced the price of property part of the trend reflects the increased earnings of the estates. There were two or three possible ways in which these could be increased. Especially in the east the owners farmed the land themselves and earned very high returns given the high prices of agricultural products. In other areas only part of the land was cultivated directly by the estate owner, the remainder being rented to farmers. There were also areas where the old estates had been divided up and the estate owner became a rent collector rather than a farmer. Whichever way the estate was run, however, a high level of prosperity could be achieved. When money was short, it could generally be squeezed out of the farmers. The unfortunate farmers were, however, unable to hand on increases in taxes to any other group.

THE GROWTH OF AGRICULTURAL SCIENCE AND AGRICULTURAL IMPROVEMENT

The eighteenth century was a period of great interest and great advance in agriculture. It marked the beginnings of a recognizable science of agriculture. The German universities began to run courses in agricultural economics and in the techniques of farming. Although the beginnings of a German scientific literature in agriculture go back to the second half of the sixteenth century, it was in the eighteenth century that the first major works, attempting a systematic appraisal of agricultural practice, appeared[102]. The major German agricultural societies were also founded in the second half of this century. Agriculture had become the major interest of the ruling classes and an acceptable topic of conversation in the highest society. They took pleasure in founding societies together in which the new methods and possibilities in farming could be discussed. In 1762 the Thuringian Society for Agriculture was founded, closely followed by the famous Celle Society in 1764. Numerous others were founded by the end of the century.

This strong interest in farming, from the King of Prussia

[101] Abel, W., *op. cit.*, 1967, pp. 330-1
[102] Abel, W., *op. cit.*, 1967, p. 275 ff.

downwards, was matched by rapid technical development. We have already noted the improvements in the three-field system with the cultivation of the fallow and also those brought about by the introduction and spread of new plants. Considerable improvements also were made in the breeding of cattle and sheep, while the introduction of the merino increased both the quality and quantity of production in Germany. However, although there were great advances towards the end of the century, others, including newly designed farm implements coming largely from England, had to wait for the nineteenth century. The freeing of the peasants in Germany also had to wait until after 1800 so that little improvement was possible in the use of labour. In short, the progress of the eighteenth century was concentrated in the fields of land use and animal breeding with few real advances in the fields of implement design, labour efficiency and capital investment.

5 Enclosure and consolidation

The technical advances in German agriculture in the nineteenth and twentieth centuries and the farm policies of the German governments of the period are dealt with adequately in the literature, both English and German[1]. We shall deal here with the most important changes in the settlement pattern and the structure of farming from the period of the enclosure of the commons to the present day. We turn first to changes in western Germany.

Enclosure of the commons

In some parts of Germany the common land had been enclosed well before A.D. 1800. In the East Friesian *Marsch* much of the common land had been divided among private individuals by the twelfth century[2]. Elsewhere there had been some division by private agreement in the eighteenth century. Nevertheless in the mid-eighteenth century there was still some common land in most parts of Germany and in the north it was very extensive.

State regulations governing the process of enclosure in the commons and the extinction of common rights (*Gemeinheitsteilung*) began to appear after 1750, and general laws were passed in most of the larger states in the first half of the nineteenth century. The driving force behind the movement was again the state. The existence of large areas of almost unused land was of great interest to rulers trying to increase the population and the tax income of their states. While the land was in the joint ownership of all the farmers of the village, however, it was impossible for the state to

[1] for instance see: Tracy, M., *Agriculture in western Europe − Crisis and adaptation since 1800*, London 1964, and Haushofer, H., *Die deutsche Landwirtschaft im technischen Zeitalter*, Stuttgart, 1963.
[2] Rack, E., 'Besiedlung und Siedlung des Altkreises Norden', *Spieker*, Vol. 15, 1967

settle any new colonists on it. In some areas the large landowners were also interested in the enclosure of the commons, for they were in a position to lay claim to the largest part. Very frequently the old, established full-time farmers were opposed to the enclosure, for they lost their rights to pasture on the commons for which the small enclosure they received did not compensate. In many cases the smallholders (the *Kötter*) were also against the division because they knew that they would be turned off their land, yet in some areas they appear to have struggled successfully to claim new enclosed plots on the commons.

The legal basis for enclosure was often not laid until the first half of the nineteenth century, but division had generally taken place far earlier. The division of the commons had started as early as 1723 in Bavaria and around 1750 in many of the other states. One of the earliest laws was passed in the Bishopric of Osnabrück where the Markenteilungsgesetz came into force in 1785. In Bavaria formal encouragement was given to the farmers to enclose the commons in an official document of 1762[3]. In Prussia the Urbarmachungsedikt passed in 1767 gave the state the right to use waste land and settle colonists on it, though the act regulating enclosure of the commons did not come until the *Regulierungsedikt* of 1811 and the *Gemeinheitsteilungsordnung* of 1821. These laws were followed by similar ones in Württemberg in 1822, Baden in 1823 and Saxony in 1832. Opinion was very favourable towards enclosure among the ruling groups in Germany in the last half of the eighteenth century. It remained favourable during the first few years of the following century in most regions; there were 921 case of commons enclosure in Bavaria between 1799 and 1804[4]. After 1815, however, especially in the south-west there was some opposition to the division of the commons even in the ruling classes and amongst the landowners. Enclosure slowed down, and in Baden and Württemberg legislation even restricted enclosure. Meanwhile in the north, in Prussia, Hannover, Mecklenburg and Oldenburg the division went ahead. By the end of the nineteenth century very little common land remained in Germany.

The social effects of the enclosure vary with the degree of success which the small farmers had in laying claim to a share of the common lands. In some parts of southern Germany the *Seldner* appear to have been treated equally with the established farmers. In Württemberg some enclosure was made in the early eighteenth century in which the *Seldner* had received land and in 1808 it had been ruled here that generally at enclosure the *Seldner* were to be treated in the same way as the farmers[5]. In the Riss valley on the Alpine foreland the smallholders were again able to establish their rights to the common lands[6]. In the north on the other hand generally only the old established farmers and the oldest group of *Kötter* received land in the commons and many of the more recent *Kötter* families and the *Heuerlinge* were turned off land they had occupied for many years or even generations. In these northern areas the smallholders lost a large part of their income through the loss of the commons and with the unfortunate decline in the rural textile industry coming at the same time, many were forced to leave for the growing industrial areas or for North America. In those regions where these groups received land on the commons, however, they were sometimes able steadily to improve their standard of living and to establish a higher social status in the village. The negative income effects of enclosure on the poor were somewhat ameliorated by the founding of new colonies and by the increase in alternative employment in factories and mines.

The effects of the enclosure on the settlement form and field pattern are perhaps obvious. In parts of southern Germany, where little common land was left to be divided at the start of the nineteenth century, these effects were perhaps slight, for the enclosure of the commons was not associated with consolidation of the strips on the open fields. In the north where there were both large areas of common and of other waste land, enclosure transformed the landscape. On the sandy heathlands and in the peat bogs settlements were founded and forest established. Hedges were planted across open land and new roads were constructed.

An interesting and instructive case of enclosure is the course of the division of the commons in the old Duchy of Oldenburg. Here the legal basis for the enclosure is the *Gemeinheitsteilungs-ordnung* of 1806. At that time there were 420 commons with an area of 187,625 ha, which is equivalent to 45 per cent of the total area of the Duchy (excluding the area of *Marsch* where the commons had been divided at a far earlier stage)[7]. In some parishes

[93] König, M., 'Die bäuerliche Kulturlandschaft der hohen Schwabenalb', *Tübinger Geog. Studien*, Vol. 1, 1958, p. 28

[6] Köhler, A., *op. cit.*, p. 125

[7] Harms, O., 'Die Teilung der Marken und Gemeinheiten in Oldenburg als landeskulturelle Massnahme im 19. Jahrhundert', *100 Jahre Verkoppelung in Oldenburg*, Oldenburg, 1958, pp. 20-24

the proportion of the land in commons was far higher – in the parish of Essen for instance they made up two-thirds of the total parish area. In addition to these areas of extensively used land, there were also large areas which were totally waste, notably the area of peat bogs west of Oldenburg. In these circumstances it is no wonder that the rulers of this small state were interested in the reclamation and settlement of as large an area as possible.

The Dukes of Oldenburg had long claimed unused land as their own. In the seventeenth century Graf Anton Günther claimed all uncultivated unhedged waste land for the state. The state was also entitled to one-third or one-tenth of the commons, when they were enclosed, although it sometimes waived this right. A large part of the waste land in Oldenburg lay on the *Geest* and in the peat bogs of the Oldenburgisches Münsterland, an area which was only given to the Duchy in 1803. The rulers of the state did not take into consideration the totally different social and economic circumstances on the *Geest*, when they drafted the order for the division of the commons. Here in the area around Vechta and Cloppenburg, the local lords had been able to keep a large amount of power in their own hands, while in the old Duchy of Oldenburg in the north the power of these groups had been broken by the state. Nevertheless through the emancipation of the farmers and the abolition of feudal rights and privileges, which occurred throughout Germany at the start of the nineteenth century, the local nobility in the Oldenburgisches Münsterland lost their special rights in the *Mark*. They became just landowners with certain rights of use in the commons. In spite of protests from the nobility, the state was able to push through the enclosure of the very large commons in Vechta and Cloppenburg as well as in the old Oldenburg areas.

The various social classes in Oldenburg received land in proportions to their status in the village. The *Vollerbe* received 40 *Jück* (17.8 ha), the *Halberbe* 20 *Jück*, an established *Kötter* 10 *Jück*, a new *Kötter* 5 *Jück* and others, including the *Heuerlinge*, nothing[8]. For the established farmers who had long protested about the use of the commons by the *Kötter*, *Brinksitzer* and *Heuerlinge*, their division was of great advantage. It meant here, just as in the other parts of Germany, a tremendous change in the methods of farming which had basically remained unchanged for centuries. No longer was the common pasture available and the sources of peat, timber and firewood were now in private ownership. Nevertheless the addition of about 18 ha of land to the farm considerably

[8] Harms, *op. cit.*, p. 21

benefited the established farmer. In many cases the farmers did not cultivate the newly acquired land until the end of the century when artificial fertilizers became available. In Cloppenburg and Vechta for instance 7,280 ha of land were newly cultivated in the period 1893-1902, and most of this land was in private ownership in the former commons[9].

On the other hand, enclosure was a bitter blow for many groups in Oldenburg. Those dispossessed of land in the commons lost part of their livelihood. For the non-inheriting sons of farmers the chance of staying in farming and living locally also disappeared. These groups made up a large part of the total population. In the Oldenburgisches Münsterland the *Heuerlinge* alone made up half the total population. At the time of enclosure summer jobs in the Netherlands became more difficult to find and the textile industry declined. As a result, a tremendous flood of emigrants left Oldenburg between 1830 and 1860, almost all of them from the *Geest* in Vechta and Cloppenburg. Alone in the ten years from 1841 to 1850 some 5,000 emigrated from this small area of South Oldenburg, approximately one fourteenth of the 1841 population[10]. The division of the commons was only one of several reasons for this large-scale emigration but was nevertheless an important reason.

The state was shocked by this loss of population at a time when it wanted to build up its population rather than lose it. It first tried negative policies such as the prohibition of American advertising which encouraged emigration, but then it turned to policies designed to encourage people to stay in Oldenburg. In Oldenburg in the nineteenth century the state was the only colonizer of waste land, and this had the advantage of reducing speculation in land values and allowed the settlement of the economically weak sections of society. In 1820 the state laid down guidelines for colonization. Commissions were sent to study the East Friesland fen-colonies and the eighteenth century Prussian and Hannoverian settlements in the vicinity and to report on the best way of colonizing the waste areas of Oldenburg. It was therefore possible for the Oldenburg rulers to learn from the mistakes of others and to improve on these procedures in their own colonies. Nevertheless it must never be forgotten that this was a commercial venture in which the state saw a good financial return. It paid to retain the

[9] Böckmann, U., ' Die sozial- und wirtschaftsgeschichtliche Entwicklung und Bedeutung der Heide- und Moorsiedlungen im Oldenburger Münsterland seit der Markenteilung ', Diss., Bonn, 1957
[10] Böckmann, *op. cit.*, pp. 25-30

population and to encourage new settlers to come in, for they all paid taxes!

And so throughout the nineteenth century there were new colonies founded on the peat bog and the *Geest* in Oldenburg, and frequently this involved the use of the *tertia* (or *decima*) *mercalis*, which the state had claimed for itself at the enclosure of the commons. A large part of this land was also used to increase the size of existing farm units and a small area was afforested by the state. At the same time the example set by the state was followed by private individuals, who cultivated small areas adjacent to their own farms. Indeed after 1890 this private reclamation and cultivation accelerated greatly as farmers saw the advantages offered by new methods of reclamation and by greater intensification of cultivation. So the process of settlement and reclamation went on into the twentieth century, unchanged in spite of the change of authority from the Dukes of Oldenburg to the new German Reich after 1871. By the beginning of the present century almost all the commons had been enclosed but large areas remained uncultivated[11].

A measure of this state and private activity is that whereas in 1869 45 per cent of the state area was uncultivated land this was reduced to 34 per cent in 1900, 29.5 per cent in 1910 and only 18.8 per cent in 1925[12]. In the period 1856 to 1892 the state gave 80,363 ha for new colonization, for additions to existing farms and for afforestation[13]. Nearly 12,000 ha went towards the construction of 233 new settlements. An example of how this state activity changed the landscape quite radically is given in fig. 23. The dominant feature of this part of Oldenburg in 1790, when the Vogtei map was surveyed, was the peat bog of Wildenlohs Moor. This was largely uncultivated, though some small patches of land were being cultivated by poor settlers from the surrounding villages on the *Geest*. The modern map of the area reveals radical changes. The unimproved peat bog has disappeared and has been replaced by the state 'fen-colonies' of Petersfehn, Friedrichsfehn and

[11] Small areas of undivided commons remain today both in Oldenburg and elsewhere throughout Germany. With the exception of the commons at Oythe, which still remain unenclosed, enclosure was more or less complete by 1900. Elsewhere some enclosure had to wait until the twentieth century, e.g. at Hestrup near Bentheim, the commons were divided in 1919

[12] Böckmann, *op. cit.*
Tantzen, R., 'Die landwirtschaftliche Siedlung im Landesteil Oldenburg', Oldenburg, 1931, unpublished

[13] Böckmann, *op. cit.*, pp. 25-30

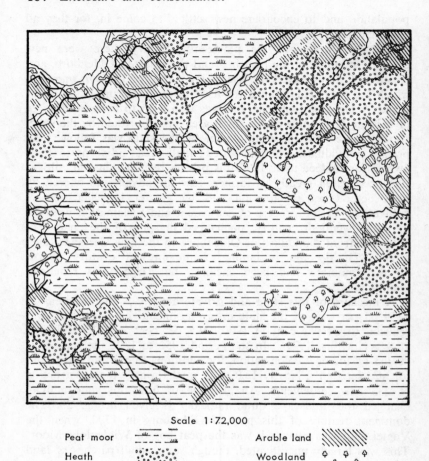

Scale 1:72,000

Peat moor   Arable land

Heath   Woodland

Fig. 23a. Wildenlohs Moor, Oldenburg before the division of the commons (taken from the Oldenburg Vogteikarte, 1790)

Moslesfehn, founded in 1847, 1847 and 1871 respectively[14]. Only very small areas of uncultivated land remain, though one or two small areas were afforested.

The colonies founded in Oldenburg were places of considerable poverty, despite their late foundation. The normal size of a plot

[14] The 'fen-colonies' of Oldenburg were cultivated using the same technique as that in the East Frisian fen-colonies, but in Oldenburg roads not canals form the main settlement axes.

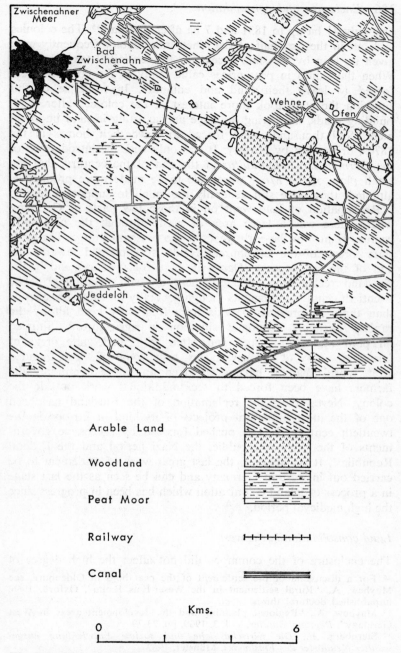

Arable Land

Woodland

Peat Moor

Railway

Canal

Kms.

0   6

Fig. 23b. Wildenlohs Moor after the division of the commons
(topographical map 1 : 50,000, no. 2914, Oldenburg)

was only 4½ ha up to 1831 and 7 ha after that date[15]. The colonies laid out in the first half of the nineteenth century frequently were given no help by the state except for the ten initial tax-free years. When the slump in peat prices came many of the colonists were forced to leave their land and emigrate. In response to this situation the state took more interest in the colonies after 1850, building roads, improving drainage and assisting in land improvement. Still thousands were forced to leave their homes in the 1870s, driven out by poverty. It was only with the introduction of the *German Hochmoorkultur* at the end of the century, that the small plots of the *Moor* were able to be made more productive, although they were still generally too small to support a family.

Reclamation of land went on in those few parts of Germany where there was a large area of waste through the nineteenth century right into the early years of the present century. The great state forests of the Lüneburger Heide were planted towards the end of the last century (Oerrel in 1876 for instance) and in the Emsland reclamation and settlement are still continuing[16]. The twentieth century settlements though generally far more prosperous than those of previous periods have frequently been hit by the rapidly changing economic situation in agriculture[17]. Situated on poor agricultural land and often with inadequate areas of farmland, many of the new farms, even some of those founded after World War II, have been given up. More commonly the farmers have been forced to seek additional work outside the colony. Nevertheless the reclamation of the Emsland has been one of the most important projects of its kind in Europe in the twentieth century. It was pushed forward by successive governments of the Weimar republic, the Nazi period and the Federal Republic[18]. It is, however, the last great work of settlement to be carried out in western Germany and can be seen as the last stage in a process of inland colonization which has been in progress since the high medieval period.

Land consolidation in the west

The enclosure of the commons did not affect the high degree of

---

[15] For a discussion of the settlement of the peat bogs in Oldenburg, see Mayhew, A., ' Rural settlement in the Weser-Ems Raum ', Oxford, 1966, unpublished doctoral thesis.

[16] Mayhew, A., ' Regional planning and the development areas in West Germany ', *Regional Studies*, Vol. 3, 1969, pp. 73-79

[17] Sternberg, F., *Die wirtschaftliche und soziale Entwicklung ausgewählter Neudörfer des Emslandes*, Münster, 1962

[18] Mayhew, A., *op. cit.*, 1966, pp. 374-443

fragmentation which existed on the arable land of the village. In western Germany the consolidation of the small arable parcels came long after the division of the commons and in some areas has still to be undertaken.

In the pattern of land consolidation, the south-western parts of Germany again stand out from those of the north. In Hannover the legal basis for the *Verkoppelung* (consolidation of land parcels) was created in 1848 and in Oldenburg with the passing of the *Verkoppelungsgesetz* in 1858. Similar laws were passed in Prussia in 1850, in Baden in 1856, Hessen in 1857, Bavaria in 1861 and in Württemberg in 1862[19]. The concentration of these dates around and just after 1848 is not coincidental. It was only after the final destruction of all feudal and communal ties to farmland in 1848 that progress in consolidation could really be made. Whereas, however, it was pushed through by state officials in the north and was generally seen there by the farmers to be beneficial, in the south the system of partible inheritance prevented any great progress being made.

In one area of Germany, however, land consolidation and the disintegration of the village had taken place far earlier. This was in the Allgäu, in the area owned by the Abbey of Kempten[20]. The oldest recorded consolidation here was in 1550 and in 1551 the first resettlements of farmers out from the village took place. This movement continued until the mid-nineteenth century, reaching its zenith in 1770. Before consolidation there had been extreme fragmentation, with plots only a few square metres in size, and the common pasture was generally a long way from the village. The way in which the movement came to Kempten is not clear, but it seems that the initiators of the individual consolidation and resettlement projects were the farmers themselves. The movement started in the small hamlets where consolidation was easy and spread to the larger settlements later. Some of these latter were only partly dealt with or were left untouched. The result of the movement was, however, to create farms, which even in modern economic circumstances can be run efficiently. Between the small hamlets today there are numerous *Einzelhöfe*, lying in the middle of their large consolidated blocks of land. Undoubtedly the great prosperity brought by the growth of dairying in this region was made possible only by this early consolidation and resettlement which created a suitable farm structure.

[19] Haushofer, H., *op. cit.*, p. 58
[20] Endriss, G., ' Die Separation im Allgäu ', *Geografiska Annaler*, Vol. 43, 1961, pp. 46-56

Elsewhere it was only in the late eighteenth century that consolidation got under way and more especially in the middle of the nineteenth century. Much of the earliest consolidation which was completed in the second half of the nineteenth century was by present standards inadequate. In those areas, notably Hannover and those parts of Prussia in western Germany, which at the time were the most advanced in agricultural improvement, secondary consolidation is having to be made at the present time. The process of consolidation was very slow even in these areas of northern Germany. It was a very complicated process and met the opposition of conservative farmers.

In Oldenburg state consolidation got under way with the scheme for the Sager Esch in 1859, though there had previously been one consolidation at Hasbergen with special permission of the state[21]. In the early scheme in Oldenburg an astonishingly high degree of consolidation was achieved; on the Sager Esch for instance only 75 separate parcels remained from the 640 which had existed before consolidation. In Sage the average size of parcels on the *Esch* rose from 0.37 ha to 3.2 ha which even by present day standards is not too unfavourable[22]. Seven farmers, including those with the largest farms, moved their farms out from the village. Unfortunately not all the schemes were so successful. The process of *Verkoppelung* (consolidation) continued in Oldenburg through into the present century and indeed today several schemes are being worked upon[23]. In all some 47,194 ha of land in 295 schemes involving 12,816 landowners were consolidated in Oldenburg between 1859 and 1958[24].

After rapid progress in the period between the founding of the Reich in 1871 and 1890 the speed of consolidation slackened. It picked up again during the latter years of the Weimar republic and the early Nazi period. Consolidation was encouraged by the

[21] Harms, O., 'Die Verkoppelung des Hasberger Kirchenesches', *100 Jahre Verkoppelung in Oldenburg*, 1958, p. 26

Reissig, H. H., 'Die Verkoppelung des Sager Esches', *100 Jahre Verkoppelung in Oldenburg*, 1958, p. 27-30

[22] Reissig, *op. cit.*, p. 28

[23] Mayhew, A., *op. cit.*, 1966, pp. 175-203 and pp. 245-315

Mayhew, A., 'Zur strukturellen Reform der Landwirtschaft in der Bundesrepublik Deutschland erläutert an der Flurbereinigung in der Gemeinde Moorriem/Wesermarsch', *Westfälische Geographische Studien*, Heft 22 1970.

Mayhew, A., 'Agrarian reform in West Germany: an assessment of the integrated development project Moorriem', *Trans. Inst. of British Geographers*, 52, 1970, pp. 61-76

[24] 'Kulturamt Oldenburg', *100 Jahre Verkoppelung in Oldenburg*, Oldenburg, 1958

passing of the *Reichsumlegungsordnung* in 1937, which for the first time gave to the authorities powers of compulsion. Several valuable consolidations were made under this order and this formed the legal base for all schemes until 1953, when the *Flurbereinigungsgesetz* (Land consolidation act) was passed. The *Flurbereinigungsgesetz* turned the simple pre-war consolidation schemes into integrated rural planning projects[25].

The *Flurbereinigungsverfahren* (consolidation plan) today deals not only with the consolidation of land parcels but also with the creation of new infra-structures in rural areas, the improvement of the land and land drainage, the resettlement of farms out from the congested villages, the enlargement and improvement of existing farms and also the replanning of villages (*Dorferneuerung*). There have been large schemes in northern Germany but undoubtedly the greatest projects have been on the highly fragmented open fields of the south and south-west. Here the schemes have often completely altered the settlement patterns, creating better working and living conditions for the farm and non-farm populations alike.

As an example we take the project in Oberaltertheim, Unteraltertheim and Steinbach near Würzburg in Lower Franconia[26]. Here before the *Flurbereinigung* the whole area of the parishes, with the exception of small patches of woodland on the steepest parts of the valley sides, was divided into incredibly small strips, most of which could only be reached by crossing those of other farmers. In all there were 35,300 parcels totalling 1,950 ha, in agricultural use, and divided among 1,372 owners. The average size of strip was therefore only 0.055 ha. Many of the farms had well over 100 separate parcels spread widely over the parish. After the consolidation many of the farmers had only one large parcel, and most had less than ten parcels. A typical farm in Oberaltertheim, which before consolidation had 14.1 ha in 108 parcels, received back after the scheme 13.6 ha in four parcels. The scale of the consolidation is enormous, though whether a 13.6 ha farm is a viable unit in present conditions is doubtful. In this scheme twelve farms could be moved out of the cramped villages and placed on the edge of the parish areas. Furthermore, the villages themselves have been provided with new facilities and new building plots for non-farm residents (fig. 24).

[25] Mayhew, A., 'Structural reform and the future of West German agriculture', *Geographical Review*, Vol. 40, 1970, pp. 54-68
[26] 'Bundesministerium für Ernährung, Landwirtschaft und Forsten', *Die Verbesserung der Agrarstruktur in der Bundesrepublik Deutschland, 1963-64*, Bonn, 1964, pp. 72-75

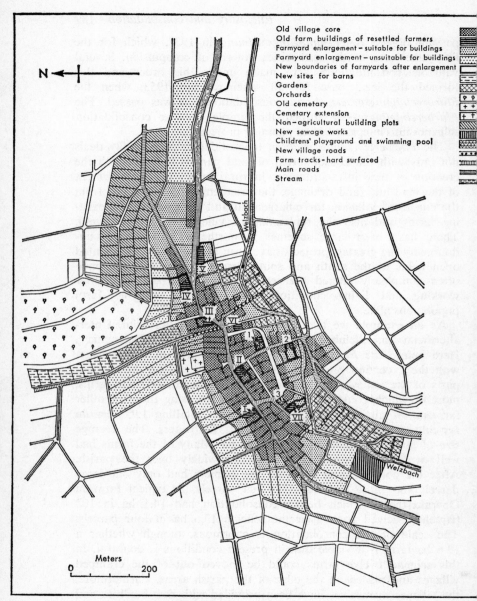

Old village core
Old farm buildings of resettled farmers
Farmyard enlargement – suitable for buildings
Farmyard enlargement – unsuitable for buildings
New boundaries of farmyards after enlargement
New sites for barns
Gardens
Orchards
Old cemetary
Cemetary extension
Non–agricultural building plots
New sewage works
Childrens' playground and swimming pool
New village roads
Farm tracks–hard surfaced
Main roads
Stream

N

Welzbach

Welzbach

Meters
0   200

Fig. 24. Village replanning (Dorferneuerung) in Unteraltertheim,
Lower Franconia.

It is not only in the modern *Flurbereinigungsverfahren* that farmers have moved out of the villages. In many of the older consolidation projects of the last century, farms were moved. The division of the commons gave the farmers land far from the village, but their valuable arable land was often still in strips close to the village. So there was often little incentive to move the farm until the arable land was consolidated. An interesting example is that of Benstrup near Löningen in South Oldenburg[27]. Figure 25 shows the settlement and field patterns created by the division of the commons in 1805 and the consolidation of the *Esch* and the meadows in 1936. Here in fact seven farmers left the village and rebuilt on their newly enclosed land in 1817 soon after the division of the commons. The land in the *Mark* which fell to the state at enclosure was used to found the colony of Steinrieden, in which each colonist received only $4\frac{1}{2}$ ha of land. After the consolidation of the *Esch* another movement of farmers from the village was generated and another five rebuilt their farms near the edge of the parish.

The changes which the *Verkoppelung* and the *Flurbereinigung* have wrought on the settlement and field patterns are very great. These changes are obvious from what has been said above. Today, throughout Germany the small strips of the open fields are disappearing and being replaced by large blocks of land. The villages are disintegrating and changing character. As the farms move out so often people without interests in agriculture move in. The village becomes a service and residential centre. New farms spring up as *Einzelhöfe* or in small hamlets outside the built-up area. New roads and improved drainage networks appear everywhere. At the same time the whole character of the rural economy is changing too, moving away for the first time from its farming base.

Today in the Federal Republic of Germany the authorities are trying to build a sound agriculture on the basis of the large family farm. Co-operation is encouraged, but essentially the system is built around the autonomy of the individual farmer. The individual, now freed of all feudal ties, makes his own decisions, right or wrong, although this is not necessarily the best way of making agriculture efficient. In eastern Germany, to which we now turn, the course of events have been very different.

[27] Diekmann, F., ' Über die Auflockerung der Ortslage bei Verkoppelungen und neuere Aussiedlungsmassnahmen in Oldenburg ', *100 Jahre Verkoppelung in Oldenburg,* Oldenburg, 1958

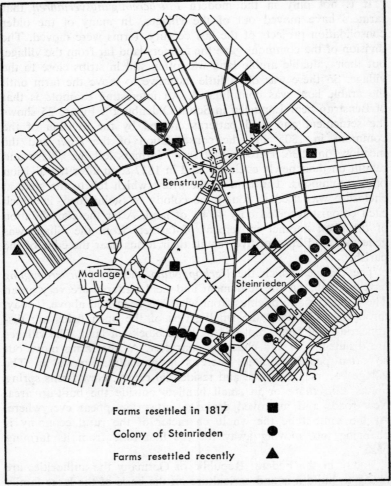

Farms resettled in 1817 ■

Colony of Steinrieden ●

Farms resettled recently ▲

Fig. 25. The enclosure and resettlement at Benstrup/Oldenburg

The farm structure in eastern Germany since 1800

In Prussia Friedrich II encouraged the so called *Separation*, through his Edict of 1751. Initially this meant the separation of the land of the estate owners including their share of the commons from that of the peasants. The estate land was consolidated but frequently the land of the peasants was left fragmented in small strips on the open fields and what remained of the commons were left unenclosed. Towards the end of the eighteenth century the land of the peasants was also consolidated in some areas. The legal basis to a regular division of the commons was laid in 1821 and to consolidation in 1850.

In Schleswig-Holstein many of the estates had been divided up and let out to farmers in the eighteenth century. In other parts of north-east Germany (especially in Mecklenburg and Vorpommern) the estates had been consolidated, and towards the end of that century the estate system had reached a totally stable state in which the peasants were legally bound as servants to the estate owner. In Vorpommern and Mecklenburg whole landscapes were occupied by the estates, with hardly any peasant land remaining. A position of absolute rule by a small élite and complete social injustice had been reached. Yet at the end of the century, with the Napoleonic revolution radically changing established political and social patterns, opinion inside Prussia began to change. Leading state officials pressed for a revolution from above to change Prussia from an absolutist state to one in which people were free and through education could become responsible citizens. One of the leaders of the reformists was Reichsfreiherr vom und zum Stein and his suggestions for reform were largely effected by a 'liberal', Freiherr von Hardenberg. These reform plans, the so called Stein-Hardenberg reforms, were put into effect during the latter years of the Napoleonic Wars. The Prussian regulations freeing the peasants were copied in many other parts of Germany and most of the old feudal ties had been broken by 1850.

After 1815 the rulers of Prussia turned once more to extreme conservatism. Most of the proposed internal reforms were abandoned and the freeing of the peasants was slowed. In fact this movement was used to strengthen the hand of the landed aristocracy and to increase the size of the estates. The peasants were forced to compensate the estate holders for their freedom both through payment in cash and through the forfeit of land. The result was the expansion of the estates and the growth of a proletariat consisting of smallholders working on the estates. This development also led to increased out-migration from the rural areas of the east to the towns and the industrial areas.

The estates produced by these reforms in Prussia were often extremely efficient agricultural units. Many of them became centres of agricultural innovation. Von Thünen on his estate in Mecklenburg is of course an extreme example of scientific endeavour on the eastern estates but is not untypical of many of the estate owners. Some of the money invested in the estates came from

N

urban businesses and from high office in the state and this was used for farm improvement, land reclamation and other measures which served to increase quality and output of farming in these areas. Theodor Fontane in his *Wanderungen durch die Mark Brandenburg* describes the rise and fall of the Gentz family at their estate in Gentzrode. Although the founder of the family fortune ' was only conceivable in the Mark and indeed perhaps only in the Ruppin area ' he was typical in his endeavour to build up the estate by improving cultivation methods and reclaiming land. In and after 1856 large areas of sand were reclaimed partly for agriculture and partly for forestry. Trials of new plants and techniques were made. Out of a wilderness the Gentz family built a flourishing estate.

The Gentz estate was built up between 1850 and 1880 during the period of German unification and the creation of the Reich. It is known in Germany as the *Gründerjahre* – these were years of great economic development, when the towns expanded very rapidly and Germany became a world power. The estate owners were frequently in a position to invest in the new industry and to become men of great wealth and very considerable political influence. They were a keystone in the political organization of the Reich under Bismarck and they saw to it that nothing hindered or threatened the development of their estates. So throughout the nineteenth century the same pattern of large, powerful estates, with many paid labourers living in estate villages with few rights, continued. This is the social situation described with cynicism and humour by the contemporary Mecklenburg writer Fritz Reuter.

There had been considerable controversy as to the amount of land which was diverted to the estates from the peasant farms through the nineteenth century reforms. Graf von Finckenstein, for instance, maintains that while the smallholders gained considerable areas of land during this century, both the larger farmers and the estates lost land[28]. Saalfeld, in an extremely careful analysis, comes to the conclusion that the reforms did not lead to very great changes in the ownership pattern, but that the thesis of von Finckenstein is not consistent with the facts[29]. Saalfeld estimates that the farmers lost 420,000 ha without payment to the estate owners and they sold a further 450,000 ha to

---

[28] von Finckenstein, Graf, H. W., *Die Entwicklung der Landwirtschaft in Preussen und Deutschland, 1800-1930*, Würzburg, 1960, p. 109 ff.
[29] Saalfeld, D., ' Zur Frage des bäuerlichen Landverlustes in Zusammenhang mit den preussischen Agrarreform ', *Ztschr. f. Agrargeschichte und Agrarsoziologie*, Vol. 11, 1963, pp. 163-71.

them in payment for the reforms. Therefore the estates gained nearly 900,000 ha from the farmers. However, the farmers also gained 600,000 ha from the division of the commons and so suffered an effective loss of less than 300,000 ha. But the estate owners were also able to claim the remainder of the commons and therefore to increase the size of their estates still further. The thesis that the reforms led to the creation of landless labourers is no longer tenable according to Saalfeld, for the majority of labourers on the estates were able to acquire small-holdings, either at the division of the commons or through purchase from the estates. According to Saalfeld the number of smallholdings increased rapidly throughout the century.

The first world war was a key event in the collapse of the estate system. In the first engagements of this war many of Prussia's estate owners and heirs to estates were killed[30]. During the war the swing towards socialism and democracy brought a social democratic government to power in 1919. No longer was Germany ruled by the *Junker* – some power at least had passed to the people. After the war and especially during the economic crisis of the '30s many estates came up for sale and were bought by the settlement associations founded after the war in order to foster the settlement of peasants on the land of the large estates. In 1926 the referendum to decide whether the German nobility should have their land confiscated without compensation brought no majority and so many of the estates were able to survive the interwar years. Nevertheless the scale of the interwar division of the estates should not be underestimated as the figures quoted by Benthien show[31]. Between the passing of *Reichssiedlungsgesetz* (Reich settlement law) in 1919 and 1932, 72,430 ha of land were settled, most of this coming from division of the estates. Further division and settlement by small farmers came under the National Socialists, during which period favourable terms were given to estate owners wishing to sell to the state.

While during the interwar period radical changes had taken place in the settlement form (through the division of estates) and in the structure of society, nevertheless a large number of the estates survived. At the end of World War II the area of the great estates fell to the communist states, with the exception of a small part which remained in Schleswig-Holstein. The areas east

[30] Rosenberg, A., *Entstehung der Weimarer Republik,* 1961 edition, Frankfurt/Main, p. 103
[31] Benthien, B., *Die historischen Flurformen des südwestlichen Mecklenburg,* Schwerin, 1960, pp. 162-7

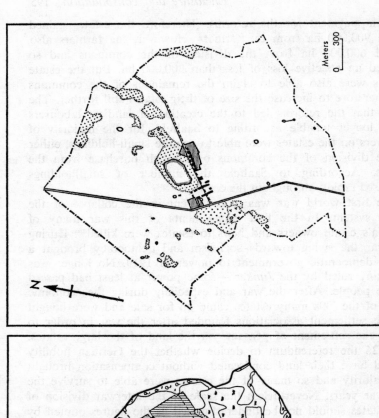

(a) Stresow in 1694 with three open-fields

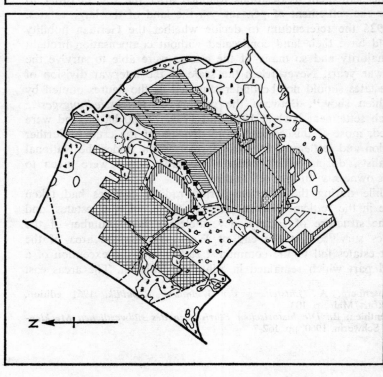

(b) Stresow in 1900, as an estate village

FIG. 26. THE DEVELOPMENT OF THE ESTATE VILLAGE STRESOW IN VORPOMMERN (AFTER BENTHIEN)

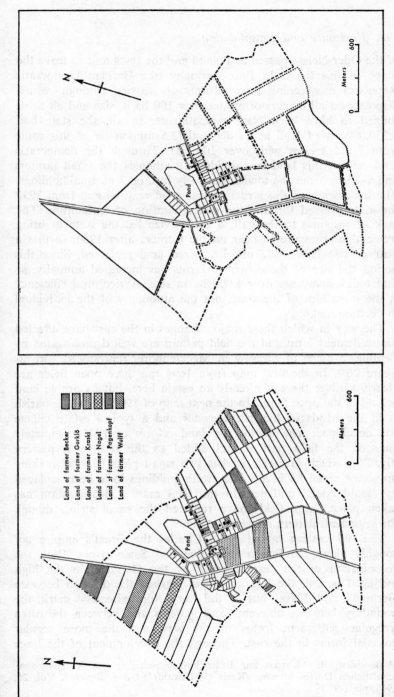

Land of farmer Becker
Land of farmer Gorkiš
Land of farmer Kraski
Land of farmer Nagel
Land of farmer Pagenkopf
Land of farmer Wulff

(c) Stresow in 1946, after the democratic land reform

(d) Stresow in 1960-61, after collectivization

of the Oder-Neisse passed to Poland and the USSR and so leave the scope of this book. In East Germany (the German Democratic Republic) a sweeping land reform was carried through, which dispossessed all owners of estates over 100 ha in size and all those judged to have been Nazi sympathizers. In all, the state had 3,220,000 ha of land at its disposal (2.5 million ha of this came from 7,112 estates with over 100 ha). Through the democratic land reform this land was divided up amongst the small farmers and workers from the towns, generally in 6 or 7 ha smallholdings. The inefficiency of this structure was soon realized and from 1952 the state pressed through the collectivization of agriculture. The lack of response to the call to collectivize led the state to bring tremendous pressure to bear on the farmers after 1960, so that a year or two later, little uncollectivized land remained. Since this period the size of the collective farms has increased annually, so that today many are over 1,000 ha in size. Agricultural efficiency is the main aim of the state, not the autonomy of the individual in decision making.

The way in which these major changes in the east have affected the settlement form and the field pattern are well demonstrated by Benthien's maps of Stresow in Mecklenburg, reproduced here as figure 26[32]. In the first map from 1694 the three open fields are clearly visible; there is already an estate here, but its arable land is held in the open fields. In the next map of 1900 the whole parish is in the hands of the estate owner and a typical estate village has developed. The democratic land reform of 1945 completely changed the field pattern and added to the settlement pattern (fig. 26c). Each farmer now has two small plots of land making up six or seven ha in all. The estate buildings have been replaced by smallholders' cottages. In the final map, collectivization has taken place, large fields have replaced the small strips, though the settlement pattern remains the same.

The old eastern boundary of Charles the Great's empire lay roughly along the line of the Elbe and Saale rivers. With the colonization of the eastern areas by the Germans in the high medieval period, the line no longer marked the division between Germans and Slavs, but it did very approximately mark the boundary between different legal systems and between the often irregular settlement forms of the west and the more regular colonial forms in the east. Through the development of the large

[32] Benthien, B., 'Karten zur Entwicklungsgeschichte des Vollgenossen-schaftlichen Dorfes Stresow (Kreis Greifswald)', *Geog. Berichte*, Vol. 26, 1963, pp. 1-9

eastern estates and the social changes which came in their wake, this boundary became the dividing line between contrasted economic and social systems. Now there is a more significant division in much the same area, though it has moved west beyond the Saale.

The 'Iron Curtain' today divides totally different political, social and economic systems. But in terms of the settlement pattern far less has changed than one might think. In the west the reforms already described are continuing but the pace of the resettlement of farmers out from the village has slowed because of the high cost. In the east the period of the 'democratization' of land ownership and farming is over and now the large collective farm is in some superficial ways similar to the old estates. There are very large farm units, efficiency in production is the main goal, and the collective farmers have only small areas of private land. But the estate owner is now the state and the peasants have some say in the running of the collective and a stake in its profitability.

Today in west and east the state is all powerful and if this book were to have a moral, it would be that this is a development from as far back at least as the ninth century. Then we saw the monastery of Lorsch colonizing and determining settlement form and field pattern. Through the middle ages it was first the territorial lords, then the local rulers who controlled new colonization and to a large extent the development of the existing settlements. In the early modern period, the state gradually took control and in the east during the absolutist period it stamped out all possible initiative from the peasantry. Rarely has the peasant been an initiator of change. This role almost always fell to the wealthy capitalist or to the state.

Bibliography

Abel, H., 'Die Besiedlung von Geest und Marsch am rechten Weserufer bei Bremen', *Deutsche Geographische Blätter*, vol. 41, 1933, pp. 56-60

Abel, W., *Agrarkrisen und Agrarkonjunktur*, Berlin, 1935; *Die Wüstungen des ausgehenden Mittelalters*, Stuttgart, 1955; 'Schichten und Zonen europäischer Agrarverfassung', *Zeitschrift f. Agrargeschichte und Agrarsoziologie*, vol. 3/1, 1955, pp. 1-19; *Agrarpolitik*, 2nd ed. Göttingen, 1958; 'Verdorfung und Gutsbildung in Deutschland zu Beginn der Neuzeit', *Geografiska Annaler*, vol. 43/1-2, 1960, pp. 1-8. Also printed in *Zeitschrift f. Agrargeschichte und Agrarsoziologie*, vol. 9, 1961, pp. 39-48; 'Die drei Epochen der deutschen Agrargeschichte', *Schriftenreihe für ländliche Sozialfragen*, vol. 37, 1962; *Die Geschichte der deutschen Landwirtschaft vom frühen Mittelalter bis zum 19. Jahrhundert*, 2nd ed. Stuttgart, 1967

Albrecht-Thaer Gesellschaft, *Die Landwirtschaft Niedersachsens 1914-1964*, Celle, 1965

Arends, F., *Ostfriesland und Jever in geographischer, statistischer und besonders landwirtschaftlicher Hinsicht*, 3 vols., Emden, 1818-1820

Arps, L., 'Der güldene Ring: Deichbau aud Landgewinn an der Nordseeküste', *Neues Archiv f. Niedersachsen*, 1952, pp. 477-491

Aschkewitz, M., 'Geschichte des Dobriner Landes', *Deutsches Archiv f. Landes- und Volksforschung*, 1943, pp. 261-316

Aubin, H. (ed.), *Geschichte Schlesiens*, Breslau, 1938; 'The lands east of the Elbe and German colonization eastwards', *Cambridge Economic History of Europe I*, pp. 449-486

August, O. and Schlüter, O., *Atlas des Saale- und Mittleren Elbegebiets*, Leipzig, 1958

Baasen, C., *Das Oldenburger Ammerland*, Oldenburg i. O., 1930; *Niedersächsische Siedlungskunde*, Oldenburg i. O., 1930; 'Das Siedlungsbild der nordwestdeutschen Flottsandgebiete', *Archiv f. Landes- und Volkskunde von Niedersachsen*, 1944

Baden, W. (ed.), *Festschrift aus Anlass des zehnjährigen Bestehens des Kuratoriums f. die staatliche Moor-Versuchsstation in Bremen*,

Hamburg, 1960 ; 'Von der Spatenkultur des Reichsarbeitsdienstes in den Emslandmooren zum voll-mechanisierten Urbarmachungsverfahren', *Jahrbuch des Emsländischen Heimatvereins*, vol. 11, 1964, pp. 16-29

Bader, K. S., *Das mittelalterliche Dorf als Friedens- und rechtsbereich*, Weimar, 1957

Bäuerle, L., 'Die Fehnsiedlungen im deutsch-niederländischen Grenzraum', *Westfälische Geog. Studien*, vol. 25, 1971, pp. 131-142

Bantelmann, A., 'Aufgaben und Arbeitsmethoden der Marschenarchäologie in Schleswig-Holstein', *Berichte zur deutschen Landeskunde*, vol. 27, 1961, pp. 240-252

Benthien, B., *Die historischen Flurformen des südwestlichen Mecklenburg*, Schwerin, 1960 ; 'Karten zur Entwicklungsgeschichte des vollgenossenschaftlichen Dorfes Stresow (Kreis Greifswald)', *Geographische Berichte*, vol. 26, 1963, pp. 1-9

Bernard, W., 'Das Waldhufendorf in Schlesien', *Veröff. d. Schlesischen Gesellschaft f. Erdkunde*, vol. 12, 1931

Bertelsmeier, E., 'Bäuerliche Siedlung und Wirtschaft im Delbrücker Land', *Arbeiten d. Geog. Kommission, Münster*, vol. 7, 1942

Bierwirth, L., 'Siedlung und Wirtschaft im Lande Hadeln, eine Kulturgeographische Untersuchung', *Forschungen zur deutschen Landeskunde*, vol. 164, 1967

Blanke, H., *Emsländischen Moorkolonien im Kreis Meppen*, Osnabrück, 1938

Blaschke, K., 'Soziale Gliederung und Entwicklung der sächsischen Landbevölkerung im 16. bis 18. Jahrhundert', *Zeitschrift f. Agrargeschichte und Agrarsoziologie*, vol. 4/2, 1956, pp. 144-56

Blohm, R., 'Die Hagenhufendörfer in Schaumburg-Lippe', *Veröff. d. Provinzialinstituts f. Landesplanung u. niedersächsische Landes- und Volksforschung Hannover-Göttingen*, Series AII, vol. 10, 1943

Böcker, F., *Die innere Kolonisation im Herzogtum Oldenburg*, inaugural dissertation University of Jena, 1913

Böckmann, U., 'Die soziale und wirtschaftsgeschichtliche Entwicklung und Bedeutung der Heide- und Moorsiedlungen im oldenburger Münsterland seit der Markenteilung', unpublished dissertation, Bonn, 1956

Boelke, W. A., 'Die frühmittelalterlichen Wurzeln der südwestdeutschen Gewannflur', *Zeitschrift f. Agrargeschichte und Agrarsoziologie*, vol. 12, 1964, pp. 131-63

Bonsen, U., 'Die Entwicklung des Siedlungsbildes und der Agrarstruktur der Landschaft Schwansen vom Mittelalter bis zur Gegenwart', *Schriften d. Geog. Instituts d. Universität Kiel*, vol. 22/3, 1966

Born, M., 'Siedlungsentwicklung am Osthang des Westerwaldes', *Marburger Geog. Schriften*, vol. 8, 1957 ; 'Langstreifenfluren und ihre Vorformen in den hessischen Berglandschaften', *Berichte zur*

deutschen Landeskunde, vol. 20, 1958, pp. 104-24 ; ' Frühgeschicht-
liche Flurrelikte in den deutschen Mittelgebirgen ', *Geografiska
Annaler,* vol. 43, 1961, pp. 1-8 ; ' Wandlung und Beharrung ländlicher Siedlung und bäuerlicher Wirtschaft ', *Marburger Geog.
Schriften,* vol. 14, 1961 ; ' Langstreifenfluren in Nordhessen? '
Zeitschrift f. Agrargeschichte und Agrarsoziologie, vol. 15, 1967,
pp. 105-133 ; ' Studien zur spätmittelalterlichen Siedlungsentwick-
lung in Nordhessen ', *Marburger Geog. Schriften,* vol. 44, 1970
Bosl, K., ' Eine Geschichte der deutschen Landgemeinde ', *Zeitschrift
f. Agrargeschichte und Agrarsoziologie,* vol. 9/2, 1961, pp.
129-43
Boyens, W. F., *Die Geschichte der ländlichen Siedlung,* Berlin-Bonn,
1959-60
Brägelmann, P., *Inwieweit kann das Heuerlingswesen einen Beitrag
zur Gesundung der landwirtschaftlichen Arbeitsverfassung leisten?*
Münster, 1958
Brand, F., ' Zur Genese der ländlich-agraren Siedlung im lippischen
Osningvorland ', *Landeskundliche Karten und Hefte d. Geog.
Kommission f. Westfalen, Reihe Siedlung und Landschaft,* vol. 6,
1967
Brand, H., ' Die Übertragung altdeutscher Siedlungsformen in das
ostholsteinische Kolonisationsgebiet ', *Schriften d. Geog. Institut d.
Universität Kiel,* vol. 4, 1933
Brünger, W., ' Das Doppelhofproblem in seinen natur- und kultur-
geographischen Beziehungen ', *Deutscher Geographentag, München,
1948, Verhandlungen,* 1950, pp. 155-77 ; *Einführung in die Sied-
lungsgeographie,* Heidelberg, 1961
Brüning, K., ' Das Hannoversche Emsland ', *Geog. Rundschau,*
vol. 10/5, 1958, pp. 161-70
Brunken, O., ' Das alte Amt Wildeshausen ', *Oldenburger For-
schungen,* vol. 4, 1938
Bünstorf, J., ' Die ostfriesische Fehnsiedlung als regionaler Siedlungs-
form-Typus und Träger sozial-funktionaler Berufstradition ',
Göttinger Geog. Abhandlungen, vol. 37, 1966 ; ' Bundesminister f.
Ernährung, Landwirtschaft und Forsten ', *Die Verbesserung der
Agrarstruktur in der Bundesrepublik Deutschland,* Bonn, 1964
Burrichter, E. and Hambloch, A., ' Das Bild der frühmittelalterlichen
Siedlungslandschaft um Münster/Westfalen ', *Abhandlungen des
Landesmuseums f. Naturkunde, Münster,* vol. 20/3, 1958
Buschendorf, H., ' Die Flurformen der Rodesiedlungen im oberen und
mittleren Eichsfeld ', *Mitteilungen d. sächsisch-thüringischen Vereins
f. Erdkunde zu Halle/Saale,* 1934, pp. 34-99
Buttkus, H., ' Die Dorfformen in den Landschaften der ehem.
Regierungsbezirks Magdeburg ', *Berichte zur deutschen Landes-
kunde,* vol. 9, 1951, pp. 382-8
Cellbrot, G., ' Die Siedlungsformen des Kreises Teschen ', *Zeitschrift
f. Ostforschung,* 1963, pp. 75-97

Christmann, S., 'Die ländlichen Siedlungs- und Flurformen im deutschen Oberrheingebiet', *Mitteilungen d. Geog. Fachschaft Freiburg,* vol. 2, 1969, pp. 1-38

Clemens, P., 'Lastrup und seine Bauernschaften', *Schriften d. wirtschaftswissenschaftlichen Gesellschaft zum Studiem Niedersachsens e. V.,* vol. 40, 1955

Conze, W., 'Agrarverfassung und Bevölkerung in Litauen und Weissrussland', in *Deutschland und der Osten,* vol. 1, Leipzig, 1940

Czybulka, G., 'Wandlungen im Bild der Kulturlandschaft Masurens seit dem Beginn des 18. Jahrhunderts', *Veröff. d. Seminars f. Staatenkunde und Historische Geographie,* vol. 3, Berlin, 1936

Dannenbauer, H., 'Bevölkerung und Besiedlung Allemaniens in der fränkischen Zeit', *Zeitschrift f. württembergische Landesgeschichte,* vol. 13, 1954, pp. 12-37; *Grundlagen der mittelalterlichen Welt,* Stuttgart, 1958

Deike, L., *Die Entstehung der Grundherrschaft in den Hollerkolonien an der Niederweser,* Bremen, 1959

Diekmann, F., 'Über die Auflockerung der Ortslage bei Verkoppelungen und neuere Aussiedlungsmassnahmen in Oldenburg', *100 Jahre Verkoppelung in Oldenburg,* Oldenburg i. O., 1958

Dittmaier, H., 'Esch und Driesch', *Festschrift f. F. Steinbach,* Bonn, 1960

Drescher, G., 'Geographische Fluruntersuchungen im Niederbayerischen Gau', *Münchener Geog. Hefte,* vol. 13, 1957

Dürig, K., 'Das Siedlungsbild der Insel Fehmarn', *Forschungen zur deutschen Landeskunde,* vol. 32, 1937

Edelman, C. H. and Edelman-Vlam, A. W., 'Studies concerning the morphogenesis of some old rural settlements in the sandy areas of the Netherlands', *Tijdschrift van het Koninklijke Nederlandsche Aardrijkskundig Genootschap,* vol. 77, pp. 312-18

Elster, P., 'Hochmoor Erschliessung im Oberledinger Land', *Beiträge z. Heimatkunde und Geschichte von Kreis und Stadt Leer,* Leer, 1961, pp. 19-35

Ellenberg, H., 'Steppenheide und Waldweide. Ein vegetationskundlicher Beitrag zur Siedlungs- und Landschaftsgeschichte', *Erdkunde,* vol. 8, 1954, pp. 188-94

Emmerich, W., 'Ergebnisse und Probleme der süddeutschen Flurforschung, vor allem hinsichtlich der Entstehung der Gewannflur', *Berichte zur deutschen Landeskunde,* vol. 29, 1962, pp. 253-72

Emsland, GmbH., *Siedlungsergebnis im Emslandplangebiet, (a.) 1945-63, (b.) 1945-65,* Meppen, 1964 and 1966

Endriss, G., 'Die Separation im Allgäu', *Geografiska Annaler,* vol. 43/1-2, 1961, pp. 46-55

Engel, A., 'Die Siedlungsformen in Ohrnwald', *Tübinger Geog. Studien,* vol. 16, 1964

Engel, F., 'Das Rodungsrecht der Hagensiedlungen', *Quellen zur niedersächsischen Geschichte,* vol. 3, Hildesheim, 1949; 'Erläuterungen zur historischen Siedlungsformenkarte Mecklenburgs und Pommerns', *Zeitschrift f. Ostforschung,* vol. 2/2, 1953, pp. 208-30

Engelhard, K., 'Die Entwicklung der Kulturlandschaft des nördlichen Waldeck seit dem späten Mittelalter', *Giessener Geog. Schriften,* vol. 10, 1967

Ernst, E., 'Siedlungsgeographische Folgeerscheinungen der Agrarstrukturverbesserung innerhalb der Dörfer', *Berichte zur deutschen Landeskunde,* vol. 40, 1968, pp. 223-37

Evers, W., 'Zum Problem der grossen Haufendörfer', *Veröff. d. deutschen Geographentages in Frankfurt,* 1951, pp. 249-58; 'Grundfragen der Siedlungsgeographie und Kulturlandschaftsforschung im Hildesheimer Land', *Schriften d. Wirtschaftswissenschaftlichen Gesellschaft zum Studium Niedersachsens e. V.,* vol. 64, 1957

Fehn, H., 'Das Siedlungsbild des niederbairischen Tertiärhügellandes zwischen Isar und Inn', *Mitteilungen d. Geog. Gesellschaft München,* vol. 28, 1935, pp. 1-94; 'Waldhufendörfer im hinteren Bayerischen Wald', *Mitteilungen d. Nürnberger Geog. Gesellschaft,* 1937, pp. 5-61

Fehn, K., 'Entstehung und Entwicklung der mittelschwäbischen Angerdörfer des 14. Jahrhunderts', *Mitteilungen d. Geog. Gesellschaft,* München, vol. 48, 1963, pp. 33-58; 'Zum Problem der mittelalterlichen Plansiedlungen in Süddeutschland', *Mitteilungen d. Geog. Gesellschaft in München,* vol. 48, pp. 193-7; 'Siedlungsbild, Wirtschaftsleben und Gesellschaftsstruktur in der mittelschwäbischen Herrschaft Welden um 1800', *Mitteilungen d. Geog. Gesellschaft in München,* vol. 49, 1964, pp. 155-80; 'Siedlungsgeschichtliche Grundlagen der Herrschafts- und Gesellschaftsentwicklung in Mittelschwaben', *Veröff. d. Schwäbischen Forschungsgemeinschaft,* Reihe 1, vol. 9, 1966

Filipp, K. H., 'Studien zur Entwicklung der Flurformen im Kreis Kirchheimbolanden', *Rhein-Mainische Forschungen,* vol. 62, 1967

Fliedner, D., 'Formungtendenzen und Formungsphasen in der Entwicklung der ländlichen Kulturlandschaft seit dem Hohen Mittelalter besonders in Nordwestdeutschland', *Erdkunde,* vol. 23, 1970, pp. 102-16; 'Die Kulturlandschaft der Hamme-Wümme-Niederung. Gestalt und Entwicklung des Siedlungsraumes nördlich von Bremen', *Göttinger Geog. Abhandlungen,* vol. 55, 1970

'Forschungsstelle für bäuerliche Familienwirtschaft', *Förderung bäuerlicher Selbsthilfe bei der Verbesserung der Landwirtschaft,* vols. 1-9, Frankfurt/Main, 1957-65

Francksen, T., 'Einige Besonderheiten des oldenburgischen Verkoppelungsgesetzes gegenüber Reichsumlegungsordnung und Flurbereinigungsgesetz', *100 Jahre Verkoppelung in Oldenburg,* 1958, pp. 12-14

Franz, G., *Geschichte des Bauernstandes,* Stuttgart, 1970

Gabler, A., 'Die alemannische und fränkische Besiedlung der Hessel-berglandschaft', *Veröff. d. Schwäbischen Forschungsgemeinschaft,* Reihe 1, vol. 4, 1961

Galluser, W., 'Die landwirtschaftliche Aussiedlung in der struktur-verbesserten Agrarlandschaft an Beispiel des Kreises Schleiden', *Erdkunde,* vol. 18, 1964, pp. 311-28

Geier, H., 'Schraubeshain – Ein Beitrag zur Wüstungskunde des südöstlichen Harzvorlandes', *Wissenschaftliche Zeitschrift d. Universität Halle,* vol. 15, 1966, pp. 31-37

Giese, E., 'Die untere Haseniederung', *Westfälische Geog. Studien,* vol. 20, 1968

van Giffen, A. E., 'Der Warf in Ezinge, Provinz Groningen, Holland und seine westgermanischen Häuser', *Germania,* vol. 20/1, 1936; 'Die frühgeschichtlichen Marschensiedlungen, die Terpen oder Warfen', *Jahrbuch d. Männer vom Morgenstern,* vol. 36, 1955, pp. 1-13

Glässer, E., 'Der Dülmener Raum, Neuere Untersuchungen zur Frage des ländlichen Siedlungs- und Wirtschaftswesens im Sand- und Lehm-Münsterland in der Auseinandersetzung mit dem Natur-raumgeschehen', *Forschungen zur deutschen Landeskunde,* vol. 176, 1968; 'Die Kulturlandschaftsentwicklung des westlichen Ruhr-gebiets vor Beginn der hochindustriellen Periode', *Berichte zur deutschen Landeskunde,* vol. 40/1, 1968, pp. 59-80

Gradmann, R., 'Das ländliche Siedlungswesen des Königreichs Würt-temberg', *Forschungen zur deutschen Landes- und Volkskunde,* vol. 21, Stuttgart, 1913

Grees, H., 'Das Seldnertum im östlichen Schwaben und sein Einfluss auf die Entwicklung der ländlichen Siedlungen', *Berichte zur deutschen Landeskunde,* vol. 31, 1963, pp. 104-150; 'Die Auswirk-ungen von Wüstungsvorgängen auf die überdauernden Siedlungen', *Erdkundliches Wissen, Geog. Zeitschrift,* vol. 18, 1968, pp. 50-67; 'Das Kleinbauerntum in Ostschwaben und sein Einfluss auf die Entwicklung von Siedlung und Wirtschaft', *L'habitat et les pay-sages ruraux d'Europe. Les congrès et colloques de l'Université de Liège,* vol. 58, 1971, pp. 179-204

Gries, H., 'Winzer und Ackerbauern am oberen Mittelrhein', *Rhein-Mainische Forschungen,* vol. 69, 1969

Grotelüschen, W., 'Rodungssiedlungen der nordwestlichen Eifel', *Rheinische Vierteljahrsblätter,* 1934, pp. 72-83

Grohne, E., 'Wurtenforschung im Bremer Gebiet', *Jahresbericht d. Focke Museums,* Bremen, 1938

Haarnagel, W., 'Die historische Entwicklung der Forschung, insbe-sondere der Wurten- oder Warfenforschung im Küstengebiet der Nordsee', *Festschrift z. 70. Geburtstag von K. H. Jacob-Friesen,* Hildesheim, 1956, p. 243ff; 'Die spätbronze-frühneuzeitliche Gehöft-siedlung bei Jemgum auf dem linken Ufer der Ems', *Die Kunde,* vol. 8/1-2, 1957, p. 37ff; 'Probleme der Küstenforschung im südlichen Nordseegebiet', *Schriftenreihe der Provinzialstelle f. Marschen- und Wurtenforschung*, vols. 1-6, 1940-57; 'Die Marschen im deutschen Küstengebiet der Nordsee und ihre Besiedlung', *Berichte zur deutschen Landeskunde*, vol. 27/2, 1961, pp. 203-19; 'Die Grabung Feddersen-Wierde und Ihre Bedeutung für die Erkenntnisse der bäuerlichen Besiedlung im Küstengebiet in dem Zeitraum vom 1. Jahrhundert vor bis 5. Jahrhundert n. Chr.', *Zeitschrift f. Agrargeschichte und Agrarsoziologie*, vol. 10, 1962, pp. 145-57; 'Die prähistorischen Siedlungsformen im Küstengebiet der Nordsee', *Erdkundliches Wissen, Geographische Zeitschrift*, vol. 18, 1968, pp. 67-84; 'Die Siedlungen im Nordseeküstengebiet', *Westfälische Geog. Studien*, vol. 25, 1971, pp. 90-112

Habbe, K. A., 'Das Flurbild des Hofsiedlungsgebietes im mittleren Schwarzwald', *Forschungen zur deutschen Landeskunde*, vol. 118, 1960; 'Die "Waldhufensiedlungen" in den Gebirgen Südwestdeutschlands als Problem der systematischen Siedlungsgeographie', *Berichte zur deutschen Landeskunde*, vol. 37/1, 1966, pp. 40-52

Haefs, J., 'Neusiedlung im Rahmen der Massnahmen zur Verbesserung der Agrarstruktur und Eingliederung von Heimatvertriebenen und Flüchtlingen', *Innere Kolonisation*, 1961, p. 97 ff.

Hambloch, H., 'Einödgruppe und Drubbel', *Landeskundliche Karten und Hefte der Geog. Kommission f. Westfalen, Reihe Siedlung und Landschaft in Westfalen*, vol. 4, 1960, pp. 40-56; 'Langstreifenflur im nordwestlichen Altniederdeutschland', *Geographische Rundschau*, vol. 14/9, 1962, pp. 345-56

Hanenkamp, H., 'Börger und seine 5 Töchtersiedlungen am Nordrande des Hümmlings', unpublished dissertation, Hamburg, 1951; 'Das Dorf Börger und seine räumliche Entwicklung', *Jahrbuch d. Emsländischen Heimatvereins*, vol. 2, 1954, pp. 96-110

Hannesen, H., 'Die Agrarlandschaft der schleswig-holsteinischen Geest und ihre neuzeitliche Entwicklung', *Schriften d. Geog. Institut d. Universität Kiel*, vol. 17/3, 1959

Harders, N., *Die Siedlungsverhältnisse in Ostfriesland*, Aurich, 1927

Harms, O., 'Die Teilung der Marken und Gemeinheiten in Oldenburg als landeskulturelle Massnahme im 19. Jahrhundert', *100 Jahre Verkoppelung in Oldenburg*, 1958, pp. 20-25; 'Die Verkoppelung des Hasberger Kirchenesches', *100 Jahre Verkoppelung in Oldenburg*, 1958, p. 26; 'Die Entstehung der Bauerschaft Wapeldorf, ein Musterbeispiel für planmässige Besiedlung', *900 Jahre Rastede*, Rastede, 1959; 'Marken- und Gemeinheitsteilungen in Oldenburg', *Allgemeine Vermessungs Nachrichten*, 1960, pp. 189-95

Hartke, W., 'Ländliche Neusiedlung als geographisches Problem', *Erdkunde*, vol. 1, pp. 90-106

Hastrup, F., *Danske Landsbytyper – en geografisk analyse*, Århus, 1964

Hatt, G., 'Das Eigentumsrecht an bebautem Grund und Boden'

Zeitschrift f. Agrargeschichte und Agrarsoziologie, vol. 3, 1955, pp. 118-37

Haushofer, H., *Die deutsche Landwirtschaft im technischen Zeitalter,* Stuttgart, 1963

Heide, F., 'Das westliche Emsland', *Marburger Geog. Schriften,* vol. 22, 1965

Heinemann, B., 'Über Aufbau und Verbreitung der Plaggenböden im Emsland', *Jahrbuch d. Emsländischen Heimatvereins,* vol. 6, 1959, pp. 62-76

Heinritz, G., Heller, H. and Wirth, E., 'Wirtschafts- und sozialgeographische Auswirkungen reichsritterschaftlicher Peuplierungspolitik in Franken', *Berichte zur deutschen Landeskunde,* vol. 41/1, 1968, pp. 45-72

Helbig, H. and Weinrich, L., *Urkunden und erzählende Quellen zur deutschen Ostsiedlung im Mittelalter,* Darmstadt, 1968

Heller, H., *see* Heinritz, G.

Herbort, W., 'Die ländlichen Siedlungslandschaften des Kreises Wiedenbrück um 1820', *Westfälische Studien,* 4, 1950

Herz, K., 'Das Lommatzer Land. Eine historisch-geographische Untersuchung', *Wissenschaftliche Veröff. d. deutschen Instituts f. Länderkunde,* Neue Folge, vol. 17-18, 1960, pp. 209-82

Herzog, A., 'Grund und Aufriss der Neudörfer im Bourtanger Moor', *Jahrbuch d. Geog. Gesellschaft Hannover,* (*Obst Festschrift*), 1953, p. 297ff.; 'Die grosszügige Siedlungsarbeit des Staates im Emsland', *Jahrbuch des Emsländischen Heimatvereins,* vol. 1, pp. 26-38; 'Dorf und Landschaftsgestaltung in den Neusiedlungsgebieten des Hannoverschen Emslandes', *Neues Archiv f. Niedersachsen,* vol. 8/2, 1955-6, p. 90 ff.

Hildebrandt, H., 'Regelhafte Siedlungsformen im Hünxfelder Land. Ein Beitrag zur Erforschung der Genese der Kulturlandschaft im ehemaligen Territorium der Reichsabtei Fulda', *Marburger Geog. Schriften,* vol. 38, 1968

Hömberg, A., *Die Entstehung der westdeutschen Flurformen, Blockgemengflur, Streifenflur, Gewannflur,* Berlin, 1935

Hövermann, J., 'Die Entwicklung der Siedlungsformen in den Marschen des Elb-Weser-Winkels', *Forschungen zur deutschen Landeskunde,* vol. 56, 1951

Hugle, R., 'Die Erschliessung und Förderung des hannoverschen Emslandes im Zehnjahresplan', *Neues Archiv f. Niedersachsen,* vol. 9, p. 72ff.; *Das Hannoversche Emsland. Ein Raumordnungsplan nach den Grundsätzen der Landesplanung,* Hannover, 1950

Huppertz, B., *Räume und Schichten bäuerlicher Kulturformen in Deutschland,* Bonn, 1939

Huttenlocher, F., 'Gewanndorf und Weiler', *Verhandlungen des 27. deutschen Geographentages in München, 1948,* publ. 1950, pp. 147-155; 'Das Problem der Gewannfluren in südwestdeutscher Sicht', *Erdkunde,* vol. 17, 1963, pp. 1-15

Imeyer, G., ' Die niedersächsische Geest zwischen Hunte und Weser ', *Schriftum zur Landeskunde und Landesentwicklung Niedersachsens,* Series A1, Hildesheim, 1965

Ipsen, G., ' Die preussische Bauernbefreiung als Landesausbau ', *Zeitschrift f. Agrargeschichte und Agrarsoziologie,* vol. 2/1, 1954, pp. 29-54

Jacob-Friesen, K., ' Der Stand der Wurtenforschung ', *Deutsche Geog. Blätter,* vol. 42, 1939

Jäger, H., ' Die Entwicklung der Kulturlandschaft im Kreise Hofgeismar ', *Göttinger Geog. Abhandlungen,* vol. 8, 1951 ; ' Methoden und Ergebnisse siedlungskundlicher Forschung ', *Zeitschrift f. Agrargeschichte und Agrarsoziologie,* vol. 1, 1953, p. 3ff. ; ' Wege der agraren Kulturlandschaftsentwicklung in den Randländern der Nordsee ', *Verhandlungen d. deutschen Geographentages, Würzburg, 1957,* 1958, pp. 386-98 ; ' Probleme und Stand der Flurformenforschung in Süddeutschland ', *Berichte z. deutschen Landeskunde,* vol. 20, 1958, pp. 142-60 ; ' Entwicklungsperioden agrarer Siedlungsgebiete im mittleren Westdeutschland seit dem frühen 13. Jahrhundert ', *Würzburger Geog. Arbeiten,* vol. 6, 1958. ; ' Die Allmendeteilung in Nordwestdeutschland in ihrer Bedeutung für die Genese der Gegenwärtigen Landschaften ', *Geografiska Annaler,* vol. 43/1-2, 1961, p. 138ff. ; *Historisch-landeskundliche Exkursionskarte von Niedersachsen, Blatt Duderstadt,* Hildesheim, 1964

Jäger, H. and Schaper, J., ' Agrarische Reliktformen im Sandstein-Odenwald in ihrer Bedeutung für die Landschaftsgeschichte ', *Zeitschrift f. Agrargeschichte und Agrarsoziologie,* vol. 9, 1961, pp. 169-88

Jakob, H., ' Wüstungstendenzen und Wüstungsursachen im ehemaligen Hochstift Bamberg, Anno 1348 ' *Berichte zur deutschen Landeskunde,* vol. 41/2, 1968, pp. 251-60

Jankuhn, H., ' Die Entstehung der mittelalterlichen Agrarlandschaft in Angeln ', *Geografiska Annaler,* vol. 43/1-2, 1961, pp. 151-65 ; ' Vorgeschichtliche Landwirtschaft in Schleswig-Holstein ', *Zeitschrift f. Agrargeschichte und Agrarsoziologie,* vol. 9, 1961, pp. 1-13 ; *Vor- und Frühgeschichte,* Stuttgart, 1969

Jesson, O., ' Niederländische Einflüsse in der deutschen Kulturlandschaft ', *Comptes Rendus du Congrès International de Géographie, Amsterdam, 1938,* vol. 2/4, pp. 127-42

Jorzick, H. P., ' Die Siedlungsstruktur der Weserniederung zwischen Hoya und Rieda oberhalb Bremens ', *Deutsche Geog. Blätter,* vol. 46, 1952, pp. 57-232

Käubler, H., ' Notwendige Bemerkungen zur " Entwicklung der Kulturlandschaft im Stift Neuzelle ",' *Wissenschaftliche Zeitschrift d. Universität Halle,* vol. 15/1, 1966, pp. 39-42

Käubler, R., ' Ein Beitrag zum Rundlingsproblem aus dem Tepler Hochland ', *Mitteilungen d. Fränkischen Geog. Gesellschaft,* vol. 10, 1963, pp. 69-81

Keil, G., 'Zur historischen Besiedlung der mittel-deutschen Löss-wälder', *Wissenschaftliche Zeitschrift d. Universität Halle*, vol. 15/1, pp. 43-56

Keuning, H., *De Groninger Veenkolonien*, Amsterdam, 1933 ; 'Esch-siedlungen in den östlichen Niederlanden', *Westfälische Fors-chungen*, vol. 1, 1938, p. 143ff. ; 'Siedlungsform und Siedlungs-vorgang', *Zeitschrift f. Agrargeschichte und Agrarsoziologie*, vol. 9, 1961, pp. 153-168

Köhler, A., 'Die Kulturlandschaft im Bereich der Platten und Terrassen an der Riss', *Tübinger Geog. Studien*, 1964

König, M., 'Die bäuerliche Kulturlandschaft der hohen Schwaben-alb', *Tübinger Geog. Studien*, vol. 1, 1958

Kötzschke, R., 'Ländliche Siedlung und Agrarwesen in Sachsen', *Forschungen zur deutschen Landeskunde*, vol. 77, 1953

Kraft, H., 'Die bäuerlichen Gemeinheitsflächen im Kriese Lüding-hausen um 1800', *Westfälische Forschungen*, 1941

Kramm, H., 'Die ur- und, frühgeschichtlichen Siedlungen im östlichen Brandenburg', *Wissenschaftliche Zeitschrift der P. H.* Potsdam, vol. 5/1, 1959, pp. 3-8 ; 'Die deutsche Ostexpansion in ihren Aus-wirkungen auf die Wirtschaft und Siedlung im Gebiet des heutigen Bezirks Frankfurt an der Oder', *Wissenschaftliche Zeitschrift der P. H. Potsdam*, vol. 5/1, 1959, pp. 9-31 ; 'Der preussische Absolu-tismus und seine Bedeutung für die ökonomische- und siedlungs-geographischen Verhältnisse im Gebiet des heutigen Bezirks Frank-furt an der Oder', *Wissenschaftliche Zeitschrift der P. H. Potsdam*, vol. 5/1, 1959, pp. 33-42

Krause, P., 'Vergleichende Studien zur Flurformenforschung im nordwestlichen Vogelsberg', *Rhein-Mainische Forschungen*, vol. 63, 1968

Krell, H., 'Die Besiedlung des Donaumooses', *Jahresschrift d. Heimatvereins Neuburg an der Donau*, vol. 104, 1940-49

Krenzlin, A., 'Die Kulturlandschaft des Hannoverschen Wendlandes', *Forschungen zur deutschen Landes- und Volkskunde*, vol. 28, 1931, 2nd ed., 1969 ; 'Probleme der neueren nordostdeutschen und ost-mitteldeutschen Flurformenforschung', *Deutsches Archiv f. Landes-und Volksforschung*, vol. 4, 1940, pp. 547-69 ; 'Zur Erforschung der Beziehungen zwischen der spätslawischen und frühdeutschen Besiedlung in Norddeutschland', *Berichte zur deutschen Landes-kunde*, vol. 6, 1949, pp. 133-45 ; 'Dorf, Feld und Wirtschaft im Gebiet der grossen Täler und Platten östlich der Elbe', *For-schungen zur deutschen Landeskunde*, vol. 70, 1952 ; 'Historische und wirtschaftliche Züge im Siedlungsformenbild des westlichen Ostdeutschland', *Frankfurter Geog. Hefte*, vol. 27-29, 1955 ; 'Blockflur, Langstreifenflur und Gewannflur als Ausdruck agrari-scher Wirtschaftsformen in Deutschland', *Abh. u. Ber. des inter-nationalen Kolloquiums f. Agrargeographie und Agrargeschichte, Nancy, 1957*, pp. 353-369 ; 'Das Wüstungsproblem im Lichte ost-

o

deutscher Siedlungsforschung ', *Zeitschrift f. Agrargeschichte und Agrarsoziologie,* vol. 7, 1959, pp. 153-69 ; ' Zur Genese der Gewannflur in Deutschland ', *Geografiska Annaler,* vol. 43, 1961, pp. 190-205 ; ' Die Entwicklung der Gewannflur als Spiegel kulturlandschaftlicher Vorgänge ', *Berichte zur deutschen Landeskunde,* vol. 28, 1961

Krenzlin, A. and Reusch, L., ' Die Entstehung der Gewannflur nach Untersuchungen im nördlichen Unterfranken ', *Frankfurter Geog. Heft,* vol. 35, Frankfurt/Main, 1961

Krüger, R., ' Typologie des Waldhufendorfes nach Einzelformen und deren Verbreitungsmustern ', *Göttinger Geog. Abh.,* vol. 42, 1967

Kryzmowski, R., *Geschichte der deutschen Landwirtschaft unter besonderer Berücksichtigung der technischen Entwicklung der Landwirtschaft,* Stuttgart, 1951

Kuhn, W., *Siedlungsgeschichte Oberschlesiens,* Würzburg, 1954 ; *Die deutsche Ostsiedlung in der Neuzeit,* 2 vols. and map volume, Köln-Graz, 1955

Kullen, S., ' Der Einfluss der Reichsritterschaft auf die Kulturlandschaft im mittleren Neckarland ', *Tübinger Geog. Schriften,* vol. 24, 1967

Kulturamt Oldenburg. *100 Jahre Verkoppelung – Flurbereinigung in Oldenburg,* Oldenburg i. o., 1958

Lamping, H., ' Dorf und Bauernhof im südlichen Grabfeld – zur Analyse der Struktur agrarischer Räume ', *Würzburger Geog. Arbeiten,* vol. 17, 1966

Lauenstein, J., ' Die ländliche Siedlungsproblematik des Emslandes. Siedlung und innere Kolonisation im europäischen Raum ', *Beiträge und Untersuchungen d. Instituts f. Siedlungs- und Wohnungswesen d. Westfälischen Wilhelms-Universität Münster,* vol. 50, 1957, p. 5ff ; ' 10 Jahre Forschung und Entwicklung in Emsland ', *Mitteilungen über die Arbeiten d. Staatlichen Moorversuchsstation in Bremen,* Hamburg, 1960, pp. 13-29

Lehmann, R., ' Siedlungsgeschichtliche Aufgaben und Probleme in der Niederlausitz ', *Berichte zur deutschen Landeskunde,* vol. 17/1, 1956, pp. 60-89

Liebich, G., ' Werden und Wachsen von Petersdorf im Riesengebirge ', *Quellen und Darstellungen zur schlesischen Geschichte,* vol. 6 Würzburg, 1961

Lütge, F., ' Die deutsche Grundherrschaft ', *Zeitschrift f. Agrargeschichte und Agrarsoziologie,* vol. 3/2, 1955, pp. 129-37 ; ' Vergleichende Untersuchungen über die landwirtschaftlichen Grossbetriebe seit dem Ausgang das mittelalters ', *Zeitschrift f. Agrargeschichte und Agrarsoziologie,* vol. 9, 1961, pp. 189-202 ; *Geschichte der deutschen Agrarverfassung vom frühen Mittelalter bis zum 19. Jahrhundert,* Stuttgart, 1963

Machens, K., ' Beiträge zur Wirtschaftsgeschichte des Osnabrücker

Landes im 17. und 18. Jahrhundert', *Osnabrücker Mitteilungen,* vol. 70, 1961, pp. 86-104

Marten, H. R., ' Die Entwicklung der Kulturlandschaft im alten Amt Aerzen des Landkreises Hameln-Pyrmont', *Göttinger Geog. Abh.,* vol. 53, 1969

Martiny, R., ' Hof und Dorf in Altwestfalen', *Forschungen zur deutschen Landes- und Volkskunde,* vol. 24, 1926, pp. 157-323 ; ' Die Grundrissgestaltung der deutschen Siedlungen', *Petermanns Mitteilungen,* (*Ergänzungs-Heft, 197*), 1928

Matzat, W., ' Alter und Funktion der Blockgemengeflur in Süddeutschland', *Berichte zur deutschen Landeskunde,* vol. 29, 1962, pp. 307-13 ; ' Flurgeographische Studien im Bauland und Hinteren Odenwald', *Rhein-Mainische Forschungen,* vol. 53, Frankfurt/ Main, 1963

Mayhew, A., ' Rural settlement in the Weser-Ems Raum', unpublished dissertation, Oxford, 1966 ; ' Regional planning and the development areas in West Germany', *Regional Studies,* vol. 3, 1969, pp. 73-79 ; ' Structural reform and the future of West German agriculture', *Geog. Review,* vol. 60, 1970, pp. 54-68 ; ' Zur strukturellen Reform der Landwirtschaft in der Bundesrepublik Deutschland erläutert an der Flurbereinigung in der Gemeinde Moorriem/Wesermarsch', *Westfälische Geog. Studien,* vol. 22, 1970 ; ' Agrarian reform in West Germany ; an assessment of the integrated development project Moorriem', *Trans. Inst. of British Geographers,* vol. 52, 1970, pp. 61-76

Meffert, E., ' Die Innovation ausgewählter Sonderkulturen im Rhein-Mainischen Raum in ihrer Beziehung zur Agrar- und Sozialstruktur', *Rhein-Mainische Forschungen,* vol. 64, 1968

Meibeyer, W., ' Die Rundlingsdörfer im östlichen Niedersachsen', *Braunschweiger Geog. Studien,* vol. 1, 1964

Meitzen, A., *Siedelung und Agrarwesen der Westgermanen und Ostgermanen, der Kelten, Römer, Finnen und Slawen,* 3 vols. and Atlas volume, Berlin, 1895

Metz, F., *Die ländlichen Siedlungen Badens,* Karlsruhe, 1925

Metz, W., ' Waldrecht Hägerrecht und Medem. Gedanken zu einer Genesis der Siedlerrechte', *Zeitschrift f. Agrargeschichte und Agrarsoziologie,* vol. 1, 1953, p. 105ff.

Meyer, K., *Ordnung im ländlichen Raum,* Stuttgart, 1964

Minssen, O., *Hooksiel, der Vorhafen der Koopstadt Jever,* Jever, 1960

Mittelhäusser, K., ' Über Flur- und Siedlungsformen in der norwestlichen Lüneburger Heide', *Jahrbuch der Geog. Gesellschaft,* Hannover, 1953, p. 236ff.

Mortensen, H., ' Siedlungsgeographie des Samlandes', *Forschungen zur Deutschen Landes- und Volkskunde,* vol. 22, 1923, pp. 283-358 ; ' Beiträge der Ostforschung zur nordwestdeutschen Siedlungs- und Flurforschung', *Nachr. d. Akad. d. Wiss. Göttingen* (phil. hist.),

1945 ; ' Fragen der nordwestdeutschen Siedlungs- und Flurforschung im Licht der Ostforschung ', *Nachr. d. Akad. d. Wiss. Göttingen,* (phil. hist.), 1946/47, pp. 37-59 ; ' Zur Entstehung der deutschen Dorfformen insbesondere des Waldhufendorfes ', *Nachr. d. Akad. d. Wiss. Göttingen,* (phil. hist.), 1946-7, pp. 76-80 ; ' Neue Beobachtungen über Wüstungs-Bandfluren und ihre Bedeutung für die mittelalterliche deutsche Kulturlandschaft ', *Berichte zur deutschen Landeskunde,* vol. 10, 1951, pp. 341-61 ; ' Zur Entstehung der Gewannflur ', *Zeitschrift f. Agrargeschichte und Agrarsoziologie,* 1955, pp. 30-48 ; ' Die mittelalterliche deutsche Kulturlandschaft und ihre Verhältnis zur Gegenwart ', *Verhandlungen d. deutschen Geographentages, Würzburg, 1957,* pp. 361-75 ; ' Probleme der mittelalterlichen deutschen Kulturlandschaft ', *Berichte zur deutschen Landeskunde,* vol. 20/1, 1958, pp. 98-104 ; ' Beiträge zur Kenntnis des nordöstlichen Mitteleuropa um 1400 ', *Zeitschrift f. Ostforschung,* 1960, pp. 333-61 ; ' Die Arbeitsmethoden der deutschen Flurforschung und ihre Beweiskraft ', *Berichte zur deutschen Landeskunde,* vol. 29, 1962, pp. 205-14

Müller, T., *Ostfälische Landeskunde,* Braunschweig, 1952

Müller-Wille, M., ' Eisenzeitliche Fluren in den nordöstlichen Niederlanden ', *Westfälische Forschungen,* vol. 16, pp. 5-51

Müller-Wille, W., ' Langstreifenflur und Drubbel. Ein Beitrag zur Siedlungsgeographie Westgermaniens ', *Deutsches Archiv f. Landes- und Volksforschung,* vol. 8, 1944, pp. 9-44 ; ' Die Hagenhufendörfer in Schaumburg-Lippe ', *Petermanns Mitteilungen,* vol. 90, 1944, pp. 245-7 ; *Westfalen,* Münster, 1952 ; ' Agrarbäuerliche Landschaftstypen in Nordwestdeutschland ', *Verhandlungen d. Deutschen Geographentages,* Essen, 1955, pp. 179-86 ; ' Siedlungs-, Wirtschafts-, und Bevölkerungsräume im westlichen Mitteleuropa um 500 n. Chr.', *Westfälische Forschungen,* vol. 9, 1956, pp. 5-25 ; ' Die spätmittelalterliche-frühneuzeitliche Kulturlandschaft und ihre Wandlungen ', *Berichte zur deutschen Landeskunde,* vol. 19, 1957, pp. 187-200 ; ' Blöcke, Streifen und Hufen ', *Berichte zur deutschen Landeskunde,* vol. 29/2, 1962, pp. 293-306

Munderloh, H., ' Die Bauerschaft Etzhorn ', *Schriften d. Niedersächs. Heimatbundes,* vol. 30, Hannover, 1955

Musall, H., ' Die Entwicklung der Kulturlandschaft der Rheinniederung zwischen Karlsruhe und Speyer vom Ende des 16 bis zum Ende des 19. Jahrhunderts ', *Heidelberger Geog. Arb.,* vol. 22, 1969

Neugebauer, U., ' Die Siedlungsformen im nordöstlichen Schwarzwald ', *Tübinger Geog. Studien,* vol. 30, 1969

Niemeier, G., ' Eschprobleme in Nordwestdeutschland und in den östlichen Niederlanden ', *C. R. du Congrès International de Géographie Amsterdam, 1938,* vol. 2/5, Leiden, 1938, pp. 27-40 ; ' Fragen der Flur- und Siedlungsformenforschung im Westmünsterland ', *Westfälische Forschungen,* vol. 1, 1938, pp. 124-42 ; ' Gewannfluren, ihre Gliederung und die Eschkerntheorie ', *Peter-*

manns Mitteilungen, 1944, pp. 57-74; 'Frühformen der Waldhufen', *Petermanns Geog. Mitteilungen,* vol. 93, 1949, pp. 14-27; 'Von Plaggen und Plaggenböden', *Jahrbuch des Emsländischen Heimatvereins,* vol. 3, 1955, pp. 15-24; 'Agrarlandschaftliche Reliktgebiete und die Morphogenese von Kulturlandschaften im Atlantischen Europa', *Geografiska Annaler,* vol. 43/1-2, 1961, pp. 229-35; 'Die Eschkerntheorie im Licht der heutigen Forschung', *Berichte zur deutschen Landeskunde,* vol. 29, 1962, pp. 280-6; *Siedlungsgeographie,* Braunschweig, 1967

Nitz, H. J., 'Regelmässige Langstreifenfluren und fränkische Staatskolonisation', *Geographische Rundschau,* vol. 9, 1961, pp. 350-65; 'Das Alter der Langstreifenfluren', *Berichte zur deutschen Landeskunde,* vol. 29, 1962, pp. 313-16; 'Die ländlichen Siedlungsformen des Odenwaldes', *Heidelberger Geog. Arb.,* vol. 7, 1962; 'Siedlungsgeographische Beiträge zum Problem der fränkischen Staatskolonisation im süddeutschen Raum', *Zeitschrift f. Agrargeschichte und Agrarsoziologie,* vol. 11, 1963, pp. 34-62; 'Entwicklung und Ausbreitung planmässiger Siedlungsformen bei der mittelalterlichen Erschliessung von Odenwald, nördlichem Schwarzwald und Hardtwald', in: *Heidelberg und die Rhein-Neckar-Lande, Festschrift Geographentag 1963,* pp. 210-35; 'Langstreifenfluren zwischen Ems und Saale – Wege und Ergebnisse ihrer Erforschung in den letzten Jahrzehnten', *Westfälische Geog. Studien,* vol. 25, 1971, pp. 113-130

Oberbeck, G., 'Die mittelterliche Kulturlandschaft des Gebietes um Gifhorn', *Schriften d. Wirtschaftswiss. Gesellschaft z. Studium Niedersachsens e. V.,* Series A, vol. 66, 1957; 'Neue Ergebnisse der Flurformenforschung in Niedersachsen', *Berichte zur deutschen Landeskunde,* vol. 20, 1958, pp. 125-42; 'Das Problem der spätmittelalterlichen Kulturlandschaft erläutert an Beispielen aus Niedersachsen', *Geografiska Annaler,* vol. 43/1-2. 1961, pp. 236-43

Obiditsch, F., 'Die ländliche Kulturlandschaft der Baar', *Tübinger Geog. Studien,* 1961

Obst, E. and Spreitzer, H., 'Wege und Ergebnisse der Flurforschung im Gebiet der grossen Haufendörfer', *Petermanns Geog. Mitteilungen,* 1939, pp. 1-19

Obst, J., 'Kulturlandschaftsveränderungen im oberen Vogelsberg – Ackerschwund-Grünfallen-Auffichten', *Rhein-Mainische Forschungen,* vol. 49, 1960; 'Das Flurformengefüge der Wetterau im 14. Jahrhundert', *Berichte zur deutschen Landeskunde,* vol. 37/1, 1966, pp. 53-63

Ohling B., *Die Acht und ihre sieben Siele,* Emden, 1965

Ostermann, K., 'Die Besiedlung der mittleren Oldenburgischen Geest', *Forschungen zur deutschen Landes- und Volkskunde,* vol. 28, 1931, pp. 153-238

Otremba, E., 'Die Entwicklungsgeschichte der Flurformen im oberdeutschen Altsiedelland', *Berichte zur deutschen Landeskunde,* vol. 9, 1951, pp. 363-81 ; 'Lange Streifen', *Berichte zur deutschen Landeskunde*, vol. 31, 1963, pp. 197-208

Ottens, B., 'Hebelermeer, ein echtes Hochmoordorf', *Jahrbuch d. Emsländischen Heimatvereins*, vol. 8, 1961, pp. 124-30

Overbeck, F., 'Zur Geschichte der deutschen Agrarlandschaft im Übergang vom Mittelalter zur Neuzeit', *Erdkunde*, vol. 15/2, 1961, pp. 136-40

Pfaff, W., 'Die Gemarkung Ohrsen in Lippe', *Westfälische Geog. Studien*, vol. 11, 1957

Pieken, H., 'Zur Entwicklung der Siedlungsformen in den Marschen des Elb-Weser-Winkels', *Die Erde*, vol. 2, 1956, pp. 129-53

Pohlendt, H., 'Die Verbreitung der mittelalterlichen Wüstungen in Deutschland', *Göttinger Geog. Abh.*, vol. 3, 1950 ; 'Die Verfehnung von Hochmoorkulturen am Beispiel von Fehndorf (Kreis Meppen)', *Neues Archiv f. Niedersachsen*, vol. 4/6, p. 120ff.

Rack, E., 'Besiedlung und Siedlung des Altkreises Norden', *Spieker*, vol. 15, 1967

Radig, W., *Die Siedlungstypen in Deutschland und ihre frühgeschichtlichen Wurzeln*, Berlin, 1955

Reinhardt, W., 'Die Grabung auf der Dorfwarf von Groothusen, Kr. Norden und ihre Ergebnisse', *Emder Jhb.*, vol. 39, 1959, pp. 20-33 ; 'Die Siedlungsverhältnisse in der ostfriesischen Marsch', *Ber. z. deutschen Landeskunde*, vol. 27, 1961, pp. 233-9 ; 'Studien zur Entwicklung des ländlichen Siedlungsbildes in den Seemarschen der ostfriesischen Westküste', *Probleme der Kustenforschung im südlichen Nordseegebiet*, vol. 8, Hildesheim, 1965

Reissig, H., 'Die Verkoppelung des Sager Esches', *100 Jahre Verkoppelung in Oldenburg*, 1958, pp. 27-28

Reusch, L., *see* Krenzlin, A.

Riepenhausen, H., 'Die bäuerliche Siedlung im Ravensberger Landes bis 1770', *Arb. d. Geog. Komm. f. Westfalen*, vol. 1, 1938

Rippel, J., 'Die Entwicklung der Kulturlandschaft am nordwestlichen Harzrand', *Schriften d. Wirtschaftswiss. Gesellschaft z. Studium Niedersachsens e. V.*, vol. 69, 1958

Ritter, G., 'Die Nachsiedlerschichten im nordwestdeutschen Raum und ihre Bedeutung für die Kulturlandschaftsentwicklung', *Ber. z. deutschen Landeskunde*, vol. 41, 1968, pp. 85-128

Röhm, H., 'Die Vererbung des landwirtschaftlichen Grundeigentums in Baden-Württemberg', *Forschungen zur deutschen Landeskunde*, vol. 102, 1957

Röll, W., 'Die kulturlandschaftliche Entwicklung des Fuldaer Landes seit der Frühneuzeit', *Giessener Geog. Schriften*, vol. 9, 1966

Roshop, U., 'Die Entwicklung des ländlichen Siedlungs- und Flurbildes in der Grafschaft Diepholz', *Quellen und Darstellungen zur Geschichte Niedersachsens*, vol. 39, 1932

Rothert, H., 'Das Eschdorf, ein Beitrag zur Siedlungsgeschichte', *Aus Vergangenheit in Gegenwart*, Münster, 1923, pp. 54-65 ; 'Die

Besiedlung des Kreises Bersenbrück ', *Veröff. d. hist. Komm. f. d. Provinz Westfalen,* Quakenbrück, 1924

Rubow-Kalähne, M., ' Langstreifenfluren in Neu-Vorpommern, eine Auswertung der schwedischen Matrikelkarten ', *Mitteil. d. Geog. Instituts d. Martin-Luther-Universität, Halle,* vol. 6, 1959, pp. 663-8 ; ' Matrikelkarten von Vorpommern 1692-8 nach der schwedischen Landesaufnahme ', *Wiss. Veröff. d. deutschen Instituts f. Länderkunde,* vol. 17-18, 1960, pp. 189-208

Saalfeld, D., ' Bauernwirtschaft und Gutsbetrieb in der vorindustriellen Zeit ', *Quellen und Forschungen zur Agrargeschichte,* vol. 6, 1960 ; ' Zur Frage des bäuerlichen Landverlustes im Zusammenhang mit den preussischen Agrarreformen ', *Zeitschrift f. Agrargeschichte und Agrarsoziologie,* vol. 11, 1963, pp. 163-71 ; ' Die Produktion und Intensität der Landwirtschaft in Deutschland und angrenzenden Gebieten um 1800 ', *Zeitschrift f. Agrargeschichte und Agrarsoziologie,* vol. 15, 1967, pp. 136-175

Saenger, W., ' Die bäuerliche Kulturlandschaft der Hohenloher Ebene und ihre Entwicklung seit dem 16. Jahrhundert ', *Forschungen z. deutschen Landeskunde,* vol. 101, 1957

Sanders, H., ' Die Besiedlung Grossefehns, ein Beispiel ostfriesischer Fehnkolonisation ', *Neues Archiv für Niedersachsen,* vol. 1/3, 1954, p. 48ff.

Schaper, J., *see* Jäger, H.

Scharlau, K., ' Landeskulturgesetzgebung und Landeskulturentwicklung im ehemaligen Kurhessen seit dem 16. Jahrhundert ', *Zeitschrift f. Agrargeschichte und Agrarsoziologie,* 1953, pp. 126-45 ; ' Kammerfluren und Streifenfluren im westdeutschen Mittelgebirge ', *Zeitschrift f. Agrargeschichte und Agrarsoziologie,* vol. 5/1, 1957, pp. 13-20 ; ' Ergebnisse und Ausblicke der heutigen Wüstungsforschung ', *Blätter f. deutsche Landesgeschichte,* vol. 93, 1957, pp. 43-101 ; ' Flurrelikte und Flurformgenese in Westdeutschland ', *Geografiska Annaler,* vol. 43/1-2, 1961, pp. 264-77 ; ' Die Bedeutung der Wüstungskartierung für die Flurformenforschung ', *Berichte zur deutschen Landeskunde,* vol. 29, 1962, pp. 215-20

Schlenger, H., ' Formen ländlicher Siedlungen in Schlesien ', *Veröff. d. Schlesischen Gesellschaft f. Erdkunde,* vol. 10, 1930

Schlicht, E., ' Die Entstehung der Moorkolonie Neurhede ', *Jahrbuch d. Emsländischen Heimatvereins,* vol. 6, 1959, pp. 10-23

Schlüter, O., ' Die Siedlungsräume Mitteleuropas in frühgeschichtlicher Zeit ', *Forschungen zur deutschen Landeskunde,* vols. 63, 74, 110, 1952, 1953, 1958

Schlüter, O., *see* August, O.

Schmidt, W., ' Landwirtschaft und Landeskultur in Oldenburg ', *100 Jahre Verkoppelung in Oldenburg,* Oldenburg, 1958

Schmitz, H., *Deutsche Kulturleistung im Netzegau,* Schneidemühl, 1939

Schneider, P., ' Natur und Besiedlung der Senne ', *Spieker,* vol. 3, 1952

Schöningh, L., 'Die Geschichte der Familie Schöningh und die Grund-
ung von Schöninghsdorf', *Jahrbuch des Emsländischen Heimatvereins,* vol. 8, 1961, pp. 57-71

Schott, C., 'Orts- und Flurformen Schleswig-Holsteins', *Beiträge zur
Landeskunde von Schleswig-Holstein, Schriften d. Geog. Inst. d.
Univ. Kiel,* 1953, pp. 105-34

Schröder, K. H., 'Weinbau und Siedlung in Württemberg', *Forschungen z. deutschen Landeskunde,* vol. 73, 1953 ; 'Die Gewannflur
in Süddeutschland', *Vorträge und Forschungen,* vol. 7, Konstanz-
Stuttgart, 1964, pp. 11-28

Schröder, K. and Schwarz, G., 'Die ländlichen Siedlungsformen in
Mitteleuropa. Grundzüge und Probleme ihrer Entwicklung',
Forschungen zur deutschen Landeskunde, vol. 175, 1969

Schröder-Lembke, G., 'Zur Flurformen der Karolingerzeit', *Zeitschrift f. Agrargeschichte und Agrarsoziologie,* vol. 9/2, 1961,
pp. 143-53

Schultz, A., 'Die Sielhafenorte', *Göttinger Geog. Abh.,* vol. 27, 1962

Schulz-Lüchow, W., 'Primäre und sekundäre Rundlingsformen in
der Niederen Geest des hannoverschen Wendlandes', *Forschungen
zur deutschen Landeskunde,* vol. 142, 1963

Schwalb, M., 'Die Entwicklung der bäuerlichen Kulturlandschaft in
Ostfriesland und Westoldenburg', *Bonner Geog. Abh.,* vol. 12, 1953

Schwarz, G., *Allgemeine Siedlungsgeographie,* Berlin, 1966 ; *see*
Schröder, K.

Seraphim, H., 'Das Heuerlingswesen in Nordwestdeutschland',
*Veröff. d. Provinzialinstituts f. westfälische Landes- und Volks-
kunde,* series 1, vol. 5, Münster, 1948

Sick, W. D., 'Zur Siedlungsentwicklung Südwestdeutschlands im
Bereich des römischen Limes', *Stuttgarter Geog. Studien,* vol. 69,
1957, pp. 151-63

Siebels, G., *Zur Kulturgeographie der Wallhecke,* Leer, 1954

Slicher van Bath, B., *The agrarian history of Western Europe,
A. D. 500-1850,* London, 1963

Spreitzer, H., *see* Obst, E.

'Staatliche Kreditanstalt Oldenburg-Bremen', *75 Jahre im Dienste
von Staat und Wirtschaft,* Oldenburg, 1958

Steffens, H. G., 'Untersuchungen über die mittelalterliche Besiedlung
des Kreises Bremervörde', *Göttinger Geog. Abh.,* vol. 29, 1962

Steinbach, F., 'Gewanndorf und Einzelhof', *Historische Aufsätze,
volume in honour of A. Schulte,* Düsseldorf, 1927, pp. 44-61

Sternberg, F., *Die wirtschaftliche und soziale Entwicklung ausgewählter Neudörfer des Emslandes,* Münster, 1962

Tantzen, R., 'Die landwirtschaftliche Siedlung im Landesteil Oldenburg', Siedlungsamt Oldenburg, 1931, unpublished ; '75 Jahre
Siedlungsamt Oldenburg', *Neues Archiv f. Niedersachsen,*
vol. 10-12, p. 257ff.

Theunisz, J., 'De Nederlandse oostkolonisatie', *Studiereeks der*

Germaansche Werkgemeenschap Nederland, vol. 1, 1943

Thorpe, H., ' The green village as a distinctive form of settlement on the North Europeon Plain ', *Bulletin de la Société Belge d'Études Géographiques,* vol. 30, 1961, pp. 5-134

Tüxen, J., ' Über einige Beziehungen zwischen Pflanzensoziologie und Siedlungsgeschichte ', *Zeitschrift f. Agrargeschichte und Agrarsoziologie,* vol. 6/2, 1958, pp. 119-22

Uhlig, H., ' Old hamlets with infield and outfield systems in western and central Europe ', *Geografiska Annaler,* vol. 43/1-2, 1961, pp. 285-313

Warnecke, E., *Engter und seine Bauerschaften,* Hannover, 1958

Weber, J., ' Siedlungen im Albvorland von Nürnberg. Ein Siedlungs-geographischer Beitrag zur Orts- und Flurformengenese ', *Mitteilungen d. Fränkischen Geog. Gesellschaft,* vol. 11-12, 1964-5, pp. 141-264

Weinrich, L., *see* Helbig, H.

Westerhoff, A., *Das ostfriesisch-oldenburgische Hochmoorgebiet, die Entwicklung seines Landschafts- und Siedlungsbildes,* Emsdetten, 1936

Weyand, H., ' Untersuchungen zur Entwicklung saarländischer Dörfer und ihrer Fluren ', *Arbeiten aus dem Geog. Inst. d. Univ. d. Saarlandes,* vol. 12, 1969

Wiegel, J. M., ' Kulturgeographie des Lamer Winkels im Bayerischen Wald ', *Mitteilungen d. Fränkischen Geog. Gesellschaft,* vol. 11-12, 1964-5, pp. 265-392

Willms, W., ' 100 Jahre Verkoppelung-Flurbereinigung in Oldenburg ', *100 Jahre Verkoppelung in Oldenburg,* Oldenburg, 1958, p. 8

Winkelmann, R., ' Die Entwicklung des oberrheinischen Weinbaus ', *Marburger Geog. Schriften,* vol. 16, 1960

Winter, H., ' Die Entwicklung der Landwirtschaft und Kulturland-schaft des Monschauer Landes unter besonderer Berücksichtigung der Rodungen ', *Forschungen z. deutschen Landeskunde,* vol. 147, 1965

Wirth, E., *see* Heinritz, G.

Wrede, G., ' Die Langstreifenflur in Osnabrücker Land ', *Osnabrücker Mitteilungen,* vol. 66, 1954, pp. 1-102

Zschocke, H., ' Die Waldhufensiedlungen am linken deutschen Niederrhein ', *Kölner Geog. Arb.,* vol. 16, 1963

Zschocke, R., ' Siedlung und Flur der Kölner Ackerebene zwischen Rhein und Ville in ihrer neuzeitlichen Entwicklung mit einem Vorschlag zur Flurformenterminologie ', *Kölner Geog. Arb.,* vol. 13, 1959 ; ' Die Kulturlandschaft des Hunsrücks und seiner Randland-schaften in der Gegenwart und in ihrer historischen Entwicklung ', *Kölner Geog. Arb.,* vol. 24, 1970 ; ' Die Entwicklung der landwirt-schaftlichen Betriebsgrössen und ihre Auswirkungen auf die Kultur-landschaft ', *L'habitat et les paysags ruraux d'Europe, Les congrès et colloques de l'Université de Liège,* vol. 58, 1971, pp. 423-42

Glossary and Index of German Terms used in the Text

Gründerjahre 194; the years of rapid economic development after the founding of the Reich in 1871

Grundzinsen 44; form of land rent payable by farmers to the land-owner after the break-up of the feudal system

Gutshof 135, 140-2; the estate farm in eastern Germany

Gutsweiler 143; the settlement of estate workers cottages in eastern Germany

Hägerrecht 77; the rights given to the farmers in *Hagen* settlements

Häusler 124, 127, 129; a cottager in southern Germany with very little land

Hagenhufendorf 76-7; a high medieval settlement in west-central Germany given special rights by the lord and with a long-strip field pattern

Hagenmeister 77; also called *Hachmeister;* the leader of the colonists in the *Hagen* settlements

Halberbe 19, 41, 181; also called *Halbbauer;* a 'half entitled' farmer—generally the result of division of a full farm unit

Haubarg 175; large square house form in the pastoral areas in western Schleswig-Holstein

Haufendorf 18ff, 39-41, 60, 77, 83, 113, 123, 126, 133-4, 144; a large, densely built up village, without obvious regularities in structure

Heuerling 19, 24, 124-5, 127, 129, 180-2; cottager settled without land in the eighteenth and nineteenth centuries in northern Germany

Hochmeister 57; head of the Teutonic Order of Knights

Hochmoor 152, 157-8, 186; raised bog on which colonies were founded in the eighteenth century (*Hochmoorkolonien*) and for which improved methods of cultivation were pioneered at the end of the nineteenth century (*Deutsche Hochmoorkultur*)

Hollandgängerei 122, 129; the seasonal migration of workers to the eastern Netherlands in the eighteenth century

Hollerrecht 49-50; Dutch settlement law applied to colonies in Germany settled by the Dutch

Hube 26; pre-fragmentation farm unit in south Germany

Hufe 24ff, 54, 58, 69ff, 78, 81, 83, 98, 161; area of farmland necessary for the support of a farmer and his family. It came to be a measurement of land area, varying regionally from about 20 to 50 ha. The Frankish Hufe became the standard farm size for the *Waldhufendörfer*

Kätner 123; regional term for cottager

Kamp 127, 129; in north western Germany an enclosure. Baasen termed the settlement associated with early enclosures a *Kampsiedlung*

Katenzeil 141; row of estate workers houses joined onto an existing settlement

Klosterhof 46; monastery farm which acted as a colonization centre in the high middle ages

Körbler 123; local term for a cottager

Kötter 19, 22, 24, 123ff, 133-4, 144, 179-182; general term for a cottager in north west Germany

Koog 160-1; the term for polder in Schleswig-Holstein

Koppelwirtschaft 170-1; complex rotation on enclosed land which developed in Holstein

Kossäten 123, 139, 140; cottagers in eastern Germany

Lagerbücher 24; record books of the early modern period

Langstreifenflur 18ff; pattern of long narrow strip fields, as was general on the *Esch*

Leibeigenschaft 143; the legal relationship between the estate owner and his workers in the east, often implying the total lack of freedom of the latter

Lokator 47, 55-9, 136, 147; village and town planner employed by the territorial and local lords in the settlement of the east

Mähder 115-6; rough meadows on the Alb in southern Germany which covered deserted areas in the late middle ages

Mark 1) 19, 22, 41, 45-6, 126, 178-186, 191; the commons
     2) 50; frontier zone in the Carolingian empire

Markkötter 124; cottager of the sixteenth and seventeenth centuries with little land

Marsch 28ff, 38-9, 42, 47-50, 61, 75-6, 146, 148, 171, 174, 178, 180; the areas of silts and clays along the North Sea coast and the estuaries of the Ems, Weser and Elbe

Marschhufendorf 71-7, 160, 165; linear settlement on or behind the dike with land in long strips at right angles to the dike

Meier 43, 160; local official of the territorial lord, cultivating his farms and collecting payments from other farmers

Meierrecht 146-7; the legal relationship between peasant and lord which developed after the end of the feudal system

Moor 151-8, 167, 168, 180ff; peat bog

Moos 161-3; peat bog in southern Germany

Nebenwieken 152, 155; Tributary canals in fen colonies

Niederungsmoor 152; eutrophic fen

Ordensstaat 54; East Prussia under the Teutonic Order
Ostpolitik 52ff; the policy of subduing and settling the eastern territories in the medieval period

Pferdekötter 124; see *Erbkötter*
Plaggendungung 20; system of manuring the Esch, involving the pasturing of sheep on the heath or peat and the subsequent cutting of sods
Polder-Färsten 160; the wealthy farmers of the polders
Priele 34, 36; small channels in the coastal mud zone
Propst 47; monastic official

Reichssiedlungsgesetz 195; imperial settlement act of 1919
Reichsumlegungsordnung 189; land consolidation order of 1937
Reutmeister 47, 83; South German term for settlement planner (see *Lokator*)
Rundling 60ff, 78, 81, 84, 141; rounded hamlet settlement form located largely around the middle-Elbe—Saale region
Rute 78; early linear measurement

Sackgassendorf 61; elongated *Rundling*
Salbücher 24; records from the sixteenth to eigthteenth centuries
Schulze 55, 64-5; local law enforcement officer and representative of the lord in the high middle ages
Schweighof 115; extensive cattle farms in south west Germany in the late middle ages
Seil 72; linear measurement
Seldengasse 127; line of *Seldner* houses joined to an existing settlement
Seldner 123ff, 144, 179-180; general term for a cottager in south Germany
Separation 192; consolidation of estate land in the east
Siedlungsgeographie 10-11; settlement geography
Sielhafen 146; small harbour in the dike
Strassendorf 77ff; street village; regular settlement form in the colonial east

Terp (Dutch), see *Wurt*

Vergewannung 26, 27; creation of a *Gewannflur*
Verkoppelung 186-192; land consolidation
Villikation 46; administrative district in the feudal system
Vöhde 86, 170; land area on which there is a rotation of arable with a long period of pasture
Völkerwanderung 11, 13, 14; the migration of the German tribes south and west before A.D. 500
Vogt 44, 59, 109; medieval local official, responsible for defence and other administration
Vogteiabgaben 44; form of tax, originally for defence
Vollerbe 19ff, 41, 179-183; also *Vollbauer*; a farmer with full rights in the commons

Waldhufendorf 67ff, 79; colonial linear forest settlement, with land in strips at right angles to the valley
Warf—see *Wurt*
Warfsleute 123; local term for cottager
Weide 115-6; pasture
Wik 36; early Frisian trading and manufacturing settlement
Wurt 28ff, 37-9, 61; artificial settlement mound in the pre-dike *Marsch*

Zehntabgabe 44; originally a church tax, which was later often collected by secular rulers

Index

GENERAL INDEX